D1593602

SLAVES,

SAILORS,

CITIZENS

A group of newly recruited contrabands in 1862. The sailors are outfitted with the standard navy uniform without any rank insignia, suggesting most of them are landsmen. Note the elderly sailor in the center foreground, a relatively common site on navy ships.

Courtesy of the New Hampshire Historical Society

SLAVES,

SAILORS,

CITIZENS

AFRICAN AMERICANS
IN THE
UNION NAVY

Steven J. Ramold

NORTHERN ILLINOIS UNIVERSITY PRESS

DeKalb

© 2002 by Northern Illinois University Press

Published by the Northern Illinois University Press, DeKalb, Illinois 60115

Manufactured in the United States using acid-free paper

All Rights Reserved

Design by Julia Fauci

Library of Congress Cataloging-in-Publication Data

Ramold, Steven J.

Slaves, sailors, citizens: African Americans in the Union navy/Steven J. Ramold.

p. cm.

Includes bibliographical references and index.

ISBN 0-87580-286-9 (alk. paper)

1. United States. Navy—History—Civil War, 1861–1865. 2. United States. Navy—African Americans—History—19th century. 3. United States—History—Civil War, 1861–1865—Participation, African American. 4. United States—History—Civil War, 1861–1865—Naval operations. 5. African American sailors—History—19th century. 6. African American sailors—Social conditions—19th century. I. Title.

E591 .R36 2002

973.7'58'08996073—dc21

2001044522

* *For Paula* *

CONTENTS

ACKNOWLEDGMENTS

• I owe a debt of gratitude to several members of the department of history at the University of Nebraska—Lincoln, specifically Professors Lloyd Ambrosius, Edward Homze, and Peter Maslowski. Dr. Keith Parker, head of the African American Studies program at the University of Nebraska, also contributed great insight into the original project. My adviser, Dr. Kenneth Winkle, provided the most help of all. I greatly appreciated his ability to compliment while giving incisive criticism. The statistical portions of the book are the best example of his influence upon me as a historian.

Professor Joseph Reidy at Howard University also deserves a great deal of thanks. He graciously permitted me to view the data he accumulated on African American sailors for the National Park Service, information invaluable to this project. I also gratefully acknowledge the assistance of the Special Collections staff of Love Library at the University of Nebraska—Lincoln, the historians of the Naval Historical Center, manuscript curators at the Library of Congress, and the courteous personnel of the National Archives and Records Administration in Washington, D.C. Most of all, I thank my wife. She tolerated research trips that she could not go on, boring discourses on things done long ago, and an occasionally cranky husband who could not get his thoughts down on paper. Because she inspires me in many ways, I dedicate this book to her.

SLAVES,

SAILORS,

CITIZENS

INTRODUCTION

- In July 1861, Commodore Silas H. Stringham was a man with more problems than solutions. Commanding the Union navy's Atlantic Squadron, Stringham had the unenviable task of blockading the Confederacy's entire eastern seaboard with a small force. The thinly stretched blockade could not cover every port or river mouth, and Confederate vessels seemed to sail at will. The shortage of ships made his blockade porous, and the prospect of reinforcements seemed dim. The Navy Department had acquired additional ships, but insufficient numbers of recruits remained a problem. News from Stringham's subordinates was also discouraging. Officers reported undermanned, poorly repaired, and inadequately armed ships. Worse still, the ships he did have on station often encountered other difficulties. From the start of the war, fleeing slaves had sought refuge aboard navy ships. While their knowledge of Confederate movements and fortifications proved invaluable, their presence placed yet another burden upon the navy. The fugitives consumed the vessel's limited stores of food, and evacuating them to a safe location meant taking the ship off blockade duty.

  Stringham's immediate concern existed aboard the USS *Mount Vernon*, Commander O. S. Glisson's ship. Already burdened by more than a dozen refugees, the *Mount Vernon* received three more the night of July 17. The men, Lewis Ransom, Robert Brooks, and Albert Hutchins, had fled from their owner, John H. Dunlavey, from nearby Mathews County, Virginia. The refugees presented a singular problem. Federal law required Glisson to return the slaves, but he declined because the slaves feared they "would be murdered." Uncertain of his authority,

Glisson appealed to Stringham for instructions.

Short of the sailors he needed, and burdened by fugitives he did not want, Stringham reached the obvious conclusion. On July 18, 1861, Stringham requested permission from Secretary of the Navy Gideon Welles to recruit among the refugees aboard his ships. "If Negroes are to be used in this contest," Stringham reasoned, "I have no hesitation in saying they should be used to preserve the Government, not to destroy it." Under pressure to find recruits, Welles could not find any logical reason to deny Stringham's request. Only four days after Stringham's note, Welles responded with a brief dispatch, only three sentences long. That short note, however, opened the door for the participation of thousands of African Americans in the Union navy. "It is not the policy of the Government to invite or encourage this class of desertion," Welles warned, "and yet, under the circumstances, no other course . . . could be adopted without violating every principle of humanity. To return them would be impolitic as well as cruel, and . . . you will do well to employ them." Instead of providing free labor, Welles later promised the refugees fair wages, stating, "If employed they are entitled to compensation."[1]

Little could Welles know the impact of his instructions to Commodore Stringham. Within months, the enlistment of thousands of African Americans, both free and slaves, transformed the makeup of the Union navy, provided an opportunity for blacks to fight against slavery, and demonstrated the courage and skill of African Americans willing to serve their country. The issue of their involvement split public and political opinion, and their presence defied the government's original stated policy of denying African Americans a combat role in suppressing the rebellion. African Americans served in every major naval battle and campaign, fought with distinction, and won the nation's highest honors. They paid for this opportunity with blood, however. Savage combat killed or wounded many that enlisted.

Many questions and issues emerge when discussing the subject of the Union navy's African American sailors, from their reasons for enlisting to their routine existence in the service. Running through all of these discussions, however, is the central theme of how the U.S. Navy perceived and treated its African

American recruits. While scholarship has revealed the intense racism and stereotyping that black soldiers overcame to serve in the Union army, the Union navy accepted African American sailors with relatively little discord. Compared with the army, the Union navy compiled a highly credible record of race relations during the Civil War. Though black troops did not appear on the battlefield in large numbers until after the Emancipation Proclamation, African American sailors fought from the start of the war. In addition to integrated crews, the navy ensured equal pay and benefits, promotion opportunities, standard of living, and health care to its African American sailors, in sharp contrast to the experience of many black soldiers. A study of navy courts-martial shows that African American defendants received equal, even preferred, treatment, and black sailors fared better in court than white defendants did. Compared with the army, racial conflicts between white and black sailors were relatively few. The sharing of a common wartime experience, along with a tradition of African American service in the navy, tended to minimize friction between white and black sailors. This does not imply that the employment of African American sailors happened without social conflict. Some incidents of racial hatred occurred, as expected in the mid-nineteenth century, but the evidence clearly shows that widespread racial harassment and persecution did not exist on the same scale as in the Union army.

Unfortunately, the achievements of African American sailors did not ensure a future in the navy. The navy instituted its policies to ensure a manpower pool required to win a war. Once the wartime crisis had passed, the navy began to restrict African American enlistment. The post-Civil War navy was no exception. By the end of the nineteenth century, few African Americans served in the navy, their wartime sacrifices long forgotten. Therefore, this book strives to reveal the actions, achievements, and service of Civil War African American sailors. The story of these largely forgotten heroes can take its rightful place in the history of the war and in the struggle for slaves and free blacks to become full citizens.

Chapter One

"AMERICA HAS SUCH TARS"

AFRICAN AMERICAN SAILORS

BEFORE THE CIVIL WAR

• Well before their massive commitment to the Civil War navy, African Americans served the navy of the United States. Beginning with the Revolutionary War, black sailors risked their lives and freedom to help subdue the enemies of the United States. African Americans, their rights unrecognized and their status as human beings questioned, still performed valuable service to the U.S. government by volunteering their effort when needed most. Unfortunately, service in early American wars did not improve the social condition of African Americans. Free black veterans remained on the fringes of white society, and many slaves in naval service remained in bondage.

African American naval service before the Civil War established a distinctive pattern repeated for nearly a century. Many African Americans, finding limited economic opportunities ashore, served in the navy because white sailors would not. This is especially true of the peacetime navy, where conditions, pay, and discipline dissuaded most whites from enlisting. The black sailors often served with distinction, reflected in the citations for bravery and demands for more black sailors by the officers who commanded them. Inevitably, however, despite their bravery and sacrifice, military service did little to change the social standing of African Americans. Small improvements manifested themselves in the aftermath of various wars, but change came slowly.

The first significant enlistment of African American sailors occurred during the Revolutionary War, when blacks served in all of America's navies. The Continental navy, funded by the Continental Congress and acting on behalf of all the rebelling colonies, recruited African Americans to fill its ranks. Although an insignificant force compared with Britain's Royal Navy, the Continental navy tried its best to combat the English blockade and attack enemy merchant shipping. With barely fifty ships, the constantly underfunded Continental navy scraped for every sailor it could muster and gladly accepted African Americans willing to serve, although a precise estimate of their numbers has never appeared. The Continental navy offered lower pay and financial reward than other naval pursuits, and the risk of battle convinced many sailors to ignore its recruiting efforts. Recruiting records seem to indicate that the navy enlisted mostly northern blacks, a trend that held through the Civil War. Massachusetts, for instance, provided many African American crewmen, including captured British crewmen willing to fight against their former masters. Once enlisted in the Continental navy, African Americans were not restricted to menial positions but held positions equivalent to those of white crewmen. The few existing ship rosters indicate African American sailors filled responsible positions equal to their representation aboard ship.[1]

More African American sailors served in the eleven state navies than in the Continental navy. While the Continental navy's recruitment of blacks was concentrated in the North, the number of African American sailors in the state fleets depended upon each state's financial ability to man its navy. The larger, more populous states attracted African Americans into service, leaving the smaller navies with fewer black sailors. Massachusetts, New York, Maryland, Virginia, and South Carolina all created navies comparable in size with the Continental navy and with a similar number of black sailors. Charged with protecting only the economic interests of their respective states, the state navies employed mostly small coastal vessels and a few larger ships. For instance, the crew of *Protector,* the largest ship in the Massachusetts state navy, included at least two African American sailors in

March 1780. A year earlier, the Massachusetts brig *Active* carried five African American sailors, all former members of the Royal Navy. Pennsylvania and Connecticut not only employed African American sailors but black marines as well. Besides boarding enemy ships during combat, marines enforced discipline among the white crewmen and performed certain duties (such as guarding the ammunition magazine and liquor room) not trusted to common sailors. Southern state navies, such as those of Maryland and Virginia, employed African Americans as pilots to escort their ships in unfamiliar and dangerous waters. At least two of Virginia's black pilots died in action with British forces. Even Georgia, a state without a significant maritime industry, employed black crewmen aboard a small squadron of galleys used for coastal defense.[2]

An important difference between the Continental and state navies was the latter's willingness to employ slaves as sailors, although the Continental navy did employ a few slaves. John Paul Jones brought along his slaves when he commanded the *Ranger,* but slave numbers seem to have remained small. The southern state navies, however, used sizable numbers of slaves sent to the service for various reasons. Some slaves entered their respective state navies as substitutes for owners wanting to do their part without risking life and limb. For instance, Lawrence Baker, a prominent Virginia slaveowner, sent his slave David to serve in the Virginia state navy in his stead. As a reward for their service, after the war the Virginia legislature freed David and all other slaves who served in their owners' absence. Other owners formally enlisted their slaves and collected their wages for themselves. Some black men fled slavery and enlisted on their own, in the hopes that naval service offered the path to freedom. Some states enlisted slaves for the simple reason that a slave offered freedom by serving the United States was one slave less fighting for freedom granted by the British. The widespread British policy of granting freedom to any slave who aided the British military effort persuaded many state legislatures to use slave sailors rather than lose them. This attitude emerged in Virginia because of a declaration by Lord Dunmore, the royal governor, offering to free all enslaved blacks "that are able and willing to bear arms, they joining his Majesty's troops . . . for the more speedily reducing this colony to a proper dignity." Some states, such as Virginia and Maryland, even purchased slaves for the sole purpose of manning their ships. Generally, these slaves faced sale on the slave market when the war ended, but two black sailors, William Bush and Jack Knight, escaped this fate. The state legislature rewarded their years of valuable service to Virginia's navy by granting them their freedom.[3]

Thousands of slaves opted to serve the British war effort, most often as coastal pilots in unfamiliar waters. Slaves fled to the British despite American efforts to halt the flow. The Virginia legislature ordered all boat owners to guard their craft lest slaves use them to escape to the British. South Carolina threatened the death penalty on any slave caught serving the British, and the state executed one black pilot as a warning to other slaves. Nevertheless, slaves in large numbers risked their lives to earn freedom. HMS *Alert*, captured by the United States in 1782, included eleven former slaves among its forty-six-man crew. The captain of the HMS *Commodore* found his black pilot so valuable he ordered him "put in a place of safety" when a battle loomed. Eager to keep skilled blacks out of the enemy's hands, in 1779 George Washington paid out "1000 dollars promised the Negro pilots" who supplied and transported his army in the Chesapeake Bay region.[4]

Another American navy of the Revolution comprised the hundreds of privateers preying on British shipping. These licensed pirates enjoyed several recruiting advantages over the Continental and state navies. Privateer crews could leave a vessel at the end of a cruise, as formal enlistment was not required, and the opportunity for financial gain was much greater than in the formal navies. Privateers did not pay wages, but the prize money from captured merchant ships could easily outstrip in a single day a year's worth of navy wages. Also, privateers had no obligation to engage enemy warships, diminishing the risk of death in combat. Fugitive slaves found privateering especially appealing. Most privateers did not question where their manpower came from, and many escaped slaves signed on raiding ships that not only carried them away from slavery but also offered the chance to make some money in the process. Many sailors, white and black, preferred the risks of commerce raiding to the established navies. One Massachusetts observer described the swarming volunteers as "grasshoppers" and found "Privateering was never more in vogue." Privateering ships multiplied rapidly (136 in 1776 alone), and by the end of the war more than fifty thousand men served on American commerce raiders.[5]

Privateers sailed with additional risks, however. Unlike captives from the Continental and state navies, the British treated privateers as pirates and punished captured privateers accordingly. African Americans, both free and slave, captured aboard privateers faced sale into slavery in the Caribbean, where backbreaking labor in crippling heat promised a quick death. The British imprisoned other captives aboard prison ships such as the *Jersey,* a floating hulk where hundreds of American prisoners died from malnutrition and disease. The captives included a fourteen-year-old free black sailor named James Forten. Captured in 1781 while serving aboard the privateer *Royal Lewis* operating out of Philadelphia, Forten endured seven grueling months aboard the *Jersey* before a prisoner exchange freed him. Forten later amassed a fortune in the shipping industry and became a prominent abolitionist.[6]

Despite their sacrifices for American freedom, the end of the Revolutionary War did not significantly improve the social lot of African Americans or ensure their right to serve in the nation's military forces. The privateers returned to commercial concerns while the state navies disbanded. Even the Continental navy disappeared after Congress eliminated its funding as a fiscal measure, with the War Department absorbing all naval responsibilities. Even without a navy, the service of African American sailors still elicited controversy. The discourse on the nature of liberty and the rights of man generated by the Revolution raised the first debates on the legitimacy of slavery. Among antislavery advocates, the issue of slaves serving in the navy so their owners could collect their wages became the first test of their ability to influence public opinion.

The most notable objection to slave sailors appeared in 1777 under the pseudonym Antibiastes. Originally printed in Philadelphia, *Observations on the Slaves and the Indented Servants, Inlisted in the Army, and in the Navy of the United States* lambasted the government for waging a war for national freedom while maintaining slavery in the conflict's aftermath. Antibiastes praised the government for its "resolve . . . for prohibiting the importation of Slaves . . . in the cause of mankind" but criticized the Continental Congress for not guaranteeing slaves their freedom as a reward for their sacrifice. Citing French and Spanish policy of freeing slave veterans, Antibiastes castigated the government because it "hazarded to employ Slaves in their wars; but immediate, or conditional emancipation was . . . held up." Quite the opposite, "the slaves . . . intrusted with arms, in the defence of their territories, were not only allowed to dispose of their whole pay as they saw fit" but risked battle for the profit of their owners. Despite pleas that the government "cannot suffer them to be ungrateful," the small social advance gained by black sailors during the Revolution disappeared with the Continental navy.[7]

New naval threats, however, revived the need for African American sailors. Growing antagonism between the United States and France in 1798 led to an undeclared naval conflict known as the Quasi-War. France's seizure of American merchant ships on the high seas forced President John Adams and Congress to create a national naval force, and on April 30, 1798, the United States Navy was born. Under the terms of "An Act to Establish an Executive Department, to be Nominated the Department of the Navy," the new Navy Department assumed all responsibilities for America's naval defense and obtained the right to build, man, and maintain a squadron of forty-five ships.[8]

Forced to build and man ships quickly, the navy again turned to African American recruits to help man the fleet. Ship rosters, including those from the USS *Constitution* and *Constellation,* show that African American sailors served the navy. William Brown, for instance, enlisted aboard the USS *Constellation* in 1798 and later received a wound in battle with the French frigate *L'Insurgente.* Another African American, George Diggs, served as a quartermaster, a petty officer, aboard the USS *Experiment* in the same year. The most daring exploits of an African American sailor belong to Moses Armstead. Captured while serving aboard the brig *Betsies,* Armstead led an uprising, killed the French prize crew, and recaptured the ship. Unfortunately, the *Betsies* fell to another French ship, and Armstead spent the rest of the conflict imprisoned in Puerto Rico. Privateers also emerged to prey on French shipping. The privateering force, nearly ten times the size of the U.S. Navy, not only seized proportionally more French vessels but probably utilized more black sailors. Prowling near the French sugar islands in the Caribbean, privateers needing replacement crewmen would find black sailors far more plentiful than white sailors. The Quasi-War ended in 1800, but, unlike the end of the Revolutionary War, African American sailors remained in the U.S. Navy.[9]

National economic growth and navy policy at the beginning of the nineteenth century also promoted the employment of African American sailors. A booming economy created a shortage of skilled merchant seamen, and the navy's recruiting woes continued into the early 1800s. The demand for merchant sailors increased as American shippers filled the international trade void caused by the Napoleonic Wars in Europe. British and French raids upon each other's shipping led both countries to use American ships in their Caribbean trade, further depleting the supply of skilled seaman. High merchant wages of thirty to thirty-five dollars per month outstripped meager navy wages, set at ten dollars per month for ordinary seamen since 1798. African Americans, searching for economic opportunities, solved some of the navy's enlistment problems.[10]

Unfortunately, the economic growth generated by American shipping companies threatened to drag the United States into the European war. In addition to restraining American vessels from carrying the goods of their enemy, the British policy of monitoring and harassing U.S. merchantmen on the high seas included random searches for deserters from the Royal Navy. Attracted by its higher pay and relatively humane discipline, large numbers of British sailors deserted from the British navy and merchant service to the U.S. Navy. Refusing to recognize the American naturalization process, the British demanded the right to search American ships on the high seas in order to impress deserters back into service. The most infamous impressment incident occurred in 1807. The USS *Chesapeake*, outfitting at the Norfolk Navy Yard in

Virginia, remained chronically short of sailors despite recruiting agents dispatched as far away as New York and Philadelphia. Eventually, the ship sailed with a crew filled out by African American seamen and three deserters from the HMS *Melampus*. A British warship, HMS *Leopard,* pursued the *Chesapeake,* and Captain Salusbury Humphreys demanded the right to search the American vessel. Commodore John Barron, commanding the *Chesapeake,* refused, and the *Leopard* fired upon the American ship, killing several crewmen, to force its consent to the search. Among the sailors taken off by the *Leopard* were the three deserters as well as another man suspected of desertion. Of the four, one was certainly of African descent while another, described as "Indian looking," could possibly have been African. Impressment of American citizens on the high seas increased military tensions between the United States and Great Britain. As a direct result of the *Chesapeake* incident, Congress forbade the enlistment of foreign nationals in the U.S. Navy, and the importance of African American sailors increased accordingly.[11]

Naval policy instituted by President Thomas Jefferson also led to the increased use of black sailors. Opposed to the massive naval spending of presidents George Washington and John Adams, Jefferson favored a system of coastal fortifications and small gunboats to defend America's maritime interests. The gunboat fleet consisted of some 177 wooden boats seventy-five feet long, propelled by oars or sails, each carrying a few cannon. Poorly designed, the overly laden and inadequately sailed vessels were difficult to handle and dangerous in anything but the most enclosed waters. Designed for forty-man crews, the gunboats during wartime frequently held nearly seventy. During peacetime, however, the navy found few recruits willing to serve on its small ships, and often states pressed militiamen into service. Desertion from gunboat service remained a constant problem. One officer lamented, "This crime happens so frequently . . . we shall never be able to put a stop to it." Hard-pressed to find crewmen for the unpopular vessels, the navy resorted to African American sailors to maintain its force structure.[12]

African Americans also found useful employment with the navy in its growing conflict with Barbary pirates in North Africa.

With naval deployments to the Mediterranean lasting as long as five years, the navy struggled to find recruits. Black sailors filled the void. The navy quickly constructed vessels suitable to fight pirates on a foreign shore, but Jefferson still opposed a large navy. Most of the new ships were small coastal sloops and gunboats. When the conflict ended, the navy had only four frigates ready for service, seven others ready only after major repairs, ten small sloops, and the gunboats of questionable quality.[13]

Despite a fervent effort to prevent war, continued British interference with U.S. shipping helped to trigger American entry into the War of 1812. Congress responded by vastly expanding the U.S. Navy. At the outbreak of war, the navy possessed only an insignificant force of ten frigates (all constructed during the Washington and Adams administrations), eight small brigantines, and seventy-two vessels of the gunboat flotilla. In comparison, the Royal Navy's American Station supported ninety-seven warships, including six ships of the line and thirty-three frigates. In addition, America's watery border with British Canada lay open, although the American and English naval forces on the Great Lakes began the war on generally even terms.[14]

There was now great demand for men to sail the navy's new ships, and sailors, as always, were in short supply. An act of Congress in 1812 allowed the navy 4,273 billets, allotting 2,987 to enlisted men. The navy exceeded that number, however, with 10,617 officers and men (including 405 sailors in prisoner-of-war camps) in the service in October 1814. Even in exceeding the manpower allotment, the navy faced constant manpower shortages. Merchant pay was high, and the navy could not match the wages. Naval service also entailed the risk of death in battle. Despite some notable American successes in single ship-to-ship duels, the British preponderance in ships and firepower soon gave them the upper hand. Sailors also refused duty on the Great Lakes flotillas. Remote and unsettled, the inland lakes offered all the possibility of death in battle with little chance of prize money or the usual seaport recreation. Fearing a British invasion from Canada, the navy took extreme measures to man the Great Lakes Squadron. For instance, in 1813 the navy transferred the entire crew, officers and men, of the USS *Congress* to the Great Lakes.[15]

Federal law banned African Americans from navy service at the time, but wartime demands overcame political opposition. Because of the unpopularity of Great Lakes duty, as many as one-half of Commodore Oliver H. Perry's men on the lakes were African American, in part lured by the 25 percent wage increase offered to volunteers for Great Lakes duty. Perry's own flagship, the USS *Lawrence*, featured men from a contingent of "three hundred and sixty colored Marines, in military pomp and naval array." Perry, like many officers, hesitated to embrace his African American crew. Perry wrote to Isaac Chauncey, his commanding officer, "The men . . . are a motley set—blacks, soldiers, and boys. . . . I am, however, pleased to see anything in the shape of a man." Chauncey replied to his subordinate: "I regret that you are not pleased with the men sent you for to my knowledge a part of them are not surpassed by any seamen we have in the fleet; and I have yet to learn that the color of the skin . . . can affect a man's qualifications or usefulness. I have nearly fifty blacks on board of this ship, and many of them are among my best men." Although initially skeptical of their ability, Perry grew to respect his African American sailors. He praised the bravery of his black crewmen during the Battle of Lake Erie, describing them as "absolutely insensitive to danger."[16]

A year later, African American sailors played a pivotal role in reversing a British incursion through Lake Champlain. One observer reported, "About one in ten or twelve of the crews were black" aboard the U.S. gunboats defending the lake. Among the sailors cited for exceptional bravery in the after-battle report was African American seaman John Day, a gunner aboard the galley *Viper*. Another African American cited for bravery was Charles Black, a former privateer who used his profits to buy his freedom. Captured on a privateer by the British, Black escaped from the infamous Dartmoor Prison in England, returned to the United States, and enlisted in the U.S. Navy.[17]

In open-ocean combat, African American sailors also demonstrated their bravery and skill. Captain Isaac Hull, commanding the famed USS *Constitution*, "Old Ironsides," credited many of his men for bravery after defeating the British frigate *Guerriere* in 1812. As a group, Hull praised the ability of his African American sailors, although using terms considered socially unacceptable to-day: "I never had any better fighters than those niggers,—they stripped to the waist, & fought like devils, sir, seeming to be utterly insensible to danger & to be possessed with a determination to outfight white sailors." The USS *Hornet,* commanded by Captain James Lawrence, defeated the HMS *Peacock* in a ship-to-ship duel with half the American crew made up of African Americans. In to-tal, the navy enlisted roughly fifteen hundred African Americans during the War of 1812, about 10 percent of its total manpower.[18]

As during the Revolutionary War, more than one navy went to war against the British in 1812. Privateers surfaced in large num-bers, and African Americans went to sea looking for profits as crewmen. Lured by the chance for quick wealth, privateer re-cruiters filled their quotas virtually overnight. One privateer cap-tain in Philadelphia filled his crew requirements "in less than one hour"; a captain in Charleston signed up 130 men in only six hours. The large numbers of privateering ships, however, soon outstripped the number of available men. In addition, many pri-vateer sailors deserted their ships after finding their romantic im-age of pirate life dispelled by the harshness of sea life. Many pri-vateers hired professional recruiting agents to find crewmen, but the agents were less than discriminating. Many privateers went to sea with illegal crewmen: British deserters, underage boys, or even drunks who passed out in taverns and awoke aboard a priva-teer at sea. Runaway slaves were another reliable source of man-power, and newspapers in coastal cities regularly featured rewards for slaves who escaped aboard privateer ships. An 1813 Baltimore newspaper offered a reward of forty dollars for the return of one escaped slave backed by a promise to sue the offending ship owner. As in the Revolutionary War, slaveowners sent their slaves to sea in order to collect their wages for themselves. Andrew Crawford, a Baltimore physician, enlisted his slave aboard the pri-vateer *Tom.* William Wade, captain of the privateer *Chasseur,* col-lected not only his prize money but also the funds of his slave, Joseph Kingsbury, a crewman aboard the vessel.[19]

Sailors serving on privateers faced serious hardships. Life aboard a privateering vessel consisted of long periods of tedium punctuated by the terrors of battle or inclement weather. Discipline was not as tight as the navy's standard of behavior, but officers expected good conduct from their men. Aboard the privateer *Yankee*, for instance, an officer accused of cowardice in battle received no worse than a stern warning only because the outcome of the battle was in the privateer's favor. However, when visiting the *Ariadne*, an American merchant ship, the captain of the *Yankee* received permission from the *Ariadne*'s commanding officer to flog a black member of his crew for mutinous conduct and insulting the privateers. The African American, only referred to as Mr Cuffy, was "tied to the windlass and each of the boat's crew as well as the *Ariadne*'s officers, gave him a dozen to teach him his duty and good manners."[20]

African American privateer crewmen also faced the possibility of fighting British sailors of their own race, as happened to the *Yankee*, cruising off the coast of Africa. After defeating the British sloop HMS *St. Iago* off Cape Verde, crewmen from the *Yankee* found among the British casualties "a black man . . . dead on the cabin floor and five others lay around him apparently dying." Elsewhere on the ship, other black sailors were in the "most dangerous condition." One black sailor, a young cabin boy, received such horrible burns an observer believed "he was literally blown out of his skin." Five of the wounded black British sailors died and received a burial at sea. Many of the English ships off the African coast were staffed by African crewmen. Several days after taking the *St. Iago*, the *Yankee* defeated the armed British merchant vessel *Andalusia* off the coast of modern-day Liberia. Africans composed half the *Andalusia*'s crew but suffered no casualties. Burdened by nearly 150 prisoners, the *Yankee* pardoned its white prisoners after exacting a promise not to fight against the United States. The ship returned its African prisoners to the mainland, but several miles down the coast because the Africans "begged us for God's sake not to put them ashore among these Anthropophagi, as King Peter [the local chieftain] would certainly kill them and eat them." The *Yankee* returned one African prisoner found on the *Andalusia*, a young man named Grand-loo, to his father, Tom Nominee, the king of the Kroomen tribe, a gesture that earned the Americans the king's gratitude. Later, the *Yankee* captured another armed merchantman, the *Fly,* manned by eleven white officers and an African crew. Again, the officers received a parole and the Africans a trip back to the mainland. *Yankee* also encountered the Portuguese schooner *Antonio de Santa Rosa de Lima,* a slaver with a full cargo. Although Congress banned the slave trade to America, these slaves were bound for São Tomé and *Yankee* had no authority to stop them.[21]

The *Yankee* was fortunate to escape from its battles with minimal casualties. Other ships lacked such fortune. Perry's Lake Erie flagship, the *Lawrence,* suffered nearly 80 percent casualties in its battle with the British, so casualties were likely among the numerous African Americans on board. Hundreds of captive African American privateers faced severe hardship after their capture by the British. Incarcerated in a segregated cellblock at Dartmoor Prison, approximately 450 African Americans suffered through months of bitter winters, poor food, and inadequate medical care. The worst eventuality for a privateer was, of course, death. Naval combat, waged at close range with little margin for error, offered the possibility for a painful, gruesome death. Crewmen aboard the privateer *Governor Tompkins* found this out in 1813 after approaching a seemingly innocent British merchantman. The easy target was actually a disguised British frigate, and the *Governor Tompkins* escaped only after a desperate gun battle. During the fight, a British shell mangled the leg of African American sailor John Johnson. Recognizing his impending death, Johnson refused medical care while cheering on his shipmates. His commanding officer, Nathaniel Shaler, praised Johnson's bravery in a letter: "While America has such tars, she has little to fear from the Tyrants of the ocean."[22]

The third navy to employ African American sailors during the War of 1812 consisted of "letters of marque" ships, armed merchant ships empowered to seize enemy merchantmen in the course of their normal trade. For various reasons, the letters of marque ships offered more opportunities to African American seamen than even the privateers. Marque ships did not actively search for enemy merchantmen. With the chances of prize money relatively slim, white sailors preferred privateers, opening billets for African American crewmen. The letters of marque ships paid regular wages, but privateers offered more of a chance for a quick dollar, luring many white sailors to privateers. Also, because the marque vessels required fewer crewmen to operate effectively, whites looking for employment turned to the privateers, which carried far more men of various experience levels. The resulting shortage of trained crewmen forced many marque ships to set sail with skeleton crews. The brig *Charles,* for instance, shipped out with only seven enlisted men, five of them African American. Another vessel, the *Courier,* sailed out of Baltimore with a crew that included an "apprentice boy of Colour" only eight years old.[23]

After the War of 1812, the United States did not fight a foreign enemy for more than thirty years. Friction generated by the American annexation of Texas flared into war with Mexico in 1846. The naval war against Mexico proved very different from earlier American wars, but participation of African Americans continued. In a changed role, the U.S. Navy, without a sizeable adversary, was the blockader tasked with strangling Mexican foreign commerce. Instead of chartering privateers, the United States hunted them. Endless, monotonous days of blockade duty replaced epic ship-to-ship duels. The nature of the conflict generated a huge demand for manpower that was never fully satisfied. Mexico possessed few major ports, and most were inland cities at the mouths of shallow rivers. Without major amphibious operations, the navy could not seize the cities, only blockade them. The navy's existing fleet of large ships could not operate in coastal waters, and the navy quickly constructed a flotilla of shallow-draft warships. Congress authorized the new warships, but finding sailors again proved a problem, partially solved by African American sailors.[24]

In August 1846, Congress authorized the navy to expand from seventy-five hundred to ten thousand men, but, owing to several factors, the navy never grew beyond eight thousand men. The Navy Department did not anticipate a lengthy war, and serious recruiting efforts did not begin until the war was a year old. With little chance for prize money, merchant sailors refused to leave the merchant service and its high wages. Improved relations with Great Britain expanded trade with Europe, and merchant sailors were in great demand. Economic opportunity in the West also drained the pool of available manpower. Rumors of gold in California were already circulating in East Coast cities, and many potential recruits preferred gold mining to naval service. The tedium of blockade duty caused many prospective sailors to turn away from naval duty and prevented the reenlistment of existing seamen. Sailors on the Mexican blockade tolerated the "parching heats of summer, and the long boisterous nights of winter" created by "northers," seasonal storms. Sailors also endured dangerous stretches of "vomito," the dreaded yellow fever. Uncertain how the disease spread, the navy was powerless to prevent it from reaching epidemic proportions in the summer months. Forced to hug close to shore to maintain the blockade, navy crews suffered heavily from the ailment.[25]

Desperate for crewmen, the navy turned to African American sailors yet again, and approximately one thousand black sailors served during the Mexican War. Black merchant sailors faced severe racial restrictions by American overseas shipping companies, and naval service provided an outlet to African American seamen seeking employment. The large numbers of African Americans, both slave and free, employed in the coastal shipping industry made them ideal for the small vessels most valuable in the war against Mexico. Many in the navy also mistakenly believed that African Americans had a natural immunity to yellow fever and other tropical diseases. Based upon this erroneous presumption, the navy sent many African American sailors to the Gulf of Mexico to replace sick white sailors. Unfortunately, the full extent of African American service during the Mexican War is difficult to determine. No one has attempted an extensive study of navy recruiting records, and a shortage of personal recollections from enlisted personnel offers little chance to identify African Americans in the narrative.[26]

The presence of African Americans in the navy during the Mexican War occurred only in the face of constant peacetime efforts to keep blacks out of military service. The first of many attempts to ban the peacetime enlistment of African Americans came with the Militia Act of 1792. Congress proposed a nationwide militia force derived from state volunteers that excluded

African Americans. The law did not have an immediate impact upon the navy, as the service disbanded after the Revolution. As part of the legislation re-creating the navy in 1798, however, Secretary of the Navy Benjamin Stoddard, following a congressional mandate, issued orders to all recruiters that "no Negroes or Mulatoes are to be admitted" into the service. Like many subsequent attempts to ban African Americans from the navy, this law proved impossible to follow. The Quasi-War created a pressing need for sailors to fight the French, and navy recruiters subsequently ignored the navy directive and enlisted African American sailors. The continued recruitment led Captain Edward Preble to remind a subordinate that he could not "Ship Black Men" in 1803, a sign that African Americans continued to serve. A more effective restriction governed the Marine Corps, however. In 1798, Major William W. Burrows, commanding the marines, prohibited African American enlistment in the corps, although he granted permission to certain recruiters to "make use of Blacks or Mulattoes while you recruit, but you cannot enlist them." The Marine Corps ban proved secure for more than a century, and the first African American marines did not appear until World War II demanded their presence in 1942.[27]

The ban on African American sailors, although ignored during the Quasi-War, remained official policy until 1807. After the incident between the *Chesapeake* and *Leopard,* Congress banned the enlistment of foreign nationals in the navy. Foreign sailors, besides triggering international incidents with the British, owed no allegiance to the United States, did not enlist on a predictable schedule, and were considered by many officers to be difficult to control. Consequently, in 1807 Congress forbade the enlistment of foreign sailors but gave the navy permission to enlist free African Americans in their stead. The new policy ensured that African Americans served the navy not only during the War of 1812 but in the years immediately after. Usher Parsons, a navy surgeon during the War of 1812 era, recorded in his memoirs that in 1816 the African Americans aboard the USS *Java* may have made up a tenth of the crew, and generally the same aboard the USS *Guerriere* in 1819. Parsons added, "There seemed to be an entire absence of prejudice against the blacks . . . [this] applies to the crews of other ships." The navy policy is in sharp contrast to the U.S. Army's 1815 decision to discharge all "soldiers of color as being unfit to associate with American soldiers." The navy could ill afford at the time to ban veteran sailors, and African Americans continued to serve.[28]

Although African American sailors manned navy ships, the institution of slavery imposed restrictions on black sailors in many southern states. In 1822, South Carolina passed the first of many state laws referred to as the Negro Seaman Acts. The bloody slave revolt triggered by Denmark Vesey had only recently ended, and frightened slaveowners sought security. Fearful that free black seamen carried insurrectionary thoughts into the state, South Carolina required free African Americans crewmembers to remain incarcerated in city jails until their ship was ready to leave port. Failure to reclaim black crewmembers could result in a maximum one-thousand-dollar fine and two months in jail for the ship owner. The jailed African American would face sale into slavery, regardless of whether the sailor was free. The law applied not only to American merchant vessels but to American warships and foreign merchantmen as well. Despite vigorous protests from the British government and a ruling by a federal circuit court that the law was unconstitutional, South Carolina defied the government and continued to enforce the ordinance. Georgia, North Carolina, Florida, Alabama, and Louisiana enacted similar laws.[29]

Despite southern efforts to restrict the movement of African American sailors, blacks continued to enlist in substantial numbers throughout the 1820s and 1830s. In September 1827, for example, a Philadelphia recruiter reported the enlistment of 102 men, among them 18 African Americans. John Amber, freed by his owner, Commodore Isaac Hull, enlisted in the navy to serve under his former owner. An English writer, touring the USS *Brandywine* at the Norfolk Navy Yard, observed approximately 40 African Americans among the crew. African American sailors went everywhere U.S. ships sailed, including Europe. The USS *Constellation* apparently carried a large complement of African Americans on its 1832 Mediterranean cruise. After observing a cutter full of African American sailors alighting in Trieste, an American observer overheard a group of Europeans conclude that all Americans must be dark skinned and the officers all English.[30]

African Americans also maintained the navy's system of yards, despite an 1818 directive not to hire either free blacks or slaves at shore facilities. The policy intended to reserve federal jobs for white applicants, but African Americans continued to work at shore establishments. Most of the laborers were slaves contracted to the navy in exchange for their wages, a sum much less than the cost of free white laborers. When constructing a stone dry dock at the Norfolk Navy Yard, for instance, the navy replaced white stonecutters, who charged $1.50 per day, with slave laborers, whose owners collected 72 cents per day. The new naval yard constructed at Pensacola, Florida, during the 1830s used predominantly slave labor because insufficient numbers of white workers applied for positions.[31]

Slaves also served aboard ships on the high seas in the antebellum period. Many officers brought their slaves with them when they went to sea, placing the slave's name on the ship's roster and collecting their salary. The navy paid lower wages to officers on shore duty than to officers of the same rank at sea. Frequently, shore-based officers compensated their lower wages by enlisting their slaves as apprentices and sending them to sea. Civilian slaveowners also continued to find maritime employment for their slaves in order to collect their salaries.[32]

The widespread use of slaves as seamen and laborers in the navy did not sit well with various political and social interests as the sectional rivalry over slavery began to heat up. The use of African American sailors increasingly became a contentious political issue that led the navy to institute restrictions and quotas. Economic interests also played a part: the panic of 1837 triggered a serious recession in the American economy, and many idle workers turned to the navy for short-term employment. To make room for unemployed whites, in 1839 Acting Secretary of the Navy Isaac Toucey restricted African American enlistment to 5 percent of monthly recruiting totals and banned the practice of enlisting slaves and sending their wages to their owners. The quota law remained in effect until 1862, and African Americans constituted only 2.5 percent of the personnel of the navy in 1861.[33]

Even with the enlistment quota, many southern congressmen sought to limit the mingling of the races aboard navy ships. In July 1839, Democrats in the House of Representatives tried and failed to pass two motions to modify African American naval service. The first, intended specifically to ban African American testimony in courts-martial, failed by a sixty-eight to sixteen margin. The second, banning outright the enlistment of African Americans in the U.S. military, also failed to achieve a majority, with a vote of seventy-three to eleven. In 1842, Senator John C. Calhoun of South Carolina failed in an attempt to restrict African Americans in the U.S. Navy by limiting their service to cooks, stewards, or servants. Calhoun argued that the interracial crews of the navy would bring white sailors "down to the footing of the negro race to be degraded by being mingled and mixed up with that inferior race." Although approved by the Senate, the measure failed in the House of Representatives.[34]

African American seamen in the antebellum period faced diverse public sentiment. The nation thanked them for their wartime service and sacrifice, but by the end of the antebellum era African Americans faced segregation and resistance from a public that chose to ignore their past collective service and saw only the color of their skin. Nevertheless, African Americans had established a tradition of naval service that would ease their integration into the Civil War navy. Although the navy struggled with public opposition to African American sailors early in the Civil War, a heritage of effective service to the United States ensured a place for African American sailors in the coming conflict and helped to open the door for the return of African Americans into the ranks of the U.S. Army.

Chapter Two

"THE WANTS OF THE SERVICE"

THE POLITICS OF

AFRICAN AMERICAN ENLISTMENT

• When Abraham Lincoln entered the White House on March 4, 1861, the nation faced the severest crisis of its history. Seven states had seceded from the Union, formed the Confederate States of America, and pledged to resist Lincoln's perceived antislavery agenda. Southern mobs seized federal facilities and armed enthusiastic volunteers for military duty to protect their new independent status. Southern states still in the Union contemplated secession, pending the actions of the new administration. Despite Lincoln's conciliatory inauguration speech calling for restraint and the rule of law, the crisis escalated with the April 1861 firing on Fort Sumter, South Carolina. With the South's firing on the flag, passions on both sides were inflamed, and Lincoln faced the reality of civil war.

Among the multitude of decisions and issues now thrust upon the president was the extent of African American participation in the war. While Lincoln tried to woo the South back into the Union by pledging noninterference with slavery, he faced considerable pressure to allow African American participation in the war. He had to wage a war that would require a tremendous amount of manpower, and African Americans were a potential source of soldiers and sailors. The president also owed his office in no small measure to abolitionist sentiment, obligating Lincoln to regard their antislavery goals. Still, Lincoln had to consider the racist attitudes of his own constituency, many of whom might refuse to serve alongside African American military personnel and were far from supporting emancipation.

Political concerns were a minor matter to the U.S. Navy, which faced a daunting mission. The navy had to blockade the three-thousand-mile Confederate coastline, pierced by no fewer than 189 ports and river mouths, to prevent the South from importing the implements of war and maintaining its economy. Union naval forces also sought to seize control of the thousands of miles of navigable southern rivers, the main transportation method of the region and routes of Union invasion. At the same time, the navy retained its prewar mission of protecting Union commerce, especially after the Confederacy began licensing privateers and constructing its own navy to raid Union commerce. Moreover, the Union navy had to rethink its emphasis. During the antebellum period, the navy protected business interests around the globe, a task that required a "blue-water," oceangoing navy of large ships. Naval operations in the South, however, required additional manpower and new types of coastal blockading and riverine ships, along with a reevaluation of navy strategy and doctrine.[1]

The navy had an imposing task to perform and little material with which to accomplish the mission. At the time of the firing on Fort Sumter, the U.S. Navy boasted only 76 ships, of which only 42 were in commission, the remainder laid up in storage. Thirty of the commissioned vessels of the navy were on foreign stations in Asia and South America or suppressing the slave trade off the African coast. Of the remaining 12, 8 were at sea, beyond immediate communication with the Navy Department. The navy faced a painful period of quick growth. Secretary of the Navy Gideon Welles scoured northern ports for vessels suitable for shallow-water blockade duty and operations on southern rivers, and the navy rapidly expanded into a potent force before the end of 1861. Within eight months, the Union navy had purchased 136 ships and contracted for the construction of 52 vessels, to be finished by the end of the year.[2]

The greatest need of the navy was manpower. The antebellum navy was restricted to only seventy-six hundred men, a small but experienced group of veterans. Within weeks of the attack on Fort Sumter, Lincoln authorized the enlistment of an additional eighteen thousand sailors for at least one, but not more than three, years. The navy expanded to more than thirteen thousand men by July 1861, but even this number proved inadequate. Ships acquired for blockade duty idled in port for want of crewmembers, forcing the navy to offer short one-year enlistments to attract recruits. Although African Americans would become an obvious source of manpower to the Union navy, the political decisions facing the Lincoln administration hindered efforts to enlist African American sailors.[3]

The first decision facing Lincoln was how to approach the conflict in terms of established international laws of war. Either the North could recognize the South's independence and wage war as two sovereign nations, or Lincoln could reject the Confederacy's claim to independence and proclaim the region in rebellion against federal authority. Both legal viewpoints had their advantages and disadvantages to the North. If the federal government recognized the South's independence, Lincoln would have full authority to raise an army, invade the Confederacy, and bring the region back into the Union by force. Lincoln could legally justify the trade blockade that the U.S. Navy was imposing upon the Confederate coast. The Confederacy's European trading partners, particularly Great Britain with its powerful navy, would be obligated to recognize the legitimacy of the blockade or risk war with the United States. Soldiers on both sides captured in battle would be regarded as prisoners of war, subject to accepted rules of treatment, handling, and exchange, whereas prisoners would have no protection in an insurrection. Recognizing the Confederacy would also free a victorious North to rewrite slavery laws in the South, an obvious desire of the abolitionists who backed Lincoln.[4]

Recognizing the South was fraught with dangers, however. A legitimate Confederacy could negotiate military alliances with foreign states, allowing European military powers to enter the war on the Southern side, especially if an invasion provoked sympathy for the Confederacy. Deprived of its access to cotton by the Union blockade of the South's ports, Great Britain might be tempted to use its naval might to relieve the economic pressure. The cash-starved Confederates might also borrow money from foreign states, thus prolonging the war beyond the South's meager financial resources. Lincoln also feared that a military invasion of the South, even if successful, would cause lasting hostility, lingering for years and inflaming future conflicts. On an ideological level, legitimizing the Confederacy would be a public admission that the South had a right to leave the Union, undermining Lincoln's stated purpose of preserving the Union with prewar institutions intact.[5]

Lincoln's other option was to declare the rebellious region to be an area in a state of insurrection, which the president preferred for several reasons. For one, declaring the South to be in rebellion denied the Confederate government any realistic chance of political legitimacy. Foreign nations would have to risk war with the United States if they engaged in negotiations with or formally recognized the Confederate government. The restriction on receiving diplomats did not deter Great Britain from recognizing Confederate representatives, prompting the 1861 *Trent* Affair. Union Captain Charles Wilkes, commanding the USS *San Jacinto*, removed two Confederate agents, John Mason and John Slidell, from the British vessel RMS *Trent* on the high seas. Wilkes became a hero, but Prime Minister Lord Palmerston threatened war over this violation of British sovereignty. While many Southerners eagerly awaited a British declaration of war, the quick release of Mason and Slidell prevented an expansion of the crisis. Many in England recognized that the profits of trading with the North greatly outweighed the benefits of obtaining Confederate cotton. Thus, European recognition remained an optimistic, but ultimately futile, aspiration of the Confederacy.[6]

Denying the Confederates political legitimacy also kept the door open for reconciliation. Lincoln hoped that, as time passed and passions cooled, moderates in the South could rally back to the Union without feeling they had betrayed a legitimate southern government. Further, the Lincoln administration favored the option of suppressing the rebellion because there was no definitive opinion in the Constitution on how rebellions were to be subdued or who had the authority to suppress them. Free from congressional powers to declare or regulate the war, Lincoln would be free to prosecute the conflict as he saw fit, although Congress would obviously have considerable influence on the process.[7]

Subduing the Confederate insurrection had its own problems, however. Without a declaration of war, the blockade of southern ports had no legitimacy, amounting to nothing more than a restriction of free trade. The British protested that, if the South was simply in rebellion, the North could not restrict honest trade in southern ports while leaving northern ports open. Moreover, international law demanded that for a blockade to be recognized it had to be "in force." Ships had to be on station to regulate the passage of merchant ships in and out of the restricted port; a paper blockade was not legitimate. Established at the 1856 Congress of Paris, the international rules for naval blockades established a legitimate means to regulate wartime trade. Although the United States did not sign the agreement, America and other nonsigning nations agreed to abide by its terms. To ensure European recognition of the blockade, Lincoln had to establish quickly a significant naval force near the Confederate coast.[8]

Also, labeling Southern troops as rebels placed them in the category of criminals guilty of treason instead of soldiers fighting for a legitimate government. The Constitution established the penalty for treason as death. Lincoln faced the quandary of imposing the death sentence on the thousands of Southerners who fought in its armies or supported its government. The Lincoln administration solved this dilemma by ignoring traditional expectations and treating captured soldiers as prisoners of war.[9]

Established federal laws, though, remained unaffected by the South's status as rebellious states. The Lincoln administration could not shape the institution of slavery by invalidating existing law and instead had to continue enforcing existing slavery measures. Chief among these was the Fugitive Slave Act of 1850, which required the federal government to return to bondage any escaped slaves under its jurisdiction. This would become a major problem when slaves escaping the Confederacy encountered Union naval forces, because many officers were strongly abolitionist or had practical reasons for resisting their return. In order to accommodate their war aims to existing slave laws, Lincoln and the Congress would have to create new legislation, advancing Union war aims while balancing the risk of backlash from Northerners opposed to equal status for African Americans.

Another restraint Lincoln faced in recruiting African Americans into the army and navy was the necessity of keeping as many states as possible in the Union. Seven states had seceded before the firing on Fort Sumter (South Carolina, Georgia, Florida, Alabama, Mississippi, Louisiana, and Texas) followed by four more after the attack (Virginia, Tennessee, North Carolina, and Arkansas). The remaining slave states forming the border between the Union and the Confederacy (Delaware, Maryland, Kentucky, and Missouri) were still noncommittal, and Lincoln feared that their secession would prove a fatal blow to the Union. Although Delaware, with its relatively small size and population, could not significantly aid the Confederate cause, it was a slave state and therefore a threat to leave the Union and deprive the North of its assets. Maryland, surrounding the District of Columbia, had to stay in the Union lest Washington become a besieged bastion deep in the rebellion or, worse, fall to the Confederacy. Missouri jutted like a knife into the regions north of the Mason-Dixon Line that did not permit slavery, a position that threatened not only Union navigation on the upper Mississippi River but future free-soil settlement on the Great Plains. Kentucky, however, was the border state most vital to the Union's future. As a Confederate state, Kentucky could restrict movement on the Ohio River, menace the western states of the Union as a base for Confederate invasions, feed the South's armies with its agricultural abundance, and transport rebel armies with its horses and mules. Lincoln better than anyone underscored Kentucky's importance when he exclaimed, "I hope I have God on our side, but I must have Kentucky."[10]

The importance of the border states in the strategic balance of the two combatants is inestimable. While the Confederacy recruited more soldiers in the border states, Union control of the states themselves more than offset that advantage, geographically and politically. Control of Maryland ensured Union dominance of Chesapeake Bay, allowing the Union navy to apply its blockade without extending patrols along Maryland's lengthy seacoast. Kentucky's river systems plunged deep into the Confederacy, forcing the South to disperse its western forces to meet any axis of Union advance. Dominance of Missouri gave the Union a foothold to threaten the trans-Mississippi southern states. Keeping the border states also had political benefits. If they had joined the Confederacy, the Union would consist of only sixteen states to rival the South's fifteen. Great Britain might conclude that the Confederacy was a legitimate government and offer formal recognition and military assistance. From Lincoln's perspective, the key to maintaining the border states in the Union was to move cautiously, avoid actions perceived as provocative, and reinforce his commitment to the prewar status quo.

Preserving the border states, however, had to balance with the efforts necessary to suppress the rebellion in the rest of the South. Lincoln had learned the hard way that what seemed to him to be a necessary measure to save the Union could have damaging outcomes. Two days after the surrender of Fort Sumter, Lincoln had exercised a 1795 law to call for seventy-five thousand state militiamen into federal service for ninety days. This seemingly innocuous action, taken as a prudent security measure, seemed an aggressive and unconstitutional threat to states' rights. In response, Virginia, Tennessee, North Carolina, and Arkansas joined the Confederate camp. Lincoln, therefore, had to step lightly around the issue of African American service in the Union military, lest fears of armed, freed slaves turn the border states to the South's advantage. Thus, the enlistment of African Americans remained a low priority.[11]

Lincoln's policy of restricting African American enlistment to avoid controversy in the border states received a test in Missouri. On August 30, 1861, Major General John C. Frémont declared martial law throughout the state, threatened summary executions for Confederate raiders, and emancipated the slaves of Southern sympathizers, justifying his actions as military necessity. By denying Missouri Confederates their property, Frémont reasoned, he could cripple their ability to support rebellion within the state, a theory that gained Frémont great praise from abolitionists and Secretary of War Simon Cameron. Frémont failed to consult Lincoln before issuing the order, and many Confederate sympathizers in Kentucky took the order as a true sign of attitudes in the North. Many of the state's citizens appeared ready to support secession. "We could stand several defeats like Bull Run," wrote one

Kentuckian to Lincoln, "better than we can this proclamation if endorsed by the Administration." Lincoln quickly revoked Frémont's edict and transferred him to a different command.[12]

A similar unauthorized situation emerged again in May 1862. Major General David Hunter, an ardent abolitionist and commander of the Department of the South (encompassing Union-held beachheads in South Carolina, Georgia, and Florida) issued a sweeping emancipation of all slaves in his department. Hunter took the additional provocative step of imposing conscription to form slave regiments, providing his African American troops with weapons and distinctive uniforms. Hunter thinly justified his actions on the premise that, in the absence of adequate numbers of white troops, black soldiers were necessary to maintain public order in the occupied regions of the South. Hunter feared that civil chaos in occupied regions would distract the Union army from military operations, and black troops could garrison posts to control the Confederate population, freeing the Union army to engage in other actions. In addition, Hunter worried that freed slaves would engage in "robbery and plunder" under the control of the first demagogue who emerged to lead them, undermining the Lincoln administration's efforts to ease the South back into the Union. Despite such arguments, the administration revoked Hunter's order and issued a public censure.[13]

While Lincoln faced considerable pressure against the use of African American military personnel, other political forces urged the president to make the conflict a war to end slavery. Abolitionist votes and political organization had been an essential component of Lincoln's victory in the 1860 election, and he could put off the abolitionists only at the risk of losing their support. As one of his most important constituencies, Lincoln needed the abolitionists, especially their newspapers, to maintain the North's commitment to the war. The Union's disastrous defeat at the Battle of Bull Run in July 1861, and the subsequent refusal of Lincoln's primary general, George B. McClellan, to engage in operations until the spring of 1862, increased Lincoln's need for public supporters.

For the most part, the abolitionists maintained their support of Lincoln, despite some antislavery advocates' view of his administration as less than committed to their political and social agenda. Especially irksome were Lincoln's actions to keep the border states in the Union, with many abolitionists complaining that the president was coddling and accommodating the hated slaveowners while ignoring the demands of those who had put him in office. "How many times are we to save Kentucky," wrote abolitionist Senator Benjamin Wade of Ohio, "and lose our self respect?" Frederick Douglass also criticized Lincoln's actions: "These Border Slave States have been the mill-stone about the neck of the Government, and their so-called loyalty has been the very best shield to the treason of the Cotton States." The revocation of John Frémont's Missouri edict contributed to the growing discord among Lincoln's political supporters. To many, Lincoln's actions appeared a clear sign of the president's unwillingness to address the slave issue or, worse, his complicity with the slaveowners still in the Union.[14]

Most Northerners, despite the attitudes of the abolitionists, supported Lincoln's policies. President only by a minority vote created by the division of the Democratic Party, Lincoln guessed correctly that the vast percentage of Unionists would not support a war for the liberation of slaves. If Lincoln attempted to force the issue, his support could quickly evaporate. Northern racists feared freed slaves migrating into the North and West, requiring difficult social readjustment and accommodation, which most in the North were unwilling to grant. Preserving the Union was an end unto itself, most still believed, with slavery left intact and unaffected. The *New York Times* wrote in April 1861, "Slavery is merely the existing . . . cause which has produced secession." A North that would not accommodate freed slaves, Lincoln fully realized, would also not fight to free them. Thus, Lincoln's goal of eventually freeing the slaves was secondary to immediate war concerns.[15]

Unfortunately for Lincoln, while abolitionists were a vocal minority in the North, their political influence was considerable. Besides important congressional abolitionists such as Senator Benjamin Wade, Lincoln faced antislavery advocates in his own cabinet. At the 1860 Republican Convention, Lincoln emerged as a dark horse for the presidential nomination. To shore up support within the party after his election, Lincoln accepted his main political rivals into his cabinet, though some of them opposed his early war policy of restraining African American enlistment in the military. Secretary of State William H. Seward of New York and Treasury Secretary Salmon P. Chase of Ohio dominated Lincoln's cabinet. Both believed they were better suited to be president than Lincoln, and each despised the other. Secretary of War Simon Cameron of Pennsylvania was a staunch Republican with a reputation for shady business dealings. His dedication to freedom for slaves depended upon the political benefits such an act would confer. Another steadfast Republican, Secretary of the Navy Gideon Welles from Connecticut, possessed a misanthropic reputation that concealed a strong dedication to Lincoln and to African American rights.[16]

Other members of Lincoln's cabinet opposed the abolitionist sentiment. Postmaster General Montgomery Blair of Maryland supported Lincoln's stated aim of saving the Union, as did Secretary of the Interior Caleb B. Smith of Indiana, nominated solely for his ability to deliver western votes. Attorney General Edward Bates of Missouri, another representative from the vital border states, also avidly supported Lincoln's early war policy. Lincoln's own cabinet divided over controversial actions like Frémont's and Hunter's emancipation orders. Seward, Chase, and Cameron supported the freeing of slaves, both as an emancipation measure and as a military blow to the South. Other cabinet members, especially southerners Bates and Blair, supported the president's decision to restrain the two generals. Lincoln's decision to revoke the emancipation orders generated dissent from his own advisors, especially Secretary of War Cameron, whose views regarding African American enlistment were to cost him later in the war.[17]

Another political pressure on Lincoln was the growing demand by free African Americans in the North to participate in the war. Many northern African Americans saw the war not only as a means of striking down the institution of slavery but also as an opportunity to press their demands for full citizenship in a reunited nation. Even in the slavery-free North, African American rights were neither consistent nor secure. Suffrage was restricted to a few New England states, African Americans generally could not testify in court against a white defendant, and economic rights were not ensured. The justification for such restrictions in the North was that these rights were reserved for citizens of the United States, which free African Americans, not to mention slaves, were not. The conflict with the South, therefore, became a venue where African Americans, by demonstrating their loyalty and willingness to sacrifice for the benefit of the federal government, could improve their social status or even gain citizenship. Many African American leaders believed blacks should deny their services to the government until offered the reward of citizenship. Frederick Douglass told a Boston crowd, "Nothing short of open recognition of the Negro's manhood, his rights as such to have a country equally with others, would induce me to join the army in any capacity." Many other African Americans, however, eagerly volunteered their services to the federal government after the assault on Fort Sumter.[18]

After the war began, hundreds of African Americans joined loosely organized military formations and presented themselves to the federal government for war service. Lincoln would have none of it. The official policy of the federal government remained, as Secretary Cameron wrote a group of African Americans volunteering for military service, one of rejecting African American volunteers: "This Department has no intention at present to call into the service of the Government any colored soldiers." Arming African Americans would destroy the president's claim of a war to preserve the Union, drive the border states into the Confederacy, and legitimize Southern propaganda depicting Lincoln as a tool of the radical abolitionists.[19]

Despite their offer to participate in the war, in spite of the obvious need for military manpower, African Americans could not join the Union armies in 1861. The Union navy, however, was quite different. Using the prewar limit of 5 percent African American enlistment per month established in 1839, the navy had quietly added more than nine hundred African American crewmen. Secretary of the Navy Gideon Welles had permitted the enlistment of African American sailors because it did not violate existing law or represent a change in federal policy and therefore did not attract the attention of either proslavery Northerners or radical abolitionists.

By early 1862, the Lincoln administration's determination to prevent African American enlistment was seriously eroding. The policy would soon be reversed, permitting full African American participation in the army and navy by the end of the year. As battle after battle occurred during the course of the year, the early expectation of a short war soon disappeared. With this discovery came the realization in the North that more manpower than originally estimated would be needed to win the war, manpower that African Americans, earlier rejected, were still willing to contribute. The securing of the border states also freed Lincoln's hands to create policy regarding African Americans. Union military victories in Tennessee and the upper Mississippi Valley and the suppression of pro-Confederate activities in Maryland firmly established the border states in the Union camp, reducing the need to placate local racist sentiment. The use of African American manpower gained support by news that the Confederates were employing slaves on military construction projects and fortifications and had armed slaves as soldiers of rebellion. The rumor gained credence on June 28, 1861, when the Tennessee legislature began enlisting free blacks into the state militia. The relatively few African American recruits were restricted to manual labor at lower pay than white soldiers, but the impression that the South would create an army of slaves continued to grow. Still, the biggest impetus to change federal policy came because of practical solutions to events unfolding far away from Washington, D.C.[20]

From the firing on Fort Sumter and the imposing of the federal blockade, fugitive southern slaves had approached Union military forces, appealing for protection. To slaves, the presence of Union troops offered perhaps a one-time chance to escape their bondage and attain freedom. While antebellum slaves had fled long distances to find liberty in the North, to slaves in the early months of the war it must have seemed the North had come to them, and the lure of freedom was too strong to resist.

Reports of the arrival of contrabands aboard navy ships soon reached the Navy Department as the number of fugitives quickly accumulated. For instance, Commander O. S. Glisson, commanding the USS *Mount Vernon* blockading the mouth of Virginia's Rappahannock River, picked up six contrabands near the Stingray lighthouse, darkened by the Confederates to impede enemy navigation. The fugitives had fled because they claimed the Confederates were "arming the negroes, with the intention of placing them in the front of the battle." The contrabands informed Glisson that the Confederate militia in the region were low on ammunition and had murdered the only "Union man" in the region, leaving his wife and children to fend for themselves. Within a few days, Glisson had received another ten contrabands, who consumed his provisions "faster than I think is desirable." Glisson requested, and received, permission to ship his passengers to Maryland.[21]

A few escaped slaves were not a great concern for the federal government. When the number became hundreds, then thousands, in a matter of weeks, the situation demanded the establishment of some official policy. Some officers refused to admit escaped slaves into the lines or aboard their ships or held the slaves for retrieval by their southern owners. An example is Major General Henry W. Halleck's General Order 3, issued on November 20, 1861. Commanding the Department of the West, Halleck ordered that no contrabands be admitted to Union lines and those already present be ejected, claiming that fugitives were hindering military operations. Among navy officers, Commander Thomas Craven, commanding the Potomac Flotilla, frequently returned contrabands from his jurisdiction to their owners. Others sheltered the slaves, reflecting their abolitionist leanings or the rationale that a slave in federal custody was a slave whose labor did not benefit the enemy. The commander of the USS *Isaac Smith* off the coast of Florida informed his commanding officer that "the whole of the banks of the river as far as one can see is planted with corn . . . If we carry their darkies off they cannot gather it; one consolation."[22]

The primary hindrance to retaining all escaped slaves was Lincoln's own opinion that the conflict with the South was a rebellion and not a war against a legitimate nation. As a rebellion, all federal laws remained in force, including the 1850 Fugitive Slave Act, obliging the federal government to return to their owners all fugitive slaves in their jurisdiction. Legally, the Union military could not shield escaped slaves from their owners, until a neat bit of legal maneuvering prevented the return of escaped slaves and opened the door for additional slaves to escape.[23]

When Virginia seceded, the Union retained strategic Fort Monroe, at the entrance to Hampton Roads, Virginia. A Union enclave deep in Confederate territory, shielded by thick walls and navy vessels offshore, Fort Monroe became a magnet for Virginia and Maryland slaves fleeing their owners. Commanding the vital location was Major General Benjamin F. Butler, a Massachusetts lawyer and politician with considerable abolitionist leanings. Less than three weeks into his command, Butler had accumulated a number of slave refugees at Fort Monroe and, lacking clear orders as to their status or disposition, determined to keep them there. When slaveowners appeared at Fort Monroe in May 1861, demanding their property, Butler refused them, claiming the slaves were "contraband of war."[24]

Contraband goods, products eligible for seizure to deny its use to an enemy, usually applied to more mundane items such as food, ships, or horses. Following the accepted rules of war, Butler believed he could seize property used to benefit the enemy. By extension, that included slaves used to build enemy fortifications and roads. The broad legal interpretation of the rules of war became accepted practice by all Union forces, and "contraband" became the universal term for any escaped slave. After Butler's actions, refusing Confederate attempts to recover escaped slaves became common, although some officers still opted to return slaves or refuse them sanctuary. Butler's policy at Fort Monroe, along with the growing number of escaped slaves lured by the opportunity of freedom, prompted Congress to pass the First Confiscation Act on August 6, 1861.

Under the Confiscation Act, an owner forfeited any claim on slaves used to construct fortifications or infrastructure for the Confederate government. Escaped slaves not used in this manner were ineligible for protection, and the navy warned captains not to accept escaped slaves from border or loyal states. It soon became apparent, however, that disproving an escaped slave's claim of being a Confederate laborer was impossible. Virtually all contrabands that reached sympathetic Union garrisons received protection. A few Union officers continued to refuse contraband access to Union lines until March 31, 1862, when the army and navy made it a military crime, punishable by dishonorable discharge, for officers to return any contrabands to the enemy.[25]

An example of the Confiscation Act at work appears in the logbook of the USS *Brazileira*, blockading Beaufort, North Carolina, on November 21, 1861. The captain of the vessel, Lieutenant Charles F. W. Behm, received on board five contrabands named Caesar Burns, Ezekiel Wallace, Jeremiah Washington, John Stanley, and Dempsey Hill, the property of James Romely, Joehl H. Davis, James Ward, Joseph Robertson, and Sally Jones, respectively. Although none of the contrabands had directly worked on Confederate military projects, all had skills potentially useful to the South. Burns was a stevedore, Wallace had aided the Confederate Coast Survey, Washington was a mason, Stanley was a carpenter, and Hill was a ship's pilot. Behm further justified his harboring of the fugitives by noting that all of the erstwhile owners were "strong secessionists."[26]

The key component of the legislation was that, while contrabands were no longer slaves under the terms of the First Confiscation Act, they were also not free. A guarantee of military protection was not an emancipation order, as the federal government was still wary of potential backlash in the North and border states created by seeming too abolitionist. As fugitives accumulated in federal custody, "contraband camps" under federal jurisdiction were created to house the escaped slaves while preventing them from migrating into the northern states, remaining for the time being in a state of legal limbo. Nevertheless, Butler's legal maneuvering was an important first step toward emancipation without violating Lincoln's political limitations; blacks escaped the status of slave property, but were not freed as people.

Many Confederates, raised on the propaganda that slavery was natural and beneficial to African Americans, could not understand the contrabands' desire for freedom. One Confederate wrote, "The temptation of cheap goods, freedom, and paid labor cannot be withstood. . . . They are traitors who may pilot an enemy into your bedchamber. They know every road and swamp and creek and plantation in the country, and are the worst of spies. If the absconding is not stopped, the negro property of the country will be of little value."[27]

Ironically, the antebellum South's own legal system aided Butler's efforts to justify the retention of contrabands. While the South defended slavery as an issue of property rights, the South's laws and legal system had granted, to a limited extent, recognition that slaves were more than mere property. Southern courts had long debated the legal status of slaves, particularly the victims of or those charged with felonies, and two divergent legal opinions developed. The first position held that slaves were the chattel property of their owners and therefore not responsible for any criminal acts they may have committed. If a slave murdered his or her owner, a slave could no sooner face prosecution for murder than could a horse that falls and kills its owner. Consequently, a slaveowner would not risk trial for the murder of a slave; the owner was simply disposing of his or her property. The second legal opinion held that slaves were human beings, aware of their moral responsibilities to uphold social standards, simply in a state of bondage. Thus, a slave faced prosecution in court for crimes he or she committed, but masters also faced trial for the abuse or murder of a slave, since it was violence against another person.[28]

Throughout most of the South, the latter legal viewpoint dominated, as reflected in antebellum law. As early as 1806, Louisiana had established laws providing for the punishment of whites who murdered slaves, and South Carolina imposed a five-hundred-dollar fine and six months in prison on those convicted of slave manslaughter in 1821. Between the Revolution and the Civil War, Virginia courts prosecuted slaveowners for excessive violence against their slaves at least thirteen times. Generally, the courts condoned violence to correct a slave's behavior, but irrational violence beyond simple punishment could lead to the prosecution of the owner. Thus, its own legal codes undermined the South's defense of waging civil war to protect the institution of slavery and sanctity of property, which granted slaves the limited status of people rather than property.[29]

Though contrabands were not welcome in the army, the navy had no such compunction. Butler's contraband policy proved to be a godsend to Navy Secretary Welles, who was grappling with the problem of fleshing out the blockade that Lincoln had ordered. With ships coming into commission but not enough sailors to man them, Welles sought to use the contrabands aboard navy ships. On September 21, 1861, he authorized naval recruiters to enlist any escaped slaves willing to join the service. Welles based his policy upon two rationales. First, contrabands sheltered by the navy were consuming navy resources without any benefit in return. Since the contrabands could not "be expelled from the service to which they have resorted," Welles believed that offering fugitive slaves an opportunity to repay the navy for its generosity was reasonable. Second, as the contrabands were no longer slaves, they "should not be compelled to render necessary and regular services without stated compensation," and Welles ordered that contraband enlistees receive fair wages for their work. Therefore, although not recognized as free men by the United States government, contrabands enlisted, trained, and served in the same manner as free seamen. Avoiding the implication that the navy recruited contrabands with status equal to white enlistees, Welles restricted contraband enlistees, despite age or previous sea experience, to the rank of "boys," with a monthly wage of ten dollars and standard navy rations. Despite the lower wages, navy service attracted large numbers of African American recruits. An army officer observed in March 1862, "A considerable number have taken service in the navy. . . . Service in the navy is decidedly popular with them . . . they get $10 a month, and are entitled to all the privileges of the ships' crews, and besides, have absolute control of the earnings of their own labor."[30]

Although criticized by some historians as a racist policy meant to deny African Americans equal status within the navy, Welles's policy was a fair balance between manpower needs and political realities. Following the lead established by the Lincoln administration, Welles was careful about the image the navy was projecting by accepting large numbers of African American recruits. Exceeding the limits established by the president had caused problems for General Frémont and others who listened too closely to the advice of radicals and abolitionists. Such independence cost Secretary of War Simon Cameron his position in January 1862. Lincoln had grown weary of Cameron's pressure to permit African American soldiers to enlist in the Union army. Aided by whispers of rampant corruption at the War Department, Lincoln removed Cameron from his office, replaced him with Edwin M. Stanton of Ohio, and shipped the former secretary off to Europe as minister to Russia. Welles faced similar replacement if his actions regarding African American enlistment surpassed the president's wishes.[31]

Further, even the meager employment of contrabands aboard ship created a legal quandary: Did the navy have the legal right to hire contrabands? Under the terms of the First Confiscation Act, contrabands were no longer slaves, but they were also not free, and their status as property or human beings remained unsettled. The navy presumed, without guidance from any legal authority, that it could hire contrabands, disregarding any property claims by slaveowners, on the premise that contrabands were wards of the federal government. Until the legal clarification of contraband status, the navy risked repercussions from Northerners who opposed extending free status to southern slaves as well as legal challenges that the navy was seizing personal property without due process.

Welles was able to elude most criticism from northern racists by the very system of naval recruiting. Unlike army volunteer regiments, organized and paid for by the states, the navy maintained recruiting as a federal responsibility. Thus, states that would not use their resources to enlist black regiments equally with white formations had no say in how the navy recruited its manpower. Since enlistees generally joined the navy at a relatively small number of urban navy yards on the East Coast, recruiting was generally out of sight and out of mind. Naval recruits would assemble within the navy yard only for a few days until distributed throughout the fleet. Their training took place at sea and on the job, out of sight of the public.[32]

Next, by granting monthly wages and rations to enlisted contrabands, the navy exceeded the benefits granted to contrabands employed by the army. Following the Confederate lead of using slaves on military projects, the army began hiring contrabands to labor for the Union. Wages varied widely between locations and were very low; some construction projects provided rations only.

Since the army hired the contrabands as laborers, employment was not reliable or consistent. The full wages and rations that came with the rank of boy at least provided the black sailor who accepted a post in the navy with a reliable, insured income. Moreover, the navy pay came with an allotment system, which forwarded a designated percentage of the sailor's pay to the crewman's family. Many contraband families, restricted to contraband camps without a means of financial support, relied heavily on allotted navy pay, especially as many contraband camps soon became a hellish place to live.[33]

Cornelia Hancock, a nurse in a contraband camp near Washington, D.C., recalled seeing twelve or fourteen people crowded into small rooms. The sole well in the camp frequently malfunctioned, leaving camp occupants to cart water in from Washington. Forced by limited space to sleep in the camp hospital, contrabands soon contracted contagious diseases to which they had no regional immunity. Rather than increase aid to the camp, the army preferred to spend its money elsewhere. Not surprisingly, given the chance to escape the horrors of the camps, contrabands accepted the offer of employment. For instance, in July 1862 the USS *Pocahontas* stopped at contraband camps at Georgetown, South Carolina, in search of replacement crewmen. The vessel's surgeon went ashore "to select such as were fit for the general service. . . . He has selected some ninety."[34]

The restriction of black enlistees to the rank of boys applied only to contrabands, as northern and foreign-born blacks were free to enlist at ranks commensurate with their skill. Moreover, recruiting records indicate that the navy enlisted contrabands at higher ranks than the secretary had authorized. Among a sample of more than 900 African Americans enlisted in 1861, only 58 (6.3%) entered as boys, with the largest percentage of black recruits, 638 (68.8%), enlisting as landsmen.[35] Of the 638 African American landsmen, 311 came from the northern states, eighteen were foreign recruits, with the other 309 originating in the South or not providing a place of origin on their recruiting form.[36]

Events in the summer of 1862 further promoted African American efforts to contribute to Union victory. Union victory at New Orleans could not offset the failure of the Peninsular Campaign, defeat at the Second Battle of Bull Run, and embarrassing efforts in the Shenandoah Valley. In addition, the horrific casualties generated by the summer campaigns prompted a new evaluation of the use of African American troops. As losses grew, more Northerners believed African American troops could die just as well as white soldiers. George H. Hepworth, a chaplain in the 47th Massachusetts Infantry Regiment, questioned why "the vast tide of death should . . . sweep away our fathers and sons, before we . . . give the black man the one boon he has been asking for so long—permission to fight for our common country." Michigan Senator Zachariah Chandler, a member of the Committee on the Conduct of the War, was particularly incensed that Michigan troops had "to dig ditches, cut down timber & do hard work." Claiming the army wasted 40,000 troops in this manner, Chandler believed slaves confiscated from rebel plantations, contrabands "who only ask freedom in return," could readily perform the task. The Union army's reluctance to employ African American personnel ("negrophoby," as Chandler labeled it) declined as the demand for troops to replenish the ranks continued to grow. Besides the need for military manpower, many Northerners desired somehow to strike back at the South if military victory was beyond the North's immediate grasp. Congress responded by enacting two additional pieces of legislation that aided African American efforts to enter military service.[37]

On July 17, 1862, following the prompting of the radical Committee on the Conduct of the War, and over the objections of President Lincoln, Congress passed the Second Confiscation Act. Meant solely to be a punishment of civilians who supported the Confederacy, the act permitted federal forces to seize any property, slaves included, in any state currently in rebellion. Contrabands were no longer required to prove they had been used as laborers on Confederate construction projects to gain entry to Union lines, and the flow of contrabands measurably increased. Moreover, the act took one of the first steps toward the emancipation of slaves, declaring that slaves confiscated under the terms of the law "shall be deemed captives of war and shall be forever free." In passing the Second Confiscation Act, Congress ignored the double standard it was creating regarding the freeing of slaves, which contradicted Lincoln's political stance since the beginning of the war. In the language of the document, the Confiscation Act seized slaves as the property of those in rebellion yet justified their freedom as captives of war. In other terms, Congress was trying to have it both ways, suppressing the Confederate rebellion using methods justified only in wars against legitimate governments.[38]

On the same day Congress passed the Second Confiscation Act, the Militia Act also became law. With hopes for a short war dashed, demands for manpower high, and the number of voluntary recruits low, the Militia Act authorized President Lincoln to draft into the army men from the Union state militias for three years of military service. The government considered any man between the ages of eighteen and forty-five a potential soldier. The Militia Act permitted the enlistment of African Americans freed by the Second Confiscation Act "for any military or naval service for which they may be found competent." The navy embraced the opportunity to enlist additional manpower, but the army found African Americans competent only as military laborers and support troops. While still not full participants in the war against the Confederacy, African Americans came a step closer to combat.[39]

Both laws corresponded closely with events in the summer of 1862 that aided the enrollment of blacks in the navy. With the exception of a small strip between Vicksburg and Port Hudson, the entire Mississippi River was in the hands of the Union navy. A region of the South where slaves outnumbered whites, the Mississippi Valley offered the navy a huge pool of African Americans to recruit under the terms of the Militia Act. Likewise, while the army's Peninsular Campaign did not meet expectations, the Union navy's operations close to the Virginia coastline gave the navy an opportunity to gather escaped slaves willing to serve. With a growing number of refugee slaves, the navy established its own system of contraband camps, which differed sharply from the squalid encampments established by the army.

Unlike the army, which concentrated its contraband camps on Union soil to supervise better their African Americans charges, the contraband camps of the navy were in the South, keeping the contrabands close to the area where they would serve.

Contrabands remained relatively close to their families even when aboard ship. Former slaves, unaccustomed to weather variations, escaped exposure to the harsh northern winters that afflicted army contraband camps and to the wide assortment of diseases for which southern contrabands had no immunity. In addition, the navy did not have to take ships off the blockade to transport fugitives north. Also, contrabands raised in the region could act as guides and pilots for Union ships unfamiliar with the local tides and rivers. Custody of contraband camps changed frequently during the war between the navy, army, or other government institutions, but in 1863 the navy operated thirteen camps with a capacity of approximately eight thousand contrabands.[40]

Camps were highly organized by the navy officers appointed as their caretakers. Contrabands at St. Simon's, South Carolina, received rigidly enforced daily rations to ensure adequate supplies for the winter, and the nearby fields were cultivated to produce food for the camp and cotton for mills in the North. Contrabands not willing to work had their rations reduced, with the worst disciplinary cases transferred to Fernandina, Florida. The occupants of the camp worked on gathering basic living materials, like lumber for shelters, and patrolling the region in search of hostile Confederate forces. Although Union gunboats were close by in case of danger, the contrabands were their own first line of defense.[41]

This is not to say that all contrabands enlisted by the navy stayed in the South. Northern navy yards required vast pools of cheap labor, and contrabands were shipped north to work on construction projects. For instance, the New York Navy Yard vastly expanded thanks to imported contraband laborers, who created new land for the confined yard by excavating the bottom of the harbor and piling the spoil to form new acreage and docks. Likewise, contrabands sent to the Portsmouth Navy Yard in New Hampshire completed new fortifications and a pier at that facility, remaining in Portsmouth after the work was completed. African American navy laborers faced severe racism in the North, however, especially among Irish immigrants, who feared contraband laborers working for lower wages would supplant them at the navy yards.[42]

Another difference between army and navy contraband camps was size. To avoid the misery of the overcrowded army camps, navy contraband camps typically held fewer than one hundred contrabands, usually extended families or slaves escaped from the same plantation, with white southern Unionists seeking protection also frequently present. The navy established small encampments of this sort, for example, at Norfolk, Virginia; Roanoke Island, North Carolina; Winyah Bay, Botany Bay, and the mouth of the North Edisto River, South Carolina; and Pilot's Island near Jacksonville, Key West, and Hurricane Island near the entrance to Tampa Bay, Florida. Contrabands in the South risked Confederate reprisal, however, so camps remained small to prevent making them an obvious military target. In July 1862, the population at the navy contraband camp at St. Simon's, South Carolina, swelled to more than one hundred. The commanding officer requested additional support, as he began to "believe it is beginning to excite the serious attention of the rebel authorities of this State."[43]

The strategy of hiding contraband camps by keeping them small did not always succeed, and local Confederate militia attacked some remote encampments. Such an attack occurred at Hutchinson Island, South Carolina, on June 16, 1862. Guided to the camp at night by an African American formerly employed on the island, Confederate soldiers opened fire on a group of sleeping contrabands. The Confederates killed and wounded several of the camp occupants, mostly women and children, before retreating when a Union gunboat arrived. One man, "literally riddled with balls and buckshot," was dead, and another man, "shot through the lungs and struck over the forehead with a clubbed musket, leaving bone perfectly bare," died soon after. The attackers wounded one woman three times and caused severe injury to a pregnant woman who escaped her attackers by leaping from a second-story window. Underscoring the brutality of the attack, the contrabands on Hutchinson Island were living on the plantations where they had been slaves, "tilling the ground for their support, which their masters, by deserting, had denied them, and who were not even remotely connected with the hated Yankees." In 1863, Lieutenant I. B. Baxter of the USS

Gem of the Sea ordered two boatloads of men up Peace Creek in search of a group of "guerillas, or regulators, as they style themselves," threatening the navy contraband camp near Charlotte Harbor, Florida. Instead of waiting for the Confederates to attack, Baxter opted for a preemptive assault. The sailors failed to make contact with the guerillas but ended the threat to the contrabands by destroying the rebel base camp. Baxter hoped the expedition "will have a tendency to break up the blockade running and stop the regulators from coming down to molest the refugees in this vicinity."[44]

Providing security for remote contraband camps remained a challenge for the navy, and arming the contrabands for self-protection was an obvious precaution, yet it was a move fraught with political dangers. The navy contraband camps were in the same region in which General Hunter had declared emancipation and raised African American troops, only to suffer rebuke. Therefore, armed slaves were only that; the contrabands were not in the navy, lacking official unit designations or even military uniforms. The navy did not publicize the arming of contrabands, and the small size and remoteness of the camps allowed the navy policy to escape public notice. Not all camps remained small, however. The seizure of Port Royal Island on the South Carolina coast by the navy in the fall of 1861, which then served as an operating base for ships blockading Charleston, led to the creation of a vast complex of encampments.[45]

To provide adequate food for a growing contraband population without overtaxing the navy's supply system, contraband camps were generally made self-sufficient. The navy provided materials to the contrabands to build shelter and engage in the growing of their own sustenance. Making camps self-sufficient also reduced the need of contrabands to pillage abandoned houses and businesses for food, a practice that intimidated whites who stayed in the occupied regions and damaged efforts to reconcile the South back to the Union. Northern efforts to stem the practice were not successful. One officer wrote: "We went up the river to enable the blacks to collect some corn. . . . I went into the creek with our boats, and finding the negroes engaged in plundering the houses instead of getting corn I ordered them off. I have endeavored to check their propensity to plunder, but with only partial success."[46]

Larger contraband encampments, like Port Royal, organized the contrabands for the task of growing cotton to feed the insatiable demand of northern textile mills, the contrabands receiving payment for their crop as well as the prospect of owning the land they worked. Camps like Port Royal also attracted a wide range of people with varying agendas, defying any attempts to determine who was in charge. Besides the navy headquarters of Rear Admiral Samuel F. du Pont's South Atlantic Blockading Squadron, the Union army created supply depots on the island while Treasury Department agents seized abandoned Confederate property for sale by the federal government. A bewildering variety of civilians also appeared, including northern agents looking to buy cotton, abolitionists documenting the plight of slaves ("collectors of negro statistics," as du Pont labeled them), missionaries ("the people of God"), and "philanthropic newspaper correspondents" looking for a story. Du Pont observed that, despite their best intentions to aid the "degraded condition" of Port Royal contrabands, "the transition state has not improved it."[47]

A second event that promoted the naval role of African Americans in the summer of 1862 was an outcome of the Militia Act. Under the terms of the law, contrabands could enlist into the service as support personnel, a delineation easy to make in the army. Armed combat troops served different functions than unarmed support troops, but naval personnel were quite different. Although manual labor, whether done by whites or blacks, was a large portion of a sailor's responsibility, separations in combat tended to become less clear. In combat, every member of the ship's crew had a post vital to the survival of the vessel, including African American contrabands shipped as boys. There was simply no way to separate the fighting sailors and noncombat laborers on a ship. Moreover, unlike the army, which had relatively few African American combat personnel, the navy could not separate free African Americans permitted to fight from contrabands that could not because of an abstract political label, and contrabands soon performed duties beyond their rank of boy.

In September 1862, Secretary Welles authorized contrabands

to perform duties above the rank of boy although contrabands could still not hold higher ranks, leaving them to perform advanced duties without additional benefits. Economics played a part in Welles's reasoning. Pay and benefits accounted for nearly 50 percent of the 1862 navy budget, and Welles saw the opportunity to expand navy manpower at no additional cost. This was an important concern to the navy, which was running out of available personnel, despite recruiting an average of fifteen hundred seamen per month.[48] Welles communicated to his blockade squadron commanders, "To supply your wants you will have to resort to the expediency of enlisting contrabands, as no more men can be sent to you. Enlistments do not keep pace with the wants of the service." Northern recruiting pools were drying up because of earlier congressional legislation. As a compensation for imposing the militia draft, the Militia Act created a bounty system for army enlistees. New soldiers would receive up to one hundred dollars in cash to avoid the draft by enlisting, making employment by the army a much more desirable choice for contrabands than navy service. Unable to match the enlistment bounty furnished only to army personnel in 1862, the navy soon saw its sources of manpower disappear as whites, free African Americans, and contrabands alike enlisted to get the immediate cash reward. For the first time, the navy had to compete with the army for African American manpower. In addition, more than a thousand white sailors refused reenlistment, preferring to accept the army's bounty. Realizing that symbolic promotions would not create recruits, Welles authorized expanded African American duties with full pay and benefits commensurate with rank.[49]

After December 18, 1862, navy officers and recruiters could enlist contrabands at the rank of landsman, one rank above first-class boy, with a monthly wage of twelve dollars. Ship captains could then use their discretion to promote the landsmen to higher enlisted ranks (up to but not including petty officers) aboard their ships, based upon the contraband's skill and ability. If a contraband sailor above the rank of landsman transferred to another ship, he returned to the lower rank. When the enlistment of contrabands with a higher rank ended, however, they retained the higher rank and the pension benefits commensurate with their position. Welles's policy was another example of the navy's compromising by meeting practical needs while not exceeding the limits established by the Lincoln administration. The prospect of higher wages attracted African American recruits away from the army, as did the expectation of doing more meaningful work than building roads and cutting down trees. The policy placed the responsibility for promoting African Americans on the individual ship captains, not on the Navy Department. Thus, Welles could avoid the implication that the government was enlisting African Americans on an equal basis with whites.[50]

Welles could also impose this policy because the Lincoln administration was moving rapidly in the last months of 1862 toward adopting the abolition of slavery as a war aim. During 1862 the Union government had authorized aid to border states that adopted emancipation, abolished slavery in the District of Columbia (with financial compensation), and eliminated slavery in the western territories (without compensation). As a further sign of Lincoln's resolve, the president chose not to prevent the execution of slave trader Nathaniel P. Gordon, the only American hanged under the 1819 law making slaving a capital offense. Lincoln further emphasized his position in June 1862, by concluding a treaty with Great Britain granting each nation the right to search each other's vessels suspected of carrying slaves. At a stroke, Lincoln reinforced his dedication to his abolitionist supporters, curtailed slave smuggling, and improved relations with Great Britain. In September 1862, Lincoln announced the impending Emancipation Proclamation, scheduled to go into effect on January 1, 1863. Supported by Northerners who wished to punish and reform the South by removing its "peculiar institution," Lincoln adopted the measure as a weapon against the South, though it also ensured political support from radical abolitionists and members of the Republican Party.[51]

Like Welles's policy, the Emancipation Proclamation itself was an exercise in practicality. The proclamation, freeing all slaves in regions of the United States in a state of rebellion, ended slavery in areas beyond the reach of the federal government at the time. Opponents charged that Lincoln was desperate to strike back at the Confederacy. The *London Spectator* criticized Lincoln's proclamation, stating, "The principle is not that a human being cannot justly own another, but that he cannot own him unless he is loyal to the United States." Despite criticism, the proclamation reflected constitutional realities. Lincoln did not have the authority to end slavery, but he could seize enemy property as a portion of his presidential war-making powers. Also, the proclamation included specific exemptions for slaves held in the border states or in regions of the South already occupied by Union troops, a response to the sensitive issue of emancipation in those politically and strategically vital regions. The Emancipation Proclamation explicitly avoided any connotation that freed slaves would engage in combat, although African Americans could garrison U.S. military installations. To temper fears that the proclamation would incite widespread slave revolts, Lincoln urged the freed slaves to "abstain from all violence, except in necessary self-defense."[52]

Even with this allowance, the acceptance of African American troops was not universal. New England states, with a long history of abolitionist sentiment, were permitted to field black regiments immediately after the proclamation, but western states, where racism was more ingrained, were restricted from raising African American troops until the summer of 1863. Although the proclamation liberated no slaves the day it became law, it stood as a symbol of the North's political and military resolve. Lincoln paid a political price for the proclamation, however, as Democrats gained thirty-four congressional seats in the 1862 elections. Despite the losses, however, the Republican majority remained strong enough to fend off any challenge to the proclamation.[53]

Perhaps the most negative response in the North to the Emancipation Proclamation came from abolitionists. The champions of African American freedom decried the administration's pledge to free southern slaves while doing nothing to ensure political and social rights for free African Americans or contrabands already in custody of the government, whose uncertain legal status remained unchanged. With the Republican Party now aligned behind Lincoln's plan to free southern slaves, the abolitionists had additional advantage to push for their goal of full African American participation in the war, as a precursor to full citizenship. The abolitionist position was aided on February 3, 1863, when Congress passed the National Forces Act, permitting Lincoln to draft into military service all men between the ages of twenty and forty-five, without having to resort to a militia draft.[54] The Supplementary Enrollment Act further defined the president's conscription powers on February 24. It removed the restriction on African Americans' becoming combat troops in army service, clearing the way for the first legitimate arming of black troops, although they would remain segregated into separate regiments under white command. From a navy standpoint, the law also permitted the enlistment of contrabands above the rank of landsman if the recruit had previous naval experience or related skills.[55]

The act also created a system of financial compensation to slaveowners in the border states or Union-occupied South who lost slaves to military service. A slave drafted into the Union military was immediately free, but the owner received one hundred dollars in compensation. If a slave volunteered for military service, the recruit was free, and the owner received three hundred dollars in compensation. The purpose of the system was to encourage slaveowners in the border states to release their slaves, lest they lose the financial windfall. The Enrollment Act also allocated funds to provide federal enlistment bounties for navy recruits, permitting the navy to retain skilled sailors rather than lose them to the army and the lure of quick cash. For unknown reasons, the navy did not benefit from the conscription system until 1864, forcing the navy to rely on volunteers and thereby reinforcing its reliance on African American manpower.[56]

The process by which African Americans gained access to Union military service reflected a variety of political and social opinions. Based on traditional viewpoints of race and status, military service seemed beyond the reach of free African Americans seeking social equality and slaves yearning for freedom. Only after the realization that the war would be a lengthy conflict, and that white blood flowed for African American liberty, did long-standing legal and social barriers begin to fall aside, gradually and grudgingly. With the final restrictions lifted by 1863, blacks entered military service, and African Americans arrived at recruiting centers to enter the Union navy.

Chapter Three

A UNIQUE SET OF MEN

THE DEMOGRAPHICS OF

AFRICAN AMERICAN SAILORS

• The actions of African American sailors in service of the
Union navy is an important part of their story, but equally important is the discussion of who they were and from where they
came. The Civil War's African American sailors did not simply
appear; they came from somewhere, and their particular attrib-
utes and backgrounds go a long way toward explaining their motivations for joining the navy. This book generally examines
African American sailors as a collective group, and this chapter
is no exception. By exploring the demographic data of African
American sailors, however, descriptions of black seamen as a sec-
tion of the American population reveal the "average" African
American sailor from a statistical standpoint. African Americans
who enlisted in the Union navy during the Civil War represent a
unique opportunity to examine a portion of the American population documented by a large amount of data. As a government
institution, the navy compiled vast statistics about its recruits, although race was rarely specified. Because of the absence of
racial classification, researching African Americans in the Union
navy is something of a guessing game, with researchers forced to
make judgment calls on the racial identity of a recruit. A comparison of African American enlistees to white sailors and
African American soldiers, focusing on such variables as date of
enlistment, state of origin, and specific regional, occupational,
administrative, and chronological categories, shows that African

American seamen form a unique demographic group, quite distinct from any of their Civil War counterparts or even black men in general. In fact, from a demographic standpoint, African American sailors had more in common with white sailors than they did with African American soldiers, particularly in occupational and geographical terms.[1]

The exact number of African American naval recruits is difficult to determine. Previous estimates of African Americans in the Civil War navy range from 8 percent to 25 percent of the total force. An examination of navy records at the National Archives conducted by Joseph Reidy of Howard University suggests it was approximately 16 percent. The biggest obstacle to determining the exact number is the navy's failure to categorize recruits by race. Throughout the Civil War, the navy did not specifically list a recruit's racial identity. The closest thing to a racial classification is the physical description generally included on the navy recruiting forms. While the recruits described as "black," "negro," "nigger," or "mulatto" are easy to enumerate as African American, recruits described as "swarthy," "dark," or "brown" are less obvious.

Despite the fact that freedom and slavery are very well defined social statuses, determining the prewar status of African American recruits is difficult. Besides not listing the race of each applicant, the navy, despite (or maybe because of) the turmoil over the issue of contraband enlistment, did not denote a recruit's prewar status. Only 4 percent of the applicants in the sample entered "slave" when asked their prewar occupation; many black recruits from southern states entered their specific slave task (e.g., field hand or blacksmith) as their occupation or left the space blank. Northern African Americans were presumably free, but the status of the remainder cannot be accurately determined. Considerable numbers of free African Americans lived in the South, and, without other means of verification, one cannot presume that a recruit who claimed a southern state as his place of origin was enslaved. The same situation exists regarding the statistics of African Americans in the Union army: a majority of black soldiers originated from the South, and former slaves made up the majority of black soldiers, although again exact percentages are unavailable. Broadly, the percentage of slave or free applicants changed relative to the status of slavery. Whereas virtually all 1861 applicants were free, the number decreased to 82 percent in 1862. The Emancipation Proclamation, however, clarified the status of future enlistees, and the number of slave recruits declined to less than 1 percent in 1865.

The year in which enlistments occurred reflects overall trends in African American recruiting. Before the war, the navy enlisted more than 400 sailors who would continue to serve the navy after the war broke out.[2] Roughly 10 percent of the African Americans in the sample pool enlisted in the navy in 1861, while the nation debated the legality and necessity of African American enlistment. A wider acceptance of African American enlistments reflected in the Second Confiscation and Militia Acts resulted in slightly more African Americans entering the navy in 1862. By 1863, however, when the Emancipation Proclamation and National Forces Act removed all barriers to black military service, African American naval enlistments soared. In 1863, one-third of the sample enlisted, followed by higher numbers in 1864, when 35 percent of the sample entered the ranks.

In 1865, however, the number of African American enlistments sharply declined. The Confederate surrender in April severely curtailed navy recruiting efforts. Also, when the Union seized the last major Confederate port at Wilmington, North Carolina, in January 1865, the navy had largely completed its mission and, in terms of manpower and ships, had reached a point of overkill. Consequently, only 2 percent of the sample entered the navy in 1865. Even extrapolated over a twelve-month period, African American recruitment in 1865 was less than the 1862 pace. Although the naval war was over for all practical purposes, the navy still needed personnel and looked to the African American community for recruits. The front page of the March 24, 1865, issue of the *Liberator*, the Boston abolitionist newspaper, featured a navy recruiting advertisement. The notice announced, "Colored men wanted for the United States Navy" and requested enlistments by "seamen, stewards, cooks, ward rooms boys, and two barbers for special service." The navy offered "large pay, bounty and prize money" to lure recruits.[3]

When a recruit enlisted, he had to commit for a set number of years, and the length of service an African American recruit was willing to spend in the navy usually reflected his dedication or optimism about the outcome of the war. In 1861, 80 percent of recruits accepted the standard three-year term of service. By 1863, however, Union battlefield losses led only a fifth of recruits to enlist for three years compared with nearly two-thirds who opted for just one year of service. The upturn in Union fortunes, however, led to a resurgence in three-year enlistments, with half of 1864 and 1865 recruits accepting the longer term of service. The rank and region of enlistment were consistent regardless of term of service. Specific regions of origin, however, showed definite trends in the length of service. Recruits from the North and the border states generally enlisted for three years while southerners tended to enlist for one-year terms. Broken down by occupation before the war, only black workers with an industrial background enlisted for one-year terms more often than for three years. Sailors with maritime experience were more likely to enlist for three-year terms, and sailors with shorter terms of enlistment were more likely to reenlist for a second term of service. Beyond the normal enlistment process are African American sailors who enlisted for the duration of the war, regardless of the length of the conflict. Most of these enlistees joined the service during 1863, enlisting mostly in the Ohio and Mississippi River valleys. Seventy-five percent of duration enlistees entered as boys, generally from the rural areas of the Confederate states. Less than 2 percent of men who enlisted for the duration had previous maritime experience and reenlisted.[4]

A study of enlistment trends must take into account the expanding system of navy recruiting centers. Early in the war, the navy only recruited African Americans at its prewar naval yards, such as Boston, New York, Philadelphia, and Baltimore. For instance, nearly 70 percent of 1861 recruits joined the service from New England and the Mid-Atlantic states. As the war progressed, however, recruits entered the navy at a variety of different locations, such as the new navy yard at Cairo, Illinois, or in temporary recruiting centers. By 1864, only a third of recruits enlisted in the Northeast, balanced by roughly the same numbers entering the service in the border states and west of the Mississippi. Recruitment centers tended to concentrate in regions the navy considered most vital. For instance, recruitment sites consistently expanded in the West until the seizure of Vicksburg in 1863 gave the Union control of the Mississippi River. After 1863, the navy concentrated on closing down the remaining blockading ports on the East Coast with a corresponding realignment of recruiting sites.

The geographical representation of African American sailors differed greatly from the approximately 178,000 blacks in the Union army, who more closely reflected the general African American population. The army recruited most black soldiers in slave states, where nineteen of every twenty African Americans resided. The border states contributed the largest number of black soldiers, with more than a third of the enlistments, followed by the Mississippi Valley, with roughly 25 percent, and the remainder came from the North. The regions generally correspond to the density of the African American population. According to the 1860 census, 20 percent of African American men between the ages of eighteen and forty-five resided in the border states, another 20 percent along the Mississippi River, 10 percent in the North, and the remaining 50 percent in the rest of the South.[5]

Because most naval recruits had to travel from their homes to their enlistment stations, a difference invariably existed between place of origin and place of enlistment. In the case of African Americans, however, the discrepancy is dramatic. In general terms, northern blacks, with a greater geographical mobility, tended to enlist in regions other than where they lived. For example, slightly more than half of Mid-Atlantic recruits originated in that region, and only 30 percent of New England, 12 percent of Midwest, and 3 percent of West recruits enlisted in their home regions. Among the African Americans who enlisted in the navy in Pennsylvania in 1861, only 45 percent were native Pennsylvanians; 19 percent were Virginians and 13 percent were Marylanders. In 1863, only a fourth of enlistees from the state of New York were native New Yorkers, with sizeable percentages originating in Pennsylvania, Connecticut, Maryland, Virginia, and North Carolina. The largest differences, however, reflect southern blacks who enlisted in the navy. Southern blacks, with less mobility, enlisted in large numbers in their own regions More than 85 percent of African Americans enlisted in the Northeast Confederacy claimed the region as their home, a pattern also noted in the Southeast Confederacy and the border states. The mobility offered to southern blacks by the Mississippi River, however, granted them wider enlistment options, with half of the recruits from the Central Confederacy and 60 percent of trans-Mississippi recruits entering the navy in other regions.

Because large percentages of African American enlistees from the South registered at northern recruiting stations, navy enlistments differ from general African American population demographics. Several reasons account for the difference, including the frequent navy practice of enlisting sailors far from the site where the recruit actually joined the service. Many sailors, especially slaves enlisted on southern shores, served significant periods of time in the navy but were not officially enlisted until the ship returned to a naval facility and filed the paperwork. Take the example of Allan Parker, a former Virginia slave, and three companions, who stole a boat and fled to the protection of a Union gunboat. The following day, one of Parker's friends, a slave named Joe, piloted the vessel to his former plantation home although he had not formally enlisted in the navy. The mission resulted in the capture of Joe's erstwhile owner, a Mr. Felton. A few days after his escape in August 1862, Parker and his colleagues formally enlisted in the navy, although New York (the vessel's home port) received credit for the enlistment instead of Virginia.[6]

Also skewing the relationship between place of enlistment and origin was the 8 percent of the sample represented by foreign blacks who joined the navy in northern ports after immigrating to America or purposely coming to the United States to enlist. An example of the former is John R. Bond. Born in Liverpool, Bond immigrated to the United States in 1862 after service aboard a British fishing boat. Although only sixteen years of age, Bond convinced recruiters he was twenty-two. Because of his previous sea experience, Bond received the advanced rank of seaman. Foreign black recruits like Bond came from every corner of the globe, most frequently the Caribbean and Africa. More than half of foreign sailors enlisted in the last two years of the war, joining the navy predominantly in the Mid-Atlantic and New England regions. A third of foreign African American sailors had previous maritime experience, leading to 89 percent of foreign-born black sailors taking positions in the deck crew (seamen and ordinary seamen). Nearly half of foreign recruits came from the Caribbean, with a quarter originating in Canada and a tenth in Europe. An obvious question is what percentage of Canadian recruits were actually born there and how many were escaped slaves returning to fight against slavery. With 70 percent of Canadian recruits under the age of thirty, one can presume a sizeable number were escaped slaves, but without more detail a closer estimate is impossible. In contrast to the varied nature of African American sailors of foreign origin, the overwhelming majority of white foreign-born sailors came from Europe. A random sample of Illinois enlistees found 22 percent of the white sailors were born overseas, all in Europe.[7]

The Lincoln administration's manpower policies also promoted a divergence between region of enlistment and region of origin for African American sailors. Many northern states actively recruited military personnel in the South, particularly after conscription went into effect. Given the possibility of finding southern replacements for their own citizens, many northern state legislatures tried to avoid the political damage of having their citizens forcibly drafted into the military. Northern legislatures hired recruiting agents in the South to find eligible draftees to fill their state's draft quota, extending further the variance between region of origin and region of enlistment among naval personnel.[8]

Another significant difference between black sailors and the general African American population is the distribution between urban and rural origins. While most African Americans resided in rural areas of the South, the largest portion of African American sailors came from an urban setting.[9] Urban recruits represented 40 percent of the sample, and only 25 percent came from rural areas. A third of enlistees did not list a place of origin, or simply entered the state or nation from which they originated. The large urban centers of the North claimed the most African

American naval enlistments. Sailors from New York City, Brooklyn, Boston, and Philadelphia combined for nearly a quarter of the sample, and Baltimore and Washington, D.C., added another 16 percent. Pockets of African American enlistments emerged in the northern industrial cities and centers of the shipping and whaling industries. The majority of urban black recruits came from states with high urban populations. New York and Pennsylvania together held a quarter of all urban recruits, with New Jersey and Massachusetts combining for another 10 percent. Two slave states, Maryland and Virginia, contained another quarter of all urban enlistments.

The importance of certain regions and states in African American enlistments grows when specific regional groups are studied. Among American enlistments, 20 percent originated in border states or the Mid-Atlantic or Northeast Confederacy regions, 10 percent from the Central Confederacy, and lesser amounts scattered among the remaining regions. In comparison, 40 percent of foreign enlistments came from the Caribbean, roughly one-quarter from Canada, 10 percent each from Europe and Africa, and the remainder from the rest of the globe. Within the United States, some states contributed more recruits than others, both in numbers and percentage of their prewar African American populations. Determining the states that contributed proportionately more African American sailors than others derives from a comparison of actual numbers of recruits (percent of state representation in the navy population) with the distribution of the African American male population in the 1860 census (percent of state representation in the U.S. population). Among northern states, only Massachusetts contributed a higher percentage of African American naval recruits (4% of the sample) than it possessed in percentage of the African American male population (3.8% of the 1860 census). The most likely explanation for the percentage margin is the active recruiting of African Americans by the Union army, siphoning recruits away from the navy. Among the slave population, however, several states (District of Columbia, Florida, Maryland, and Virginia) are overrepresented in the sample. Maryland, holding only 2 percent of the male slave population in 1860, contributed 15 percent of the Union navy's African

American recruits, and Virginia's 18.2 percent of the sample is greater than its 11 percent share of the 1860 male slave population. The largest statistical change appears among the slave recruits from the District of Columbia. Containing only one half of one percent of the nation's male slaves, natives of the capital composed 3 percent of the navy's African American recruits.

The expanding system of recruiting sites created a changing demographic picture of African American sailors as the war progressed. With most recruiting sites in the North, half of all 1861 recruits came from the North. As navy recruiting shifted to the West and South, however, recruiting in the North diminished relative to the rest of the country, declining to only 18 percent in 1864. Meanwhile, the South's contribution increased from a quarter of 1861 recruits to half of all recruits in 1863. Recruits from the border states remained generally consistent, contributing about one recruit in eight throughout the war. The biggest change, however, occurred among foreign-born black sailors. About a tenth of 1861 recruits came from foreign shores, shrinking to only 4 percent in 1863, but a year later nearly one in eight was a foreigner.

The expansion of navy recruiting into the predominantly rural regions of the West and South affected the urban/rural demographic picture of African American recruits. More than 60 percent of 1861 recruits were urban, but only 30 percent of 1864 enlistees came from American cities. The percentage of rural enlistees also slightly declined from 1861 to 1865. As the war progressed, more and more recruits listed only their state of origin or did not list a place of origin at all. Only a tenth of 1861 enlistees were unknown in their urban/rural demographic; by 1864, nearly half of all black recruits did not identify an urban or rural background. More than 80 percent of those simply listed the southern state where they originated, possible evidence that by 1864 most southern recruits were formerly rural slaves.

Upon enlisting in the navy, recruits received a rank based upon their age, previous naval experience, and peacetime employment. The most common rank, regardless of race, was landsman. An unskilled recruit over the Navy Department's mandated minimum age for enlistment of eighteen, landsmen received a salary of twelve dollars per month. With no previous naval experience, landsmen expected to learn advanced naval skills on the job, because the navy did not operate any dedicated training facilities during the Civil War. Below landsman was ship's boy, with third-class boy (at six dollars per month) the lowest rank, behind first- or second-class boy (ten and eight dollars monthly pay respectively). Boys performed light labor aboard the ship, acted as servants for the officers, and carried ammunition during battle. Above landsmen were ordinary seamen, sailors enlisted in the navy at least two years or who returned to the navy after a short period out of the service. Ordinary seaman, making fourteen dollars per month, supervised landsmen, manned the guns, and operated the ship's boats under the supervision of the coxswain, a petty officer. An ordinary seaman who showed skill and good judgment could expect promotion to full seaman, the highest enlisted rank among deck crews. Seamen, paid sixteen dollars per month, performed the most advanced tasks a ship required—handling the sails and rigging, steering the vessel, and providing leadership to the rest of the enlisted men. Other enlisted ranks, firemen and coal heavers, worked in the ship's engineering department. Firemen (either first or second class) tended the boilers, monitored the steam pressure, and repaired the machinery under the supervision of the chief and assistant engineers. Making thirty or twenty-five dollars per month, firemen performed a specialized task requiring years of experience. Coal heavers ensured the even distribution of loaded coal among the ship's bunkers and fed coal into the boilers using shovels and wheelbarrows, an exhausting task performed in hellish temperatures.[10]

Among African American rank distributions only a few trends are identifiable. First, the importance of African Americans in the engineering profession increased while their importance in the lowest ranks varied. In 1861, less than 1 percent of African American recruits occupied the engineering ranks, but the number grew consistently until 8 percent of 1865 recruits held engineering ranks. At the same time, the percentage of African American recruits in the lowest ranks fluctuated during the war: 4 percent of

African Americans recruited in 1860 held the rank of boy, increasing to 44 percent in 1862 before declining to 14 percent in 1865. The percentage of African Americans enlisted in the deck ranks fluctuated in response to the growth in the boy's ranks. Nearly all recruits in 1860 were hired as deck crew, but the number declined to roughly half of 1863 enlistees before rising to three-fourths in 1865. The increase in the number of blacks recruited as boys and the decrease in deck crew corresponded to the growing enlistment of unskilled former slaves. Of those recruited as boys in 1862, 74 percent originated in the South and another 10 percent came from the border states. The enlisted ranks of the navy can be separated into the categories of skilled or unskilled. Skill ranks (petty officers, medical personnel, cooks, stewards, firemen, seamen, and ordinary seamen) required an advanced knowledge of naval operations commensurate with previous naval service; unskilled ranks (coal heavers, landsmen, and boys) reflected little or no previous experience at sea. About one in seven African American recruits entered the navy in one of the skill ranks. Almost half of those black sailors who received skill ranks originated in the North. The border states and the South each contributed about 15 percent, and the remaining quarter of skilled enlistments were filled by foreign-born blacks, mostly from the Caribbean.

Interestingly, the percentage of African Americans holding skill ranks is consistent with rank allocations to white sailors, owing to the increased demand for lower ranked personnel caused by the advent of steam power. Earlier sail-powered ships, with vast stretches of sail and miles of rigging, required a large number of experienced crewmen to operate effectively, and usually seamen composed more than half a ship's complement. The transformation from sail to steam power, however, changed radically the skill level of navy personnel, just as steam had altered the makeup of the American work force. Similar to how steam-powered factories eliminated craft workers in American industry, the arrival of steam-powered ships led to the "de-skilling" of navy crews. Because steam engines were occasionally unreliable and coal was expensive, ships still carried a spread of sail, but the number and size of sails were much less than purely wind-powered vessels. Some seamen still handled the sails, but the number of experienced personnel (seamen and ordinary seamen) fell to less than half a typical ship's crew. The remainder consisted of landsman and ship's boys, whose level of experience better suited the manual labor needed to operate steam-powered ships. Such tasks included the exhausting and dirty process of refilling the ship's coal bunkers and necessary military tasks like standing watch and manning the guns. The need for unskilled labor in the navy was so acute that by 1863 the navy hired professional civilian recruiters to find men willing to enlist. The recruiters received three dollars for each seaman or ordinary seaman but ten dollars for each landsman or coal heaver they could locate. A ready source of African American recruits came from the segregated boarding houses frequented by merchant sailors between voyages. Many African American landlords, such as William P. Powell of New York, moonlighted as recruiting agents, finding employment for their tenants and receiving a recruitment fee in return.[11]

The de-skilling of navy enlisted crews paralleled the decline of professional merchant seamen, particularly among African Americans engaged in the sea trade. As steam power removed the need for large numbers of experienced sailors and American economic interests turned to the West, the number of professional merchant seamen invariably grew smaller as the importance of America's merchant marine force declined. Historian W. Jeffrey Bolster concludes that the number of professional black merchant sailors had steadily declined since 1800. In the 1830s, 24 percent of African American merchantmen sailing out of Providence, Rhode Island, made at least three voyages in a seven-year period, but by the Civil War only 7 percent had made an equal number of trips. Merchant sailors tended to be, as Bolster labels them, "transient" seamen—crewmen who would sign on a merchant vessel for one or two voyages because of unemployment on land or for the promise of youthful adventure. Only the whaling industry, the least desirable of the merchantman professions, retained large numbers of African American crewmen in the antebellum period. Thanks to the emergence of kerosene, however, the whaling industry was also in decline, and wages were dismally low. Evidence of these short-term seamen emerges in the occupational descriptions of African American sailors. In various navy paperwork, roughly 10 percent of African American sailors listed different occupations at various times. For instance, a sailor might list one occupation on his enlistment form but list other occupations on subsequent muster rolls. Many sailors possessed a wide range of occupations, on both land and sea.[12]

These sailors, Bolster's "transient" seamen, possessed their own unique demographic profile. With jobs in the merchant service, they tended to enlist later in the war. The Mid-Atlantic and New England regions, the center of the commercial shipping industry, enlisted two-thirds of the part-time sailors who joined the wartime navy and only 40 percent of those without previous maritime experience. Searching for long-term employment, more than half of the sailors with maritime experience enlisted for three-year terms in the service, compared with only 40 percent of those without previous sea service. The need for long-term employment also led 11 percent of experienced sailors to reenlist in the navy during the war while only 5 percent of inexperienced sailors re-upped. With their acquired ability, experienced sailors filled most of the skilled ranks upon enlistment. Nearly half received a skill rank upon enlistment, compared with only 10 percent of inexperienced sailors. As a result, less than a tenth of sailors with previous experience enlisted as boys; a third of those without experience entered the navy at that level. Predictably, owing to the North's control of merchant shipping, more than half of sailors with maritime experience originated in the Union states and foreign regions, while half of the inexperienced sailors originated in Confederate states. The slow professional demise of merchant sailors was a blessing to the U.S. Navy, however, and was an essential element in gaining African American naval enlistments during the Civil War. Without access to the draft system and cash bounties until 1864, the navy could not compel experienced mariners to join the service. The only financial lure to join the navy was the opportunity for prize money. Without employment opportunities in the merchant service, the navy gave merchant sailors, black and white, an outlet for their maritime skills.

Many commanding officers with experience in the merchant service readily accepted African American merchant seamen into the Union navy. With large numbers of vessels coming into commission, the demand for experienced officers also grew, but Congress proved unwilling to authorize additional officer commissions to the navy. Fearful of a postwar navy top-heavy with officers it could not employ, Congress restricted the navy to 711 commissioned officers. In July 1862, Congress authorized 9 rear admirals, 18 commodores, 36 captains, 72 commanders, 144 lieutenant commanders, 144 lieutenants, 144 masters, and 144 ensigns. There was no restriction on the number of petty officers. Also, the navy could enlist 200 surgeons with an equivalent officer rank. To augment the officer corps, the navy temporarily granted commissions to merchant ship officers, denoting their status with the title of "acting," e.g., acting master or acting chief engineer. In 1861, Gideon Welles reported the appointment of 993 acting commissions, including 25 acting lieutenants, 433 acting masters, 209 acting master's mates, and 61 acting assistant paymasters. The balance was mostly acting engineers and assistant engineers. During the war, approximately 7,500 acting officers served in the navy. The use of temporary civilian officers was vital to the enlistment of African American sailors because a prewar relationship existed between white merchant officers and black crewmen. Commanding African American sailors was a less novel experience to acting officers than to commanders in the regular navy, so the acceptance of large numbers of African American sailors occurred with less dislocation than if sufficient navy officers were available.[13]

Another consideration when issuing ranks was the budgetary burden on the navy. The navy's budget grew tremendously during the war, but its resources were limited. Besides paying for the operations of existing ships, the navy had to acquire new vessels, operate its system of supply bases and navy yards, and feed, clothe, and pay its personnel. Although the difference in pay among the enlisted ranks was not great, when distributed among thousands of crewmen the amount was considerable. Therefore, to save money, the navy was inclined to enlist personnel at the lowest rank possible and to restrict promotion to only the most capable sailors. Expecting a small postwar navy, the service did not have to worry about retaining large numbers of experienced personnel beyond their enlistment period, and the department simply enlisted or drafted personnel at lower ranks to save money. The navy's budget and number of personnel grew steadily during the war, but the percentage paid as wages consistently declined. In 1861, the navy employed 7,600 sailors of all ranks, but quickly expanded to 22,000 personnel by December of that year, increasing to 28,000 at the end of the following year. The number escalated to 34,000 in 1863, peaking at 51,000 in 1864 before declining to 9,000 seamen by December 1865. Emergency funding after the Fort Sumter attack swelled the navy's 1861 budget to nearly $31 million, of which the navy allocated $7 million as crew pay. The navy budget continued to grow, to $143 million in 1863 and $281 million in 1864, before declining to $24 million in 1865. The fraction allocated to crew pay generally declined as the war progressed, from 14 percent in 1863 to only 8 percent in 1864 before ending the war at 40 percent of the budget. The percentage allocated for pay in 1865 was high because the navy rapidly demobilized, requiring the payment of all wages and prize money due the departing seamen.[14]

Further evidence of this policy exists in a study of enlistments of African American and white seamen in Philadelphia and Cairo, Illinois. The navy tended to grant higher ranks to newly enlisted sailors early in the war. In 1861, nearly one-third of the recruits at Philadelphia enlisted as seamen and nearly 60 percent as ordinary seamen, compared with less than 10 percent as landsmen or boys. By 1863, less than a quarter of Philadelphia recruits were seamen and ordinary seamen compared with 60 percent landsmen and boys. At the Cairo Yard, 90 percent of 1862 recruits enlisted as sailors. In 1864, only one-third of Cairo's enlistments joined as seamen and landsmen, and the remainder enlisted as boys. Among white recruits in Philadelphia the percentage of enlistees receiving seaman and ordinary seaman ranks declined from more than 90 percent in 1861 to less than 25 percent by 1864. The percentage hired as landsmen and boys increased from 5 percent to 30 percent in the same years. African American sailors recruited in Philadelphia had different statistics. In 1861, all black recruits were either ordinary seamen or landsmen. By 1864, however, 5 percent of black Philadelphia enlistees were seamen, with more than 90 percent landsmen.

Landsman John Lawson of the USS *Hartford*. Lawson received the Medal of Honor in 1864 for conspicuous bravery at the Battle of Mobile Bay. *Courtesy of the Naval Historical Foundation, photograph no. NH 79929*

The crew of the USS *Kearsarge* poses for a ship's portrait upon their return from European duty in 1864. The African American sailor in the center foreground is possibly Joachim Pease, the Medal of Honor winner.
Courtesy of the Naval Historical Foundation, photograph no. NH 52097

The tinclad USS *Fort Hindman* in 1863. A lightly armored riverine warship, the *Fort Hindman* was typical of the navy vessels engaged in deadly close combat on southern rivers. *Courtesy of the Naval Historical Foundation, photograph no. NH 61569*

The USS *Red Rover*, the navy's first hospital ship, in 1863. A captured Confederate steamer, the vessel provided medical care to the Mississippi Squadron, utilizing a number of African American nurses. *Courtesy of the Naval Historical Foundation, photograph no. NH 49980*

(right) Sailors aboard the USS *Hunchback*. A number of African American sailors pose in this 1864 portrait of the crew at leisure, which includes a banjo and a variety of reading material. Note the cluster of ship's boys at the left front of the picture. The large number of sailors in bare feet implies it was summertime. *Courtesy of the Naval Historical Foundation, photograph no. NH 59430* (left) Sailors of the USS *Miami* relax on deck in 1864. The crewmen (including about a dozen African Americans) are engaged in a variety of pursuits: checkers, reading, playing music, and mending their clothes. Many of these men became casualties when the *Miami* clashed with the CSS *Albemarle*. *Courtesy of the Naval Historical Foundation, photograph no. NH 60873*

A typical mess preparing a meal aboard the USS *Monitor* in 1862. A ship's duty schedule, not personal choice, determined more often than not with whom a sailor dined. The uniforms suggest the sailors served in several different ship departments. *Courtesy of the Naval Historical Foundation, photograph no. NH 73688*

A group of African American sailors aboard the USS *Sacramento* in 1867. Although this photograph was taken after the Civil War, the uniforms and equipment are typical of the wartime navy. The image also demonstrates the persistence of African American sailors after the war. *Courtesy of the Naval Historical Foundation, photograph no. NH 45376*

Similar divergences exist among Cairo recruits. In 1862, every single white recruit at Cairo entered the navy as a seaman, but by 1864 white recruits had separated evenly into the ranks of seaman, landsman, and boy. African American recruits at Cairo in 1862 were lumped entirely into the rank of first-class boy, which changed little by 1864, when black recruits were roughly 10 percent seamen and 90 percent boys. Early in the war, the primary determinant for rank allocation was previous naval experience, with veterans returning to the service receiving the higher ranks. In 1861, only a third of the enlistments at Cairo and Philadelphia had previous naval experience, but they filled most of the seaman ranks. By 1863, only one-fifth of the recruits had served in the navy, but they still held the majority of the skill ranks. The decrease in monies paid as wages at a time when the number of personnel increased reflected a navy policy of lowering enlistment ranks for all recruits, regardless of race.[15]

The percentage of African American recruits receiving skill ranks decreased as the total number of black enlistments increased. In 1861, approximately one out of every five African American recruits received a skill rank, declining to one in seven by 1862 and one in eight in 1863. The number rebounded slightly to one in five in 1865. When the navy needed personnel early in the war, offering higher ranks was a means of luring recruits, but when the number of potential enlistees increased the navy rescinded the enticement of higher ranks. Also, since the army did not compete with the navy for African American enlistments in the early years of the war, black sailors took whatever rank the navy saw fit to offer, especially if the sailor was an unemployed merchant seaman. Another factor in the fluctuation in skill rank allotments was the expiration of enlistments. The standard length of a prewar enlistment was three years, a practice the navy tried to continue once war began. Initially, the navy was successful in getting three-year recruits, as patriotism drove northerners to accept the government's call to service. Many did not expect the war to last but a few months, and most enlistees considered serving a full three years (or the duration of the war for some ardent recruits) an unlikely possibility. As the war dragged on, however, the surge of patriotic enlistments waned, and the navy had to offer two-year enlistments to attract recruits and even one-year terms for especially skilled seamen and firemen. Evidence of this resides in the analysis of recruits at Cairo and Philadelphia. In 1861, virtually all enlistees signed on for the standard three-year term, declining to three-fourths in 1862, half in 1863, and ending at only one-third in 1864. At the same time the number of recruits signing on for the duration of the war increased from none in 1861 to one in ten in 1863, with most of this group comprising African American recruits at the Cairo Yard. Thus, by 1863 and 1864, beyond the normal recruiting to fill additional ships, the navy had to replace thousands of sailors whose two- and three-year terms had expired. In those years African American replacements receiving unskilled ranks overwhelmingly outnumbered skilled sailors, with a huge majority of unskilled men ranked as landsmen.

The Union army, in comparison, had no system of skilled versus unskilled ranks. The broadest equivalent to a skilled rank was the status of noncommissioned officer, but rising to that rank in the army was a circumstance largely beyond the common soldier's control. A black soldier could attain the rank of sergeant based upon good conduct observed by a commanding officer, but only after serving at least some time as a private. In the navy, an African American sailor with prewar maritime experience could skip the lower ranks and enter the service as ordinary seaman or seaman. Even if the black sailor enlisted as a boy or a landsman, promotion was reasonably inevitable, as higher-ranked enlisted men left the naval service at the end of their terms. Although a vast majority of black soldiers never changed ranks, promotion was possible for African American sailors if they avoided disciplinary problems.

Petty officers form one particularly important rank group of African American sailors.[16] These men, who skipped the enlisted ranks, performed highly specialized tasks (e.g., gunner or sailmaker) or headed specific task groups aboard ship (quartermaster or coxswain). Within the general African American sample, petty officers had specific backgrounds and experiences that marked them for intermediate rank. More than half enlisted early in the war, joining the navy predominantly in the Mid-

Atlantic states and New England. A third of African American petty officers originated in the North and another ten percent from foreign regions. With a highly desirable skill, half of black petty officers enlisted for the standard three year term of service, but only 2 percent reenlisted. One-third of African American petty officers had previous maritime experience. Blacks held a variety of petty officer ranks, but the largest group were quartermasters, responsible for the procurement and storage of foodstuffs and other supplies. Black petty officers were overwhelmingly urban in background, and much older than the average recruit, with half over the age of thirty. No petty officers were slaves, with 70 percent of the group free before the war, and the status of the other 30 percent unknown.

Cooks and stewards, who made up about 5 percent of the sample, also composed a well-defined skill group. While seemingly simple occupations, cooks and stewards required advanced skills. With meals as the only common luxury aboard ship, good cooks were essential for maintaining morale. Stewards performed many duties similar to domestic servants for officers (e.g., serving as waiters or clerks), but they also managed many of the shipboard accounts requiring cash transactions, such as purchasing small-order supplies or assisting the paymaster with monthly stipends. Thus, cooks and stewards received higher wages than deck crewmen. Because their skills were not as specialized as petty officers, the background of cooks and stewards is closer to the general African American sailor sample pool. Half of the cooks and stewards in the sample enlisted in the Mid-Atlantic states or in the trans-Mississippi region. Despite the large number of recruits from west of the Mississippi, half of the cooks and stewards were from cities. Another third did not define their urban/rural status, but most were probably rural, as the Confederate states contributed the largest percentage of cooks and stewards. Half of all cooks and stewards served for only one year, and a third for three years, but only 3 percent reenlisted for a second term. Most cooks and stewards were in their twenties when they joined the navy, but 15 percent were over the age of forty. Because so many of their tasks were similar to domestic work, it is not surprising that nearly half of cooks and stewards worked as domestics before the war while only 13 percent had previous maritime experience.

The ages of African American sailors are another intriguing and distinct demographic factor. As expected, naval service in the Civil War was a young man's profession, but the great demand for manpower pushed the boundaries of what was considered appropriate age for military service. Although enlistments below the age of eighteen were supposedly illegal, about one in ten black sailors were younger than that. As per navy regulations, most enlistees under the age of eighteen received one of the boy ranks, but a small percentage enlisted at higher ranks. Young men filled the bulk of the black enlistments of the navy. About two-thirds of African American recruits were between the ages of eighteen and twenty-five. Recruits between twenty-six and forty years of age composed another 25 percent, with men over the age of forty amounting to only 4 percent, including Henry Hill, who enlisted at Cairo, Illinois, in December 1862 at the age of seventy, the oldest African American sailor on record. Small numbers of recruits over the age of fifty enlisted early in the conflict, but none joined in the final two years of the war. Small percentages of African American enlistees between the ages of forty and fifty, however, appeared in every annual recruiting total, despite an 1864 navy recruiting regulation forbidding the enlistment of men over the age of thirty-eight without special permission of the Navy Department.[17]

Age also played a key part in determining rank. The mean age of the black sailors in the sample was 24.1 years at time of enlistment. Generally, all of the skill ranks were held by men older than average, landsmen were of average mean age, and unskilled ranks were younger than average. While the navy granted some skill ranks to young recruits, age and experience generally determined rank. Age differences also exist relative to the place of origin of black recruits. Only the northern recruits were younger than the mean average of 24.1 years, with foreign-born blacks the oldest recruits.

An African American recruit's prewar occupational group also provided insight into their demographic makeup. The largest group of African American sailors encompassed domestic workers, both private (butlers or valets) and public (porters or carriage drivers). Approximately one-third of the sample either did not list or did not have a prewar occupation. One can presume that most of the enlistees without a listed prewar occupation were escaped slaves, as nearly half claimed the South as their place of origin and 20 percent came from the border states.[18]

The distribution of skilled laborers—the North contributed a quarter of skilled laborers, and nearly half originated in the South—implies that African Americans were vital to the Confederate war effort and that African American enlistment in the Union navy denied the South large numbers of skilled laborers. Among recruits from the South, half worked in the construction industries, with a third in service occupations and a fifth in the industrial occupations. In comparison, about two-thirds of skilled workers recruited in the North came from the service and industrial occupation groups. Another category with a large African American presence was the maritime trade. New England led the shipping and whaling industries, but most experienced mariners enlisted from other areas: the Mid-Atlantic region led the way, followed by the Northeast Confederacy, New England, and the border states with sizeable percentages. In addition, foreign sailors, mostly from the Caribbean, composed approximately a quarter of recruits with maritime experience. African American recruits from the remaining employment categories hold smaller percentages of the total sample: agriculture 11 percent, slave 4 percent, and commerce 1 percent.

For obvious reasons, prewar occupation played a significant role in the rank African American recruits received at enlistment. Boys tended to come from the domestic and agricultural occupational groups, and deck crewmen originated from the domestic and maritime industries. Recruits assigned to the engine room had a background in the industrial and domestic labor fields. Nearly half of those ranked as cooks came from the domestic fields, and most stewards previously worked in the domestic and maritime fields. The significant number of African American recruits enlisted as petty officers (e.g., quartermasters, gunners, or crew captains) originated in the maritime and construction industries.

As the war progressed, the data on occupational categories of the black recruits changed considerably. For example, the elimination of slavery after the Emancipation Proclamation altered two occupational categories. The percentage of slave recruits, which hit a high of 6 percent in 1863, declined to less than 1 percent by 1865. The end of slavery in the South also clarified the status of recruits whose occupational status was unknown. Whereas half of 1861 enlistees did not list a prewar occupation (and were presumably escaped slaves), only 16 percent of 1865 recruits did not have an occupation. The demand for skilled sailors also influenced occupational categories. Only 10 percent of 1861 African American enlistees came from the maritime industries; by 1865, that number had risen to 18 percent.

Rather than simply a parallel group to the large numbers of African Americans in the Union army, black sailors possessed a distinct demographic identity. More urban, northern, and professionally oriented than African American soldiers, blacks in the Union navy were a unique group of Americans. The age of recruits relative to their rank and region of origin also defined the particular demographics singular to African American naval enlistees. By skillfully executing the responsible tasks of leadership, African Americans were allowed to serve in the petty officer ranks. The navy also attracted large numbers of foreign sailors willing to risk their lives, whether for steady employment, prize money, or to prove their worth as men. While engaged with thousands of others fighting to save the Union, African American sailors had backgrounds quite distinct from other military recruits, white or black. Once in the navy, they would continue to distinguish themselves.

Chapter Four

"SICK OF THE SEA"

EVERYDAY LIFE IN THE

UNION NAVY

• African American military service in the Civil War displayed a unique and, at times, paradoxical relationship between freedom and equality. Early in the conflict, the government denied free blacks the social equality of military service, just as slaves freed by the war failed to receive equal social status after the Civil War. But the African Americans who enlisted in the Union navy experienced the flip side of the paradox, giving up civilian freedoms for the restrictions of military service but finding in the naval bureaucracy and in the exigencies of naval life an equality that had eluded them. In terms ranging from financial compensation for military service to the attitudes of officers who commanded them, African American sailors received generally equal treatment and lived through the same trials and triumphs as white sailors during the war. The navy's attitudes, however, did not reflect any specific policy or decision. Nowhere are memos or orders detailing the Navy Department's attitudes regarding its black enlistees. Rather, the navy's attitudes demonstrated its prewar familiarity with African American crewmen, its constant demands for manpower, and, most of all, its desire to win the war. The means to this end was the fair employment of African Americans during the war years, although the postwar navy would soon revert to the prewar status quo.

Monthly pay to African Americans was the most obvious measurement of navy egalitarianism relative to the Union army. Navy pay had three important differences from the army. First, the pay scale reflected the diverse navy rank hierarchy. Because of the relatively high level of skill required to fill many navy positions, wages reflected a sailor's ability and standing in the ranks. While the army paid all its privates the same wage (depending on race), the navy rewarded skill and promotion in the enlisted ranks with increased pay. African American sailors, therefore, could expect financial compensation as their skill level increased (e.g., from boy to landsman to ordinary seaman) while army troops received additional pay only if promoted into the non-commissioned officers' ranks.

Second, navy pay was generally consistent with civilian wages, particularly wages in the maritime industries. In 1860, a typical wage was one dollar per day for an unskilled laborer, or about twenty-five dollars per month. Farm laborers received slightly less (fifteen dollars per month), and skilled laborers, such as blacksmiths, earned about thirty-one dollars per month. The landsman's wage of twelve dollars per month was well below the national average, but sailors also received free meals, clothing, housing, and medical care (as well as a liquor ration in the first months of the war). Considering that the standard navy ration was valued at about 20 cents per day in 1863, the wage balance, including other benefits, adds in favor of the sailor. Moreover, the relatively low wages of the maritime industry (eight dollars per month for sailors on whaling vessels) clearly show that navy seamen were more than adequately compensated despite the fact that navy wages had not changed since 1854. The standard pay for white army privates (thirteen dollars per month) was more than a landsman's wages but less than an ordinary seaman's. Soldiers also received the same general benefits as sailors, but the delivery of army benefits was frequently unreliable. The reliable access to associated benefits was a hallmark of the navy's supply efforts, and one the army could not always match.[1]

Significantly, navy wage rates applied equally to all, regardless of race. The navy had a relationship with black sailors going back to the American Revolution. Unlike black soldiers serving in the army, black sailors were a common presence on U.S. warships, and years of familiarity had led to an understanding that competent African American sailors deserved equal pay. Also, the public did not consider granting equal compensation to black sailors a socially elevating act. The public considered naval service an unfit occupation for respectable members of society, suitable only for the dregs of humanity. It was common for restaurants in coastal towns to feature the sign "No Dogs or Sailors Allowed," and society segregated naval and merchant mariners (regardless of race) into a social class of their own. Hence, northern racists did not perceive equal pay and benefits to African American sailors as elevating black sailors to a status equal to whites. Service in the U.S. Army, however, was different. Although not considered an ideal profession, the army at least had a history of reputable service familiar to most Americans. While the navy had a few heroes in the American pantheon, the army claimed George Washington, Andrew Jackson, William Harrison, and Zachary Taylor, who had not only excelled on the battlefield but had risen to the presidency. Not only did many in the Union oppose using black troops early in the war, but when African Americans were enlisted few favored granting them equal wages and thereby elevating African Americans to any perceived equal status with white troops.[2]

When black troops did enlist in 1863, they received significantly less pay, ten dollars per month compared with thirteen dollars for white troops. Also, whereas white troops received free clothing and medical care, black troops had three dollars per month deducted from their pay for these services, further reducing their financial compensation. Only after vigorous protest were army wages equalized in June 1864, but only for African Americans who were free before the war, retroactive to January 1, 1864. While northern blacks in the Union army received back pay and equal wages thereafter, southern African Americans did not benefit from the wage adjustment. The act insulted the thousands of contrabands that fled to Union lines to enlist in the Union army.[3]

The navy's equal wages are all the more remarkable because the department could easily have imposed different pay scales.

Rather than issue cash on paydays, paymasters entered wages into the ship's ledger book on the first day of the month, with the sailor receiving his accumulated wages upon discharge from the service. Sailors did not receive cash for several good reasons, including the lack of sufficient cash to pay monthly wages. Ships carried only a limited amount of cash to pay for additional supplies and repairs in the field. Cash distributed monthly would also be an invitation to trouble, by sailors' gambling away their wages or by theft. The navy also withheld wages until discharge to prevent crewmen from deserting. If sailors received currency, money would be available to finance an escape from their service obligation. As it was, a deserting sailor forfeited all of the pay accumulated since his enlistment. The only cash allocated to sailors was a small amount of spending money (no more than five dollars) to those granted liberty or shore leave. As cash did not change hands, it would have been very easy for naval paymasters to enter different ledger amounts based upon the sailor's race, but the navy paid its sailors their fair wage. Even a navy consistently granting lower ranks to its enlistees as the war progressed in order to save money resisted the lure of paying its black sailors less than their white counterparts. In comparison, the army paid its soldiers in cash (scrip used as legal tender in the army's area of occupation rather than paper money or gold), maintaining two pay systems, one for whites and one for blacks.[4]

Changing circumstances led to some adjustment of navy pay during the war. The most notable was the end of the liquor ration. The daily gill of hard alcohol, served first thing in the morning and again with the evening meal, was seen by most in the navy as a welcome respite from the rigors of sea life, but to civilian reformers it was an assault on the spiritual well-being of American sailors. Temperance advocates had long pressured the navy to end the daily imbibing of alcohol on the grounds that sobriety would improve discipline among the ranks. Secretary of the Navy Gideon Welles responded to these complaints and ordered an end to the liquor ration, with the "last call" coming on August 31, 1862. To quiet complaints about the action, the navy compensated its sailors with an additional five cents a day in pay. Though no large protests erupted over the new prohibition, sailors often went to great lengths to smuggle liquor onto navy ships and installations. At the naval hospital in New York a surgeon reported finding bottles of liquor concealed in "a loaf of bread and . . . a roast chicken."[5]

Another circumstance that led to pay adjustments occurred on the South Atlantic Blockading Squadron in the summer of 1863, when many sailors refused to serve aboard ironclad warships. Traditional sailors considered the vessels abominations unsuitable for human inhabitation and balked at spending a broiling southern summer encased in an iron vessel, or feared that ironclad ships would be in the vanguard of any naval assault. Rather than force reluctant sailors aboard the vessels, the navy granted a 25 percent pay raise to any sailor, including numerous African Americans, who volunteered for ironclad duty.

Another increase in pay came about in 1864, when because of increasing monetary inflation in the North sailors received their first pay raise in ten years. Wages increased two dollars per month for most rankings. First-class firemen now made thirty dollars per month, second-class firemen twenty-five dollars, coal heavers twenty dollars, seamen twenty dollars, ordinary seamen sixteen dollars, landsmen fourteen dollars, first-class boys twelve dollars, second-class boys ten dollars, and third-class boys eight dollars.[6]

Besides their monthly pay, African American sailors enjoyed other opportunities for financial benefit from the war, especially the seizure of vessels attempting to run the Union blockade, which were susceptible to seizure. The Prize Law of the navy, enacted in 1798, defined which enemy vessels were liable for seizure, the procedure for capturing and impounding suspect vessels, the auction and sale of prizes, and the distribution of the proceeds. After the deduction of court costs, the Navy Department claimed half the profits, the squadron commander received five percent, and the commander of the capturing vessel received ten percent. The other officers and crew of the capturing vessel divided the remainder. As with pay, sailors received portions regardless of race. Outgoing blockade-runners, laden with cotton, were particularly valuable catches, and a sailor could very quickly amass a small fortune at relatively little danger to himself.[7]

In 1864, for instance, the USS *Eolus* captured the blockade-runner *Hope,* earning each of the first-class boys $532, more than four years' pay. Later in 1864, the USS *Connecticut* ran down the *Greyhound,* a prize valued at $497,859. After adjudication costs ($12,897), squadron commander Rear Admiral Samuel P. Lee received $12,124, *Connecticut's* captain earned $24,248 (nearly ten times his annual pay), with each lieutenant getting $6,366, every seaman $733, and the first-class boys $407. Several factors restrained the financial windfalls of prize money, however. Navy rules stipulated that if more than one ship participated in a capture the reward went to all participating vessels. Vessels within signaling range of a captured blockade-runner counted as members of the capturing party and were eligible for a share of the proceeds. Also, sailors on swifter vessels on blockade duty collected more prize money than slower vessels (which could not catch the fast runners) or smaller navy vessels operating on the Mississippi and other rivers (which had few opportunities for prize captures). The squadron in which a sailor served also determined the frequency of prize catches. The North Atlantic Blockading Squadron, with many Confederate ports in its jurisdiction, had a large traffic of blockade-runners while the East Gulf Blockading Squadron, patrolling the sparsely populated coast of western Florida, had very few. For instance, Rear Admiral Stephen P. Lee, who only briefly commanded the North Atlantic Blockading Squadron, amassed $125,000 in prize money while Vice Admiral David G. Farragut, commanding the West Gulf Blockading Squadron for most of the war, earned only $50,000.[8]

Despite the disparities between prize opportunities, the chance for quick money offered to all sailors, regardless of race, remained unmatched by the army. Soldiering offered the possibility of pillage only at the risk of criminal prosecution. In 1861 and 1862, some contrabands serving aboard navy vessels failed to receive shares of prize money since their full enlistment in the navy was not certain. In 1878, however, Congress appropriated twenty thousand dollars for the payment of prize money to those African Americans who did not receive shares during the war. Congress approved an additional eight thousand dollars the following year to settle all prize claims. The seizure of blockade-runners even occasionally garnered the navy new recruits. After seizing the schooner *Baltimore* in October 1861, the captain of the USS *Stars and Stripes* received permission to enlist "a colored boy (free) from the island of St. Martin's . . . desirous to serve aboard this vessel."[9]

Another means for African Americans to improve their financial lot in the service was by promotion. Again, the navy's personnel system provided outlets for promotion unavailable to blacks in the army. Whereas army privates held that rank unless suitable for promotion to the noncommissioned ranks, the navy's system allowed small promotions within the enlisted ranks (boy to landsman to ordinary seaman). African American soldiers received advancement only within the segregated black regiments, limiting the number of positions available for promotion. Promoted African American sailors, however, could transfer to any ship with an open position, creating many more advancement possibilities. Evidence even suggests that black sailors received promotions at slightly higher percentages than did white sailors. In a sample of sailors recruited from Massachusetts, 25 percent of the African American sailors moved up in rank, compared with only 22 percent of the white sailors. Seventy-four percent of black sailors remained in their enlistment rank for the duration of their term of service, compared with 69 percent of whites. The navy demoted 1 percent of the African American sample and 2 percent of the white sample. Instead of race, the most common determinant for promotion was length of service. Nearly 85 percent of the sailors who received promotion enlisted for three or more years, compared with only 6 percent who enlisted for one year. Most sailors moved up only a single rank (e.g., from landsman to ordinary seaman). Two African Americans in the sample, however, became petty officers, and one moved from second-class fireman to acting third assistant engineer, a temporary officer's rank.[10]

There is no mention of African American officers in any Civil War naval history, but a black officer among the engineering ranks should not be surprising. African Americans were frequently engineers and firemen on the Ohio and Mississippi Rivers, so their collective technical expertise could conceivably lead to an officer's promotion for some black firemen. Line officers had long objected to granting officer ranks to engineers, believing them to be mere mechanics that maintained the steam plant. Only in 1859 did engineers receive equivalent ranks. Therefore, while line officers would be extremely resistant to African Americans in their ranks, an African American engineering officer would meet less resistance. African American line officers were absent from the prewar navy for two reasons. First, Americans recognized military service as an obligation of every American citizen, but American society had denied African Americans full citizenship in the antebellum period. Second, the abundance of civilian merchant officers removed the necessity of promoting competent African Americans to officer rank. The navy could avail itself of a merchant officer's experience and then release him when the war was over, a preferable arrangement, as the navy presumed it would revert to a minimal postwar force after the South's defeat.[11]

One group of African Americans held posts similar to, and just as important as, an officer's rank. Both officially and unofficially, African Americans served the navy as pilots on rivers and coastal waters. Some black pilots served unofficially for short-term operations because they knew the local waters. African American guides compensated for the navy's unfamiliarity with the region and the Confederates' destruction of navigational aids to hinder U.S. Navy operations. As early as January 1862, officers on the blockade requested permission to hire local African American pilots. In that month, the captain of the USS *Seminole* received permission to embark a contraband named Isaac as an ordinary seaman, "on account of his knowledge of the inlets along the coast." In 1863, Rear Admiral Samuel F. du Pont reported to the secretary of the navy that he "made use of the services of certain contraband pilots, and have authorized the payment to them sometimes of $30 and sometimes $40 per month. . . . They are skillful and competent." Two African American pilots received official recognition in the navy records for their efforts to aid the South Atlantic Blockading Squadron: Isaac Tattnall guided the USS *St. Marys* off Georgia's coast, and Prince was the pilot assigned to the USS *Uncas*. During combined operations with the army in Cape Hatteras in 1862, navy reconnaissance patrols followed "a Negro boy named Tom Robinson who had lived on the island for years."[12]

The most famous of the navy's unofficial African American pilots was Robert Smalls. On May 13, 1862, Smalls stole the Confederate steamer *Planter* and brazenly sailed the ship past the Fort Sumter batteries to join the Union blockade, carrying his and the other African American crewmen's families. As capturing officer, Smalls received fifteen hundred dollars in prize money. Smalls served as the master of the *Planter* for much of the war, although the vessel joined the army's fleet of supply vessels. Smalls also piloted both army and navy ships along the South's Atlantic coast, including the naval assault on Charleston, South Carolina, in April 1863. Guiding the ironclad USS *Keokuk*, Smalls escaped with his life when the *Keokuk* sank under intense Confederate shelling. Later, Smalls served as a South Carolina state senator and member of Congress from 1876 to 1884 and retired from the South Carolina state militia as a major general.[13]

Other black pilots served in a more official capacity, because of the navy's desire to have permanent pilots available for duty. On June 9, 1863, Gideon Welles authorized navy recruiters to hire full-time pilots at the rate of one hundred dollars per month, and one dollar per day for food. Late in the war, on January 17, 1865, the hired pilots formed a semiofficer class, with the temporary rank of acting master pilot (at fifteen hundred dollars per year) or acting ensign pilot (twelve hundred dollars). The former rank was equivalent to a master's rank, and the latter equaled an ensign, the two lowest officer ranks. Among these professional pilots were at least seven African Americans: William Ayler, William Debrech (also spelled in the records as Debrish), Nicholas Dickson, Stephen Small, James Taliafaro, William Tulson, and one who went by the name Mazalina. Among these pilots, Taliafaro certainly received the rank of acting master pilot, and the others most likely held that title. In April 1863, William Ayler died in the service of the U.S. Navy from wounds received while guiding the USS *Coeur-de-Lion*. A Confederate shell severed Ayler's leg, and the pilot died before medical help could arrive. In March 1862, Confederate militia in Florida captured and murdered an unknown African American pilot. Wounded in an ambush, the pilot and several other Union seamen fell into Confederate hands. The Confederates lynched the wounded pilot as a warning to other blacks should they aid the Union.[14]

In addition to wartime financial compensation, African American sailors could also expect recompense later in life. Early in the war, the federal government, to induce enlistments from those with financial concerns, established a pension system to care for veterans crippled by the war as well as widows and orphans of slain servicemen. Enacted by Congress in July 1862, the Pension Act granted monthly payments to ill or injured veterans in the enlisted ranks or to their families if the serviceman died in battle. The pension reflected the recipient's rank at the time of the veteran's death or release from the service. Retroactive to March 4, 1861, the law imposed no restrictions on pensions to African Americans, who shared pension opportunities equally with their white counterparts. Initially, the minimum monthly pension for army privates and navy boys and landsmen was eight dollars, and senior enlisted personnel garnered up to thirty dollars, but Congress adjusted the amounts after the war. After July 1866, widows received an additional two dollars per month for each child, and in June 1878 Congress granted an appropriation of seventy-two dollars per month to any veteran blinded or denied the use of hands or feet during the war. The Dependent Pension Act of 1890 increased the minimum pension payment from eight to twelve dollars for veterans in the lowest enlisted ranks. The act also granted pensions to veterans whose disability was not attributable to war service, and any veteran unable to work was eligible.[15]

Funds for the new pension system came from a revised Prize Law enacted in July 1862. Under the earlier law, the half-share of every prize case claimed by the Navy Department had to supplement the navy budget. Under the new Prize Law, the navy used its share to establish a pension fund for navy veterans. Hunting blockade-runners meant not only immediate cash benefits but also an investment in the individual sailor's future financial security. The $14 million in prize money collected by the navy during the war became the source of postwar pension relief. In 1865, the interest on the navy's money amounted to $292,783, and the department divested only $248,529 as pensions.[16]

African Americans receiving pensions after the war, however, faced some peculiar problems if they or their spouses were former slaves. Because prewar pension laws required extensive paperwork proving one's identity, postwar pension regulations were drafted to permit payment to veterans or their families who, owing to the lack of records regarding slaves, could not produce the usual sources of evidence. Because states did not recognize African American slave marriages, Congress granted pensions to African American widows who could not produce a marriage license. Under the terms of the Supplementary Pension Act, enacted in July 1864, an African American widow simply had to prove at least two years of cohabitation with a veteran in lieu of the previously required documents. The government considered all offspring produced during the cohabitation legitimate children.

Two years later, in June 1866, the two-year cohabitation minimum was itself removed. African American widows only had to provide evidence (usually in the form of a written testimony by the minister who wed the couple) that the couple had lived together as man and wife for the marriage to be valid. By 1873, Congress further relaxed the restrictions, with African American widows simply testifying that they had married a veteran in some ceremony "deemed by them obligatory." The question of African American citizenship, still undecided until the passage of the Fourteenth Amendment in 1868, did not influence the granting of pensions. Congress determined in June 1866 that African Americans who could not prove they were free before the war were still entitled to enlistment bounties or pensions granted after the war. The only requirement for financial support was proof of veteran status.[17]

Most African American navy veterans took advantage of the pension system, appealing to the government for financial assistance in their later years. A random sample of African American naval recruits shows that 78 percent of the veterans received a pension; the navy rejected or did not receive applications from the other 22 percent.[18] There are several possible reasons for a pension denial, but the most common were that applicants could not prove they were in the navy or could not demonstrate (before 1890) that their injury or disease was war-related. The sample also shows a direct relation between the year of enlistment and approval of pension funds, with the years having the highest level of African American enlistment also having a higher percentage of approved pension applications. Among 1861 applicants, 71 percent received approval, dipping slightly to 69 percent among 1862 recruits, rising to 84 percent of 1863 sailors and 81 percent of 1864 mariners. Because the war was winding down by 1865, only 50 percent of 1865 applicants in the sample received a pension, as veterans enlisting in that year had a much lower chance of combat injury or death compared with earlier years. The 78 percent of African American navy veterans compares favorably with the number of white veterans, both army and navy, who received pensions. David Shaffer has demonstrated that, among a sample of African American veterans, regardless of their branch of service, 83 percent received a postwar pension.[19]

Applying for and receiving a pension was a relatively simple process. The easiest means was to produce the discharge certificate granted to each veteran as he left the service, which virtually assured the granting of a pension if the sailor left the navy because of a disability. If a veteran did not have his discharge certificate, he filed a pension application form with the Bureau of Pensions. The bureau would then gather information from the Navy Department or adjutant general of the state in which the pensioner resided. Essential supporting documentary evidence included medical care given to the applicant as proof of wartime injury or disease. If evidence was not immediately available, the applicant would be required to send legal affidavits from his physician or others who could provide testimony on the legitimacy of the claim.[20]

For African Americans other problems relating to the application process emerged. Information such as age or place of birth was unavailable or withheld by former slave owners because the applicant no longer had contact with the owner or because of lingering grudges against former slaves. Unscrupulous pension agents who specialized in compiling information needed for a successful pension application preyed upon the poor by charging exorbitant fees in return. Illiteracy also hindered many

African American applicants who relied on others to fill out forms and compile data. Donald Shaffer's samples demonstrated that 91 percent of literate African American applicants received pensions compared with 80 percent of illiterate veterans. Appli cants from certain areas of the country were also more likely to receive pensions. Veterans from the North were more likely to receive financial support (88 percent) than were those from the Upper South (84 percent) and Lower South (77 percent). Urban African American veterans received pensions at a higher rate than rural applicants (88 percent to 80 percent).[21]

Shaffer also provided sampled statistics for pensions granted to African American widows from the general veteran population. Again, the general percentage of widows receiving pensions was high, 63 percent, with African American navy widows receiving a higher percentage of approved pension applications, 75 percent.[22] The relatively high percentage of widows receiving pensions is notable because of the additional proof needed to acquire pension funds. Besides proving their husbands were veterans killed or infirmed in the service, widows also had to prove their marital status. For instance, the widow of Thomas Hayden, who died of dysentery soon after his enlistment, did not receive her pension because the navy produced documents proving her husband had contracted the affliction before enlisting. The widow of Joseph Henson did not receive a pension because she could not prove her marriage to the veteran, who may have used an alias in the service. Fellow crewmembers recalled a man named Summerfield Henson, and the widow initially claimed the name of "Hinson," further confusing the legitimacy of her claim. The widow of Lyman H. Hyde did not receive a pension because of a confused claim. She claimed that Hyde, on his way to St. Thomas for treatment of the malaria he contracted while in the navy, died aboard the vessel taking him to the island and received burial at sea. Without proof of the marriage, evidence that Hyde contracted malaria in the service, or remains to confirm his death, Hyde's widow failed to receive compensation.[23]

A final form of financial compensation to African American sailors was the chance of gaining entry into one of the Soldiers' and Sailors' Homes established and subsidized by the federal government after the Civil War. Before 1861 the only retirement housing available to career enlisted sailors was the Naval Asylum in Philadelphia, a small antiquated facility near the Philadelphia Navy Yard. Besides being rather dilapidated and poorly funded, the asylum was also not large enough to accommodate all applicants, and many sailors in dire financial straits failed to find a place until the death of an occupant created a vacancy. After 1865, however, the federal government established a series of Soldiers' and Sailors' Homes and subsidized comparable state facilities. African American sailors found equal access to these homes, even those located in the South. For example, in 1890 twenty-one of the approximately three hundred navy veterans residing in the National Home for Disabled Soldiers in Elizabeth City, Virginia, were African Americans, along with an unknown number of army veterans.[24]

In addition, many states funded homes and shelters for indigent veterans and their families. In 1869, for instance, the state of Pennsylvania renovated a defunct college into the State School-Home for Colored Soldiers' and Sailors' Orphans. The facility housed 133 orphans in October of that year and was anticipating the arrival of an additional 159 children. Applicants had to be at least four years old and would receive "board, lodging, clothing, medical attendance, a good English education, including Sunday-School instruction and proper care in all respects at the expense of the State, until they are sixteen." Other states provided similar facilities, funded by state governments or local charities, giving veterans and their families some form of compensation years after the war had ended. Illinois, for instance, funded the construction of a state Soldiers' and Sailors' Home in Quincy, Illinois, in addition to the federally funded Home for Volunteer Soldiers and Sailors in Danville.[25]

Besides pay and other forms of financial compensation, black and white sailors received basically equal treatment, and their quality of life was far better than that found in the Union army. The navy standard of living compared with the army is succinctly addressed by an 1862 navy recruiting advertisement proclaiming,

"The pay of the sailor is somewhat more liberal than that of the soldier, and his duties include no long marches or wet encampments. He gets his meals and his grow with unfailing regularity and has always, besides, a dry bed—luxuries which a soldier can seldom count on."[26] Among the navy benefits, food was perhaps the most important. Mealtimes were usually the only leisurely moments a sailor enjoyed during his long days at sea and were a respite from what often proved to be a monotonous existence. All sailors received a relatively healthful, if not particularly varied, diet that had not appreciably changed since the navy's Bureau of Provisions and Clothing established the basic dietary requirements in 1842.[27] In a year a sailor could expect to consume 318 pounds of biscuit, 104 pounds of beef, 156 pounds of pork, 78 pounds of preserved meat, 52 pounds of flour, 26 pounds of rice, 13 pounds of dried apples, 26 pounds of pickles, 45 pounds of sugar, 6 pounds of tea, 23 pounds of coffee, 13 pounds of butter, 10 pounds of desiccated vegetables, 10 gallons of beans, and 3 gallons of molasses and vinegar each. To vary the diet, the navy disbursed various foods on different days according to regulations. For instance, meals featured fresh beef only on Tuesdays and Fridays, fresh pork on Mondays, Wednesdays, and Saturdays, with canned meat on Sundays and Thursdays. Rice came only on Sunday, and molasses appeared only on Thursdays. Hardtack, coffee, and the spirit ration were the only provisions issued every day. In addition to the established diet, the navy issued additional foodstuffs, such as pickles or canned fish, when the service could purchase a sizeable amount at a reasonable price. Seasonal foods, like fresh fruit, reached navy crews at the appropriate time of year.[28]

The navy diet varied only slightly from that issued to army troops (including African American soldiers), but sailors enjoyed a more reliable supply system. Whereas army regiments on the march often outstripped the ability of their quartermasters to supply them, navy vessels, on relatively stable patrol stations and operating out of secure supply bases, more often than not received supplies on a regular schedule. Besides the Navy Department's supply ships, squadron commanders would frequently designate a vessel a supply ship for their particular region. In

1861, for instance, the USS *Brandywine* became the general supply and receiving ship for the North Atlantic Blockading Squadron. In 1863, the navy added the chartered freighter *New Berne* to the squadron's supply fleet. In addition, the navy converted the USS *Supply, Rhode Island,* and *Connecticut* into logistics vessels capable of transporting frozen beef, considered vastly preferable to the canned variety (called "salt horse" by sailors).[29]

Rather than resupply at northern ports, the navy established supply stations at Beaufort and New Bern, North Carolina, after the capture of Pamlico Sound. The latter port was the home base for the *Massachusetts,* the supply steamer for the South Atlantic Blockading Squadron, distributing its load of "fresh meats, vegetables, fruits, etc., and in summer ice in moderate supply." The squadron also supported the old sailing vessels *Arletta, William Badger,* and *Release,* which were demasted and tied together to serve as a vast floating warehouse. The Mississippi Squadron drew its supplies from the new navy yard at Cairo, Illinois, and from New Orleans, the supply base for the West Gulf Blockading Squadron. The East Gulf Blockading Squadron opened a logistics facility at Key West, Florida. The supply schedule did occasionally fail to meet its intended rounds, forcing ships to prepare whatever provisions were available. One ship suffered through a period of "pea soup day, bean soup day, hardtack and cheese day, followed by soup day" before a supply ship arrived. When replenished, ships transferred food in bulk. For instance, on March 28, 1863, the Mississippi River ironclad USS *Carondelet,* manned by a crew of roughly fifty officers and men, received on board "32 barrels of biscuit, 8 barrels of beef, 9 barrels of pork, 9 barrels of flour, 4 barrels of rice, 4 1/2 barrels of dried apples, 4 barrels of sugar, 1 1/3 barrels of coffee, 5 barrels of beans, 3 barrels of molasses, 1 1/2 barrels of vinegar, and 2 kegs of pickles."[30]

Navy ships could also accommodate a larger amount of provisions than soldiers could carry on their backs, ensuring not only a food source but a reasonably diverse one as well. The logistical system was especially valuable during the holiday season, when ships sought to provide a more elaborate bill of fare, evident in the Christmas meals served aboard the USS *Florida.* On the menu was "roast turkey, roast beef, chicken pie, broiled chickens, roast ducks, clam pie, quails on toast, giblet stew—beets, sweet and irish potatoes, onions, green corn, & peas, asparagus, cranberry sauce, currant jelly." In addition, the United States Sanitary Commission, a civilian charitable organization, pro vided foods meant to prevent scurvy and other diseases caused by deficient diet. In June 1864, for instance, the USS *Saugus*'s supply officer reported receiving from the Sanitary Commission "1 box potatoes, 50 cabbages, 25 bushels of radishes, 1 cake of tea, 1 box preserved tomatoes, and 1 box lemons."[31]

African American sailors, integrated among the navy crews, did not suffer unequal provisions or substandard rations, as did some segregated African American regiments in the army. Besides receiving obsolete weapons and inadequate uniforms, African American troops were also frequently last to receive basic supplies and rations. African American sailors, however, integral to ship operations, could not be so readily segregated in regards to provisions, a clear benefit over conditions in the Union army.[32]

The sailors usually prepared meals themselves under the supervision of the ship's cook. Sailors were organized into messes, usually not more then twelve men, and prepared and ate their meals together, with one sailor designated as the mess cook, responsible for drawing the daily rations for his mess and preparing the meals. A sailor with culinary skill might always garner cooking duty, or the mess members would rotate the duty among themselves. Messes accommodated the ship's watch schedule. The official navy day began at noon with the afternoon watch lasting four hours, followed by two "dog" watches of two hours each until 8 P.M., when the "first watch" would go on duty until midnight. The final portion of the day was divided into the midnight to 4 A.M. mid-watch and the 4 to 8 A.M. morning watch, with the fore noon watch ending at 12 P.M. Sailors would alternate watches, being "on duty" at their watch stations or performing ship maintenance or sleeping on the alternating watches. The dogwatches allowed a rotation of the schedule, so a sailor's watch schedule changed every day.

The watch schedule provided meals as crewmembers came on or went off duty, so sailors would not have to leave their stations to eat and meals would not have to be constantly prepared.

Therefore, a sailor's watch schedule determined whom he ate with, rather than a sailor's personal preference. Crews organized messes along rank and department lines. Coal heavers and firemen would organize engineering messes among themselves, and experienced seaman and ordinary seamen would try to separate themselves from the landsmen and boys. Both groups of enlisted men were separate from the officer and petty officer messes.[33]

As navy food could be monotonous, sailors sought to diversify their menu, and an obvious source of food were the ocean and rivers. Men aboard the USS *Mystic*, for instance, collected more than eight hundred fish in one afternoon's work off Cape Fear, North Carolina, and coastal waters throughout the South yielded shad, herring, shrimp, and shellfish to hungry navy crews. Key West provided sea turtles, a local delicacy many sailors were willing to try in order to avoid the usual diet. Hunting also added to the sailor's diet, although occasionally the navy's choice of weapon left something to be desired. In January 1864, the USS *Silver Cloud*, with Major General William T. Sherman and his staff aboard, left Memphis for Vicksburg. To provide fresh provisions for their distinguished guest, the *Silver Cloud* used its forward pivot gun to shell a small island in the Mississippi River, killing forty-three birds. While the ducks and geese were welcome additions in the officer's wardroom, the sandhill cranes with a "rank flavor," were given to the crew to eat, and needed "to be boiled . . . to get this flavor out somewhat, so that they could be afterwards roasted."[34]

Foraging for food ashore also expanded the menu to include crops from southern fields or captured Confederate supplies. After seizing a town on the Roanoke River in North Carolina, a sailor reported "quantities of fresh beef, pork and flour, which the rebs had left in their flight, were found. It was an amusing sight to see the crew come over the side of the gun-boat on their return, some with huge bags of flour on their shoulders. At the close of their labors each might have been very appropriately called 'The flour of the navy.'" Foraging had risks, however. Besides the danger from Confederate troops and militia, some forage had a mind of its own. A herd of Florida cattle proved to be a match for a group of navy foragers in 1863. While the navy men "did not lack in courage in battle," the mostly urban sailors were hesitant to pursue the fleeing animals into the brush for fear "the cattle turning on them at any minute, leaving no chance of escape from their rage, except that of climbing a tree." Attempts to dispatch the animals with bayonets utterly failed, "stampeding the cattle in every direction." Frustrated sailors and marines finally resorted to shooting the cattle, "without any regard whatever to the position of his fellow hunters, thus rendering it extremely dangerous to be anywhere within gun-shot distance of this extraordinary scene."[35]

A final means of expanding the navy diet was trade with the local population. With high levels of antagonism and distrust between the navy and white Confederates, African Americans in the South became the navy's primary trade partners. Besides improving the navy diet, bartering also provided much needed capital and employment to former slaves without any other form of permanent subsistence. In the midst of a hostile land, former slaves were often the first and only friendly faces navy personnel encountered, as the arrival of navy vessels would prompt "a lively trade in eggs and poultry, exchanging in barter, tobacco and cast-off blue flannel shirts." Contact with former slaves was especially common on the Mississippi River, the densest concentration of antebellum slaves. Trade with local blacks was as close as the riverbank, and soon after their liberation African American trade with the navy was in full swing: "the boat was thronged all day with negroes who brought various articles of food such as corn and apples, muscatines, sweet potatoes, quinces, &c, &c. We had finally to forbid any more negroes coming on board, notwithstanding they swarmed along the bank by the dozen. The chief articles we give in exchange for provisions are tobacco, coffee, and flour, all of which they crave with staring eyes." The same vessel returned a few days later to replenish its food supplies from the local population, which had "already been bringing in supplies of sweet potatoes, butter, eggs, chickens, corn meal, &c, &c, for which we exchange coffee, tea, flour, and spices. . . . We require a beef every few days, and whenever they come within convenient range of the vessel, we confiscate one."[36]

Purchases ashore could get out of hand, and one ship had to

ban trade with contrabands ashore after the crew purchased all the African Americans had to offer, leaving little for the wardroom cook to purchase. Besides provisions, African American civilians also provided other services to navy personnel. Blockading the Mississippi south of Vicksburg in support of Major General Ulysses S. Grant's siege in the summer of 1863, the USS *Lafayette*'s crew, holding a relatively stable station for several weeks, frequented African American prostitutes ashore. Although initially refused permission for shore leave, the *Lafayette*'s officers frequently consorted with the "colored females in fashionable dry goods" ashore, the "octoroon Maria" being the most popular. The presence of "ladies of ill-fame" led to "scandalous rumors . . . of the laxness of morals among the officers."[37]

The close integration of navy crews also worked to limit racial discrimination when supplying other accoutrements, such as uniforms. Whereas distinct African American army regiments usually had to accept substandard clothing, strict navy regulations maintained a fair distribution of clothes and shoes. Each sailor received two full uniforms per year, along with one pair of shoes. At weekly inspections, the crew would turn out in their best uniforms for examination by the ship's executive officer. If found without a suitable uniform, a sailor would be obliged to purchase replacement uniform parts from the ship's stores, with the cost deducted from his pay balance kept by the vessel's paymaster. Thus, navy regulations ensured that African American sailors received adequate uniforms. To avoid paying for replacement uniforms, many sailors turned to contraband slaves for assistance. In addition to the foodstuffs they provided, former slaves also provided a tailor service to navy crewmen, repairing uniforms to avoid replacement or even fashioning completely new uniforms, both less expensive than navy issue. Fortunately, most navy officers did not strictly apply naval regulations about their crew's choice of dress, and individual sailors introduced personal touches and designs to their contraband-produced uniforms.[38]

Another major form of compensation that favored African American sailors over their army counterparts was the medical care they received. Like the Civil War soldier, the biggest medical threat to sailors was disease. Frequently operating in unfamiliar climates rife with diseases to which northern sailors were not accustomed, the navy struggled to control ailments that contemporary medicine barely understood. Without a significant Confederate naval force to oppose them, the climate of the South and occasionally insufficient provisions were more of a medical burden to the Union navy than combat casualties. Indeed, illness often did more to hamper Union naval operations than their Confederate adversaries did.

In the summer of 1864, a yellow fever epidemic decimated the South Atlantic Blockading Squadron. With too many sailors ill to remain on station, seven blockading ships retreated to ports in the North for medical care, weakening the naval noose about the South's neck. The USS *Alabama* suffered so much from the ailment that the navy ordered the vessel and its entire complement to Portsmouth, New Hampshire, where the crew remained in quarantine, their ship decommissioned, for three months. At one point, the USS *Chambers* had only two healthy officers aboard, "the Captain and the executive officer being down with fever," leaving Acting Ensign William J. Eldredge in command. After the death of twelve crewmen and the commanding officer, leaving the ship without "enough men to man one boat or gun," Eldredge took the responsibility for taking his ship north without the permission of the squadron commander. *Chambers* returned to its station at the mouth of the Indian River after the vessel was reequipped with "a surgeon, medical supplies, ice, and eight acclimated Negroes."[39]

Health conditions were no better on the Mississippi River. In the summer of 1863, USS *Lafayette* suffered the ravages of disease (mostly malaria and heat exhaustion) while on blockade duty near Vicksburg. On June 5, eighteen crewmen and seven of the vessel's officers were on the sick list, including the surgeon (the only medical officer aboard). With the ravages of disease increasing, on June 9, 1863, the surgeon requested that the commanding officer, Captain Henry Walke, send the ship north. Two days later, landsman Patrick Dolton died of heart disease. By June 13, with two more sailors dead and more than thirty ailing crewmen filling the sick bay, Walke ordered the conversion of a coal barge alongside the ship into a hospital. By June 22, forty-one crewmen were stricken before the *Lafayette* left for medical care in New Orleans. Disease claimed lives even on oceangoing ships, as discovered aboard the *City of New York*, a navy-chartered ship used to transport army troops during combined operations. Leaving New York on March 23, 1862, with the 13th Connecticut Infantry Regiment aboard bound for New Orleans, the first man died of "delirium tremens" only four days out. Another crewman died April 1, followed by others on the sixth and the seventh. Two more men passed away on the eighth, and another on the tenth.[40]

Although disease, injury, and death were far too common in the Union navy, sailors of all races benefited from an advanced navy medical system that the army could not match. Conscious of the need to keep the manpower it had, the navy had maintained a high standard of medical care since the inception of the service. In 1799, Congress established the Hospital Service Act to care for ailing sailors in civilian hospitals, funded by a twenty-cent-per-month fee deducted from enlisted and officer pay alike. With civilian hospital care proving too expensive, in 1811 the navy established its own hospital fund, hiring civilian doctors to treat navy personnel at navy yards. In 1830, the navy freed itself of civilian medical treatment by opening its first hospital at the Norfolk Navy Yard, still funded by the monthly pay deduction. The navy trained physicians at its own medical school, opened in 1823, at the Philadelphia Navy Yard. Navy medical training consisted of thirty-two weeks of schooling and three years as an intern under the direction of a licensed physician, followed by oral examinations and the writing of a competent medical treatise. By 1861, naval hospitals existed at navy yards at Portsmouth, Boston, Brooklyn, Philadelphia, and Washington, D.C. In contrast, the only army-operated hospital available at the time was at remote Fort Leavenworth, Kansas.[41]

In 1842, the importance of medical care to the navy became apparent by the creation of a separate Bureau of Medicine and Surgery, equal to the other navy bureaus. Under the authority of the secretary of the navy, the bureaus were responsible for different aspects of naval administration. In 1861 the navy consisted of the Bureau of Yards and Docks; Bureau of Construction, Equipment, and Repairs; Bureau of Provisions and Clothing; Bureau of Ordnance and Hydrography; and Bureau of Medicine and Surgery. The bureau system persisted until the merging of the armed forces in 1947 under the secretary of defense. Naval medicine became truly an independent institution with the opening of the naval laboratory at the Brooklyn Navy Yard. The laboratory freed the navy from purchasing drugs and medicines from civilian suppliers, ensuring cheaper costs and reliable standards of quality.[42]

With high standards of navy medical professionalism present before the war, African American sailors benefited from a better medical service than black soldiers could expect. Comparing the casualty statistics of the army and navy, as well as those of black soldiers and sailors, demonstrates the competency of navy doctors. The Union army suffered a total of 286,484 fatalities, imposed upon the 2,778,304 enlistments in the Union army.[43] The average Union soldier, then, had a roughly one in nine chance of dying during the war and a one in forty-five chance of dying in action with the enemy. African American troops had even higher casualty rates. Among the 178,975 African American enlisted men, 36,847 died, a ratio of one in five. In comparison, the estimated 118,000 naval enlistments suffered 1,805 killed or mortally wounded in battle among a total of roughly 7,031 casualties, a killed-in-action ratio of one in sixty-five and a casualty ratio of one in seventeen. The impact of disease was even greater on the Union army, with nearly one of every fifteen enlistees dying of disease (183,287), and one in seven African American soldiers succumbing to various ailments (26,211). The navy, with superior medical services and generally better living conditions, lost only about 3,000 men to "disease and accident," a ratio of one in forty.[44]

Despite a high level of medical care, African Americans were still more likely to perish in the service. A sample of recruits from several northern states found that 8 percent of the African American sailors died during their term of service, compared with only 5 percent of white seamen. In every state sample a larger percentage of African Americans died in the service, and some states exhibited dramatic differences. Ohio had the lowest percentage of African American deaths (5 percent compared with 3 percent of white sailors), followed by Massachusetts (5 percent for both races), Rhode Island (7 percent to 6 percent), Connecticut (8 percent to 4 percent), and Illinois (14 percent to 10 percent). Illinois had the highest death rate for both races, both because of the high percentage of former slaves enlisting in Illinois and because many Illinois sailors were sent into the Mississippi Squadron, which engaged in close-order fighting and suffered disproportionate casualties.[45]

The effectiveness of navy medicine was even more evident later in the sailor's life, as seen in the census of Civil War veterans conducted in 1890. Twenty-five years after the war, 51 percent of Union and 49 percent of Confederate white veterans were still alive, compared with only 29 percent of African American veterans. This is attributable to a life full of hard labor, if the veteran was a former slave, and a generally poor diet and unhealthy living conditions as members of the lower class after the war. Before 1890, 45 percent of African American veterans who applied for pensions died of respiratory diseases, followed by infection or parasitic disease. Pension applicants after 1890 died of more long-term ills, such as circulatory ailments. African American navy veterans, however, seemed to suffer fewer major ailments compared with their white counterparts.[46] They had a lower disability percentage than whites (17 percent compared with 23 percent) as well as lower percentages in most disability categories. African American veterans suffered from a higher percentage of disabilities due to wounds (6 percent to 4 percent) but had a lower percentage of ailments attributable to physical injuries (5 percent to 7 percent) and disease (6 percent to 11 percent) than white navy veterans.[47] Another loose generalization about African American navy veteran mortality emerges from the lower percentage (9 percent) of 1890 census information on African American veterans provided by their widows, compared with 10 percent for white veterans. Being alive in 1890 to provide census data implies a lower mortality rate, although this is admittedly a rather generous presumption.[48]

There were several reasons to account for the higher standard of medical care in the navy. First, the naval medical school turned out enough doctors to equip the navy as the war progressed. When the war began, the navy had 69 surgeons and 80 assistant surgeons, increasing to 80 surgeons and 118 assistants a year later. Moreover, during the Civil War the navy hired 245 acting assistant surgeons, civilian physicians plying their trade in the military service. Enough doctors meant that nearly every vessel, with the exception of the smaller gunboats, and shore station had an able full-time medical officer present. The Union army, on the other hand, constantly faced a shortage of medical personnel and was forced to retain some doctors of questionable ability. Also, fast moving army units could easily outstrip their medical teams, leaving decent medical care far behind. The segregated African American regiments in particular suffered from inadequate medical support. Few white doctors were willing to treat black soldiers, and the army commissioned only 8 African American physicians, assigning 6 of them to the army hospital in Washington, D.C. Poor medical care led to extremely lopsided casualty rolls. The 5th U.S. Colored Heavy Artillery suffered 829 fatalities during the war, including 124 in battle and 697 to disease and accidents. The 65th U.S. Colored Infantry (never tested in battle) suffered 755 fatalities, all to illness and accident.[49]

The navy's skilled physicians also went to sea with a wider variety and greater amount of drugs and medicines than their army counterparts. The naval laboratory at Philadelphia expanded along with the medical service, proving the latest treatments to navy doctors, permitting them to dispense with many old and ill-advised methods of treatment. John V. Lauderdale, a doctor attached to the Mississippi River squadron, was a good example of the highly capable doctors available to navy personnel. Treating wounded army troops for diarrhea, Lauderdale commented, "we use only a few simple remedies, [and] never give mercury, they have generally been mercurialized enough when they come on board." This advanced knowledge of contemporary medicine contrasted sharply with medical care in the merchant service. In 1851, Ned, a slave aboard the merchant steamer *Vanleer*, died of cholera despite efforts to save him such as "rubbing him with brandy, cayenne pepper and . . . Dr. Cannon's anti-cholera preparation." Unlike army doctors, whose stock of supplies was limited to ensure mobility, navy doctors usually had enough space to take to sea sufficient stocks of medicine to care for the crew. The additional storage permitted surgeons to include remedies that army doctors often lacked, such as more exotic drugs, anesthesia (the navy preferred ether but usually used chloroform because it was nonflammable), and liquor for "medicinal purposes." Navy drug treatments were so effective that scurvy, an ailment usually associated with the navy, was a greater burden to the army. The army suffered an average of thirteen cases of scurvy per thousand men (one-tenth of all army disease-related fatalities) compared with the navy's four cases per thousand.[50]

Despite the navy's excellent medical system, sailors sometimes treated themselves with patent medicines acquired through the mail or provided by concerned families. After the crew had consumed tainted water, Stephen Blanding, a petty officer aboard the USS *Louisiana,* treated the crew with doses of "Perry Davis' pain killer," a patent medicine received in the mail. The sailors proved very fond of the remedy, especially when mixed with a little water, and ailing crewmen constantly pestered the officer for a spoonful to calm their stomachs. The concoction was almost certainly alcohol-based, and Blanding suspected the deck officers "kept a supply, if not of Perry Davis' pain killer, something fully as strong, and not always to be used in case of emergency."[51]

The navy also lowered mortality by expanding its medical facilities. In addition to its six prewar hospitals, the navy added health centers at Memphis; New Orleans; Portland, Maine; Cairo, Illinois; Pensacola and Key West, Florida; and New Bern, Washington, and Plymouth, North Carolina, although the new hospitals varied in quality. While the Plymouth and Memphis hospitals featured large recovery bays and plenty of hospital staff, the New Bern facility housed only twelve patients in an uncultivated wood described as a "wilderness." For African American sailors, medical care suffered when navy hospitals were not available. Black sailor Robert Bond, wounded in the chest by a Confederate ambush, received his first medical care at the army's Hammond Hospital in Beaufort, North Carolina. Segregated into a separate "colored" ward, Bond's health suffered. In May 1864, however, Bond entered the navy hospital at Norfolk, Virginia. The racially mixed wards, segregated only by rank, featured more physicians, better food, and superior facilities, including flush toilets. In the superior navy facilities, Bond's health improved, and he went on to live a long life.[52]

In addition, the navy had access to dedicated hospital ships on the Mississippi River, the region where close clashes with Confederate forces were most likely. In December 1862 the navy placed a captured Confederate steamer in commission as the USS *Red Rover*, the first dedicated hospital ship in American naval history. A former passenger liner, *Red Rover* featured two operating rooms, a separate surgery space for amputations, filters on the windows to keep soot from the smokestacks out of the recovery wards, an elevator to shift patients between decks, and several flush toilets. The vessel listed another first when it took female nurses aboard for the first time in a navy ship. The nurses, nuns from the Order of the Holy Cross in South Bend, Indiana, aided a professional medical staff of seven surgeons caring for as many as one hundred patients. The support staff comprised several "colored laundresses" who performed much of the manual labor and complemented the nurses. Formally enlisted into the navy and paid ten dollars per month, the African American laundresses were perhaps the first women inducted into the U.S. military. Navy doctors could also rely on hospital ships operated by the Union army to transport wounded and ailing troops and sailors to hospitals in the North, and navy doctors frequently treated patients aboard army ships and vice versa. The North Atlantic Blockading Squadron temporarily converted the hulk *Ben Morgan* into a floating hospital in March 1862, followed by the captured schooner *Comet* in March 1864, a quarantine ship for smallpox cases. Lacking a dedicated hospital ship, Vice Admiral David G. Farragut, commanding the West Gulf Blockading Squadron, temporarily converted the sidewheel steamer USS *Tallahatchie* into a hospital ship for the Mobile Bay operations in 1864.[53]

The nature of navy life also aided in better health. Whereas army troops often slept on the ground in the open air, navy crews enjoyed properly sheltered sleeping arrangements. Army troops far from their supply lines contrasted sharply with sailors eating regular (if not occasionally monotonous) meals of reasonable healthiness. Sailors also had a greater opportunity to bathe and wash their clothes. Hot water was always available from the ship's boilers. Many commanding officers regularly set aside a day for the crew to do their laundry (usually Saturday), although wartime conditions made this practice sometimes uncertain. Steam-powered ships also had the intrinsic health benefit of clean drinking water. Salt water, or unclean river water, was highly corrosive to a ship's boilers, so steam ships were equipped with condensers to distill water for the boilers, with the excess clean water available for crew consumption. Providing pure water eliminated many of the parasite-related diseases, such as dysentery, that plagued army troops consuming water from tainted sources.[54]

The racial tolerance of the navy bureaucracy is clear, but personal relations between African American and white sailors could not be mandated by the Navy Department. The attitudes of officers commanding black sailors, for instance, varied widely, but generally depictions of African Americans by white officers ranged from positive to ambivalent, with few instances of overt hostility or racism. Some officers expressed openly abolitionist opinions, speaking highly of African American contributions to Union victory. Robert Critchell, an acting master's mate aboard the USS *Silver Cloud,* recounted his first prewar contact with slavery: "I attended several slave auctions and felt disagreeably the constantly asserted claim of superiority by the slave holding community." Israel E. Vail, the paymaster's clerk on USS *Massachusetts,* also openly expressed his disgust of slavery when encountering an elderly slave couple left behind by their fleeing owners to fend for themselves: "It was a pitiful sight indeed, and we were deeply impressed with the loneliness and hopelessness of those aged people. . . . I was impressed with the ingratitude and wrong that was shown, in [the owner] abandoning these aged and decrepit servants, whose years of labor had made him rich . . . to subsist on what their weak and trembling hands could dig from the ground."[55]

Still, paternalistic and condescending opinions regarding African Americans were common among navy officers. It was a widely held belief among Union sailors that freed slaves were like children free from their parents, in need of supervision. Aboard the USS *Florida,* officers depicted a thirteen-year-old African American third-class boy named Columbus as "a perfect monkey, eternally grinning or cutting up some shine." Other accounts comment with patronizing amusement on the enthusiasm of slaves, especially their cultural propensity for group singing and dancing to celebrate significant events, a common sight in the presence of Union gunboats, a sure sign that freedom had arrived. One man recalled passing "a saw mill, where there were about a dozen negroes of all dimensions, dancing and going though many ludicrous gymnastic exercises, which they intended as manifestation of joy on their part and afforded no little amusement to us." Some Union officers, encountering African American culture for the first time in their lives, were curious, even fascinated. In many written accounts, officers carefully and accurately recounted the slave dialect they encountered when speaking to African Americans or listening to their songs. Other officers distinctly remembered the physical descriptions of African Americans who persisted in their memory, such as the local woman who cooked for the ship: "She was about as broad as long, short and dumpy, and had thick, fat hands, a broad face, large eyes, an extremely broad and flat nose, . . . thick, wooly hair, which she wore in stubby curls all over her head. . . . It was like striking a solid mass of India rubber to butt against old Aunt Phebe."[56]

Many officers grew to respect the African American seamen under their command, favorably referring their crewmen in many reports and memoirs. Stephen Blanding, supervising repairs on a ship, "had four men from the 'Louisiana' to help me. . . . Besides these I had twelve contrabands, most of them quite good ship carpenters." A. J. Hopkins, an engineer at the Washington Navy Yard, conducted major repairs on a frigate's steam machinery in a few days with "only the aid of three or four contraband negroes." The attitudes of other officers changed after receiving valuable information from escaped slaves. African Americans provided the navy with updates concerning the construction of the Confederate ironclad CSS *Virginia.* Escaped slaves were instrumental in curtailing Florida's salt-making industry, guiding Federal forces to saltworks. Florida produced most of the salt, vital to the preservation of food, used in the Confederacy. (The navy became so successful in restricting the enterprise that salt became a significant portion of blockade-runner's cargoes. English salt, fifty cents a sack before the war, sold for $140 per sack in Atlanta by October 1862.) Contrabands fleeing to the USS *Massachusetts* reported that the vessel had crippled the CSS *Florida* in an earlier exchange of fire, information of which the Union commander was ignorant.[57] African Americans provided the officers of the USS *Huron* with information about the defenses at the mouth of the Stono River in South Carolina, data highly detailed because the slaves "helped to build it." When the *Huron* engaged the fortifications, "contrabands come aboard every day & tell us just where our shot strike & where the new guns are placed." In June 1862, information from a contraband led the navy to the schooner *Southern Belle* loaded with three thousand bushels of rice, which provisioned the nearby navy contraband camp at St. Simon's, South Carolina, for some weeks.[58]

Other officers owed their lives to slaves offering useful information. An officer conducting shore reconnaissance in North Carolina encountered "a colored man who told us we had better be careful, as there were rebel cavalry in the town." Separated from his shore party in hostile territory, Commander George H. Perkins relied on a local slave to "drive me, in any sort of vehicle he could get, down the levee road to our lines . . . at the negro's earnest entreaty, I put on my uniform coat wrong-side out, that it might not attract attention . . . [the driver] whipped up his mule till we were safe beyond their reach." In December 1864, navy Lieutenant William Cushing, attempting to capture General Louis Herbert, the commander of the Confederate garrison at Smithville, North Carolina, received the assistance of several local slaves who guided Cushing and his party to their target and then escaped with the Union party. Although Cushing captured the wrong officer, any success would have eluded him without the help of the local African Americans.[59]

Not all slaves were willing to aid the Union cause, however. A raid on Confederate salt works in September 1862 led to the destruction of the salt kettles and the capture of two African American carpenters hired to maintain them. The carpenters refused to leave the works, forcing the Union sailors to confiscate their tools as contraband useful to the enemy. In December 1862, a local African American refused to pilot a navy vessel near Apalachicola, Florida. The man refused on the grounds he owed his allegiance to the state of Florida, and the pilot was returned to his home with a certificate for the Confederate authorities expressing the fact the man had not aided Union forces.[60]

Other African Americans, either by force or by free will, aided the Confederate cause. In October 1861, Commander O. S. Glisson of the USS *Mount Vernon* reported the arrest of two men crossing the Rappahanock River in a canoe, a white man named Conolly Johnson and "a free Negro named George Moss." The men had thrown their cargo overboard as the Union vessel approached, and their suspicious behavior convinced Glisson that the two men were "engaged in illicit trade with the rebels." Near Winton, North Carolina, in February 1862, the USS *Delaware*'s lookout observed "a negro woman . . . motioning the boat to approach." Taking the motion as a friendly gesture, the *Delaware* pulled close to shore, where a Confederate ambush opened fire on the vessel, but no sailors were injured. When captured the next day, the woman claimed the Confederates had forced her to be the lure for their trap. In April 1862, the officers of the USS *Louisiana* arrested and searched an African American civilian seen fishing near the vessel on several occasions, suspecting him of spying for the enemy.[61]

Aboard Union vessels, it is clear that racism did exist, and some officers did little to disguise their attitudes. An officer aboard the USS *Hartford* believed African Americans to be "more of an encumbrance than an article of use, aboard a man-of-war, and . . . I wish we were rid of them. . . . they are a nuisance not to be tolerated. . . . a white man cannot speak to one of them and receive a civil answer. . . . I pity them, because they have not good sense, for if they had, they would never leave a plantation (a good home during their whole life, and a kind master,) to cast themselves adrift upon . . . a cold, unfeeling world. I know many will . . . wish themselves back from whence they were foolish enough to run away." Some officers, however, underwent a change of heart regarding their racist attitudes. Early in the war, Robert Critchell considered the black sailors aboard his vessel "always lazy, and hard to manage," but when his vessel discovered the massacre of African American troops at Fort Pillow, Tennessee, in April 1864 Critchell joined in his black crewmen's desire for revenge. Submitting a report of the incident to his congressman, Critchell voiced his expectation of retribution: "I now write to you with reference to the Fort Pillow massacre, because some of our crew are colored and I feel personally interested in the retaliation which our government may deal to the rebels."[62]

Contrary to the varied attitudes of officers, the opinions of white enlisted sailors on black mariners are muted. Relatively few enlisted men had their diaries or memoirs published, and those in print are predominated by tales of travel to exotic lands, not descriptions of their innermost thoughts regarding their shipmates. Other works on the subject of African American sailors have claimed a high level of racism by white sailors toward their black counterparts, but many of their examples are perhaps misinterpreted. One historian claimed, "The white attitude towards blacks created a hostile barrier between the races . . . and hostilities were bound to occur." Rather, there exists very little evidence of widespread racism on the part of white enlisted men, and certainly not enough to support a thesis of active discrimination. This is not to imply that racial harmony existed aboard navy ships, but there is not enough proof to allege institutional racism on the part of the navy establishment.[63]

One of the most persistent pieces of "evidence" to prove navy racism is the memoir of Rowland S. True, a lieutenant aboard the USS *Silver Lake*. True mentioned that the African American sailors aboard the vessel had their meals provided from a "mess and mess cook . . . entirely separate from ours," implying that the black sailors were segregated from the white crewmembers. The implication, however, is misplaced. Messes in the nineteenth-century navy were not places where one ate (a twentieth-century definition) but whom one ate with based upon watch schedule and where the sailor worked. True mentions that the African American sailors were members of the engineering division, so their

presence in a separate mess is no surprise. Also, True remarked
that the *Silver Lake* had five separate messes. What True was actually observing was that black crewmen were in a different mess
than his, not a separate mess from the whites.[64]

Another commonly cited example of racism among the enlisted men is the practice of dressing white sailors in blackface
for makeshift minstrel shows aboard ships, suggesting that whites
were lampooning African Americans by perpetuating the
"Sambo" stereotype. Again, this is a twentieth-century misinter-
pretation of a common form of entertainment from the nineteenth century. The Sambo stereotype had been a familiar feature of popular theater well before the Civil War, catering mostly
to the working class. Some historians have argued convincingly
that, far from satirizing African Americans, the Sambo stereotype was a manifestation of working class angst amid a changing
world. New technologies, urban life, and the professionals who
dominated the workingman's life were all targets of satire, an
outlet from an increasingly confusing world. The character of
Sambo did not necessarily portray African Americans. Since the-
atergoers were whites from an increasingly industrial society, a
polar opposite character, one in blackface, represented the pro-
gressively more alien agrarian ideal of the past. When similar
shows appeared aboard navy ships, the productions served the
same purpose for enlisted men: an outlet for complaints about
the food or the boredom of blockade duty, and an opportunity
to ridicule the officers. While some sailors may not have grasped
the subtlety of the production and perceived only the strange
behavior of "black" performers, it is difficult to call minstrel
shows racist when African American sailors themselves enjoyed
performing in them (see chapter 7). Importantly, even if the
shows organized by the sailors themselves had a racist motivation
at their conception, the navy as an institution was not involved.[65]

Still, the lack of institutional racism from the U.S. Navy
could not prevent individual bigotry among its crewmen, inevitable in the race-conscious American society. A glaring example is the diary of a marine, Miles M. Oviatt, aboard the USS
Vanderbilt. Granted liberty, Oviatt was disgusted to discover who
his liberty companions were: "we wer hurried into a boat, and

as there was some Niggars going, we had their company . . .
having to be put off with the niggars, had rather got the best of
my better nature . . . consequently was in no humor to enjoy
liberty." Another example of possibly racist attitudes was an officer aboard the USS *Silver Lake* who punished unwashed sailors
by having the offended "Stripped and scrubbed with hickory
brooms, in the hands of two strong Negroes. It wasn't often a
man needed a second scrubbing." The embarrassment of a
public bathing was increased in this case by African Americans
forcibly bathing the white offender in front of the entire crew,
using the racial perceptions of the crew to aid in their discipline. In March 1863, Thomas Wilton confessed to attempted
desertion from the South Atlantic Blockading Squadron.
Drunk on a shore party, Wilton refused to return to the USS *Se-
bago*, stating he "didn't believe in fighting for niggers." Wilton
received a year of hard labor in a state penitentiary. Aboard the
USS *Nahant*, a crewman described the officer's cook as "about
the 'plainest' negro I have ever met, and, like most negroes, he
had no love for an Irish boy, which Barney certainly was; but I
was just plain Yankee, and cook and I had no frictions."[66]

There are several possible reasons abject racism by white
crewmembers was minimal. Old salts from the prewar navy had
served side by side with African American crewmen for years,
and the experienced sailors served as role models for inexperienced recruits and draftees, demonstrating a racial tolerance
rarely found in civilian life. Second, most black sailors quickly
adapted to their new military role, perhaps earning a measure
of respect from their white counterparts. A more likely reason
for the scarcity of overt racism, however, is the fact that black
and white sailors shared in a common existence. They ate the
same food, shared common sleeping areas, and together fought
the most dreaded enemy of Civil War navy service, the mind-
numbing tedium of daily repetition.

Navy life left little time for individual leisure, and existence
became very monotonous. The tedium was worst on vessels on
blockade duty. Riverine warships at least had some change of
scenery to vary the day, but blockaders endured day after day of
the same schedule, same people around them, same vista. One

bored sailor lamented, "I have seen enough of the sea. I am not sea sick, but I am sick of the sea." While larger ships had bands or even libraries, crewmen on smaller vessels had to make do with their imaginations to amuse themselves. After all the stories were told, songs sung to their exhaustion, and newspapers read, sailors became desperate to break the tedium. Some men turned to religion: "Read a few chapters in the Bible for we have been taken with scripture reading since we came to sea." Sailors resorted to the "alternative of seeking amusement in such simple games and pastimes as we had abandoned upon reaching maturity . . . the games of childhood are entered into with as much avidity as when indulged in at the time for which they were intended." Boredom led to disciplinary problems, as sailors frustrated by weeks of inactivity became short-tempered. As an officer described the surliness of his crew, "Jack is full of fight, and when he cannot fight his enemy, he will get in a quarrel with his own friends. . . . Secesh [the Confederates] will not give Jack a chance to show his powers of endurance and he is sick at heart, and he wants to go home." The desperation to escape sea duty led one sailor to envy the crew of a vessel heading north to repair battle damage: "What luck some people do have! If one of the shells had only hit us the other day we should be going home to glory, cool drinks, and our best girls."[67]

The African Americans who enlisted in the Union navy faced many daunting tasks. Sailors dealt with combat, illness, and the repetition of daily life. Yet the problems confronted by black sailors were the same faced by whites. If shared burdens and benefits measure equality, then the U.S. Navy deserves commendation for dispensing equality in fair measure to its African American personnel. Although the benefits granted to African American sailors were only temporary, they attracted to the navy a large number of men willing to put up with the drudgery of everyday life at sea in exchange for a chance to prove themselves.

Chapter Five

"ENERGETICALLY AND BRAVELY—

NONE MORE SO"

AFRICAN AMERICAN SAILORS IN COMBAT

• While African American sailors enjoyed the relative equality of life in the U.S. Navy, such participation came with a price. The navy recruited African Americans to help win a war, and the risk of death and injury always lurked just around the corner. Casualties never reached the shocking levels of the Union army, but naval combat was just as deadly. Naval battles during the Civil War resembled the Mexican War more than earlier American conflicts. The Confederacy attempted to assemble enough vessels to challenge the U.S. blockade, but ship-to-ship duels remained rare. Instead, the Union navy patrolled hostile rivers, raided shore installations, and bombarded targets on shore in support of the army. Whatever the point of conflict, sailors found naval warfare during the Civil War a deadly business. Aside from accidental injury or death, sailors could meet their end by hidden snipers, concealed artillery in riverside ambushes, rifled guns carried by virtually impervious ironclad warships, or submerged mines.

Despite the considerable risks, African Americans equally shared the dangers of Civil War combat with their white shipmates. On a practical level, keeping African American seamen out of harm's way was an impossible task. Once combat commenced, no place on a ship was safe, and every sailor became a potential casualty. The assignment of battle stations and combat duties, though, reflects how much the navy trusted and relied on its African American sailors. In this regard, the navy was as equally liberal as it was with its pay, benefits, and medical care. Unlike the army, which often hesitated to place African American troops into combat and preferred to use them only as service troops, the navy trusted black sailors in combat, expecting them to perform just as other crewmen. In describing the experience of African American sailors in combat, several categories of examination emerge, such as the treatment of black soldiers in comparison to African American sailors. Just like white sailors, African American seamen committed conspicuous acts of bravery under fire, earning the praise and rewards of the navy. Black sailors suffered serious wounds and combat fatalities. Other sailors were captured, potentially a fate worse than death. By accepting the challenge of combat, African American sailors risked death and injury, but proved their mettle as men worthy of freedom and the rights of citizenship.

African American sailors participated in naval combat from the very first battles. The army, though, was unwilling to allow black soldiers to fight. U.S. Army officials shared the widely held opinion in the North that the conflict should be fought with the preservation of the Union as the primary military objective; African American participation, they believed, was an irrelevant distraction. The fight was between white northerners and white southerners to decide political, not social, questions, and the debate over slavery was best left alone. With no plan to change the status of slavery in the South, the army initially ignored requests to use African American troops. Furthermore, any sign of organization by African Americans attracted negative responses from public officials made nervous by blacks drilling for armed action. Public officials in Cincinnati stopped one such attempt with the rebuke, "We want you d——d niggers to stay out of this. This is a white man's war." The public had considerable concerns about a war for slave liberation. Industrial workers feared an influx of freed slaves offering cheap labor for northern factories. Public officials imagined poor houses filled with African Americans unwilling to work unless forced. Farmers, already worried about competing with slave labor in the agricultural markets, saw freed slaves as competition for land on the frontier. Social critics warned of a "bastardized race" created by widespread miscegenation. Even some who wanted an end to slavery objected to

African American participation in their white crusade. The religious mission to destroy slavery was for the pure of heart and spirit. Hence, they believed it "unworthy of a civilized or a Christian nation to use in war soldiers whose skin was not white."[1]

Once African American troops did enter service, the army did not automatically grant acceptance. Racial stereotypes especially slowed the use of African Americans in combat. Some officers believed that soldiers of African descent were naturally inclined toward a "subservient status" that made them poor soldiers. Others thought blacks incapable of the physical regimen of army life, a strange attitude considering the backbreaking labor imposed upon slaves. The stereotype of African Americans as incapable of complex thinking also hindered enlistment. Officers, not speaking from experience, considered blacks incapable of close-order drill, much less the operation of the tools of war. Before the war, General Benjamin Butler described African Americans as childishly "horrified of firearms," frightened by the flash and bang.[2]

In 1862, however, Butler, the military governor of newly captured New Orleans, asked the other question dogging African American troops: Would they fight? The army wondered whether former slaves, cowed by generations of slavery, could destroy the slaveowning South. Even if African American troops would fight, no one in the Union army readily believed they could stand the rigors of combat. Supposedly lacking the will and discipline of white troops, black soldiers suffered the expectation that they would run from the battlefield at the first sound of firing. Predisposed to the opinion that African Americans did not have the mental capacity to be soldiers, white officers hesitated to lead black troops into battle. Consequently, the regiments of the U.S. Colored Troops (USCT), formed after the Emancipation Proclamation, found themselves in an army unwilling to let them fight.[3]

Instead, the army assigned many USCT regiments to rear-area garrison duty or, much worse, to the hard labor needed to maintain an army in the field. Manual labor, or fatigue duty, might include clearing forests, mounting guns, building roads, digging entrenchments, or unloading supplies. Whatever the labor, fatigue duty was hard, monotonous, and potentially dangerous work. Without facing the enemy, USCT regiments lost men to accidents and exhaustion, as the labor damaged the health of many men. Black units also lost personnel because of the drudgery. Many black soldiers, tired of the repetitive work instead of fighting the enemy, decided to desert rather than squander their time and health in pointless labor. White combat units were often punished with fatigue duty, and the lack of status in performing the task full time destroyed the morale of many USCT units. Moreover, the constant fatigue duty denied black troops the time to drill and train. When these poorly prepared troops did fight, they almost inevitably fared poorly, reinforcing the stereotype that African American soldiers were unreliable.[4]

The army never properly utilized its black troops. Benjamin Butler decided his black troops would dig rather than fight. An officer under Butler's command wrote, "The colored troops will probably be kept near and used . . . for fatigue duty, such as making roads, building bridges, and draining marshes; they will seldom put into battle." Appeals from the commanding officers of USCT regiments too often went unheard. The 34th U.S. Colored Infantry assisted in the capture of Morris Island, South Carolina, in the summer of 1863. Immediately afterward, however, the troops labored "to mount guns, haul cannon and mortars, and were kept constantly and exclusively on fatigue duty of the severest kind." This labor lasted for six months, restricting, in the words of their commanding officer Colonel James Montgomery, "my opportunities . . . to make soldiers of my recruits." Even efforts by senior Union generals did not halt the excessive fatigue duty for African American troops. Major General Quincy A. Gillmore, commanding the Department of the South in 1863, issued a general order demanding a halt to the use of black troops to "prepare camps and perform menial duty. . . . Such use of these details is unauthorized and improper." The army's perception of African American soldiers as only laborers reached its peak in 1864 when the service created seven USCT regiments for the sole purpose of carrying out fatigue duty in their combat areas. Although these units did see some combat, they spent their term of service almost entirely on fatigue duty.[5]

USCT regiments also suffered inadequate logistics and equipment. Many units lacked proper shoes and uniforms, and many went into battle with substandard firearms. This does not mean, however, that no USCT unit fought well. By the end of the war, African American troops collectively demonstrated their skill and bravery on the battlefield. But, for every distinguished combat action, such as Milliken's Bend, in the history of the Civil War, there exists a disastrous event, such as the Petersburg Crater, where inexperienced and ill-equipped black troops sacrificed themselves with little to show for their efforts. In a desperate battle at Milliken's Bend, Louisiana, in June 1863, three inexperienced African American regiments defeated a Confederate force. One of the black regiments, the 1st Regiment Mississippi Infantry (African Descent), had received their rifles only one day before the battle. Nevertheless, the 1st Mississippi and the other units, at some points bayonet-to-bayonet, fought the Confederates to a standstill. Captain Matthew Miller of the 9th Regiment Louisiana Infantry (African Descent) bragged after the battle, "I never more wish to hear the expression, 'The niggers won't fight.'" The scandalous waste of black troops in July 1864 during the siege of Petersburg, Virginia, however, offsets that milestone of African American achievement on the battlefield. Mired in a stalemate, Union engineers devised a plan to break the impasse. Union engineers tunneled under the Confederate lines and packed a chamber with gunpowder, hoping the resulting explosion would open a gap in the enemy lines the infantry could exploit. A division of African American troops under Brigadier General Edward Ferrero trained specifically for the mission, but Lieutenant General Ulysses S. Grant ordered a division of white troops substituted for the black troops at the last minute. Unprepared for the assault, the white troops, commanded by Brigadier General James H. Ledlie, attacked into the explosion's crater instead of around it and found themselves hopelessly trapped. Ferrero's troops rushed to their aid, but their assault came too late, and the Confederates massacred many of the black troops after they surrendered.[6]

Combat for African American sailors, however, began with the war's earliest conflicts, and the navy entrusted black sailors with vital combat roles instead of shunting them into minor, subservient tasks. Integrated crews faced the perils of battle in equal measure. Far from protecting them in the relatively safe areas of the ship, the navy thrust African American sailors into the fray. Black sailors served in vital stations during combat, as emphasized by the battle stations aboard USS *Saugus*. The vessel held seventy-seven officers and men on January 1, 1865, including fourteen African Americans. Six black sailors served on the gun crews while another seven, mostly the coal heavers, manned the magazine or passed munitions, leaving the engineering officers to shovel coal themselves during battle. One black first-class boy served in the pilothouse to pass messages from the captain to other parts of the ship.[7]

The first major combat operation undertaken by the navy during the Civil War, the capture of Hatteras Inlet, North Carolina, in 1861, featured a sizeable number of African Americans. The steam frigate USS *Minnesota*, flagship of Commodore Silas H. Stringham, had several African Americans among its gun crews, including an all-black detachment manning the aft pivot gun. Instead of dropping anchor and shooting from a stationary position, Stringham formed his ships into a line ahead and fired from a circular course. The tactic gave each ship a clear shot at the enemy on the inbound leg of the circle and time to reload on the outbound. As *Minnesota*'s only gun aimed at the enemy during the reloading leg of the circle, the aft pivot gun and its crew held considerable responsibility for maintaining pressure on the Confederate garrisons defending the inlet. Although the navy suffered no combat casualties during the battle, the strain of combat led the navy to medically discharge several of *Minnesota*'s crew in the months after the action, including several African Americans. A few months later, *Minnesota* was again in action, this time at Hampton Roads, Virginia, in support of the blockade. The Confederate ironclad, CSS *Virginia*, accompanied by three smaller craft, attacked the Union squadron blocking access to the sea. Maneuvering to avoid the *Virginia*, the *Minnesota* ran aground and for the duration of the battle the aft pivot gun, manned by its African American crew, remained its only means of defense from the Confederate vessel. *Minnesota*'s casualties from the battle included two wounded African Americans, brothers Joyce and Elis Moore. All of *Minnesota*'s African American sailors received special praise. "The Negroes fought energetically and bravely—none more so," wrote their commanding officer. "They evidently felt that they were thus working out the deliverance of their race."[8]

Including African American sailors in battle reinforced their bravery as men, but it also placed them at dire risk. Although the number of lives at stake never reached the levels of land battles, naval combat was deadly serious business, and death loomed around every bend in the river or coastal inlet. Riverine warfare was especially hazardous, with a constant risk of ambush from shore. On Virginia's York River in May 1864, while investigating a farmhouse, a boat crew from the USS *Mystic* came under fire from Confederate snipers. A bullet claimed the life of William Wilson, an African American first-class boy, "the ball passing through his heart." Forced to leave Wilson's body in the water, the boat crew retreated to the *Mystic* for reinforcements. Returning to the shore, the Union sailors recovered Wilson's remains, drove the Confederate snipers away, and burned down the farm in retaliation.[9]

A sniper also claimed the life of first-class boy James Lloyd of the USS *Ellis*. A captured Confederate blockade runner converted into a Union gunboat, *Ellis* ran aground in the Neuse River, North Carolina, in October 1862. Confederate forces converged before the ship's crew could refloat the vessel, and Lloyd suffered a mortal wound while abandoning the *Ellis* with the rest of its complement. An ambush in the same region proved deadly to the crew of the USS *Hunchback* in October 1862. Operating in support of army troops near Plymouth, North Carolina, *Hunchback* fell prey to a Confederate ambush on the Blackwater River. Maneuvering around the immobilized USS *Perry*, the *Hunchback* received several damaging hits from Confederate artillery pieces concealed in the underbrush. One burst of canister killed two of *Hunchback*'s crew, James Ritchie, a boatswain's mate, and a contraband named Frank Davis. Southern forces withdrew upon the arrival of the USS *Whitehead*.[10]

Confederate ambushes also plagued the Mississippi Squadron. In May 1864, the USS *Juliet*, a thinly armored "tinclad" operating in support of the Union Army's campaign up the Red River to seize Shreveport, Louisiana, underwent a harrowing odyssey. Ambushed at a narrow bend in the Red River, *Juliet* returned fire. Its consort, the USS *New Champion*, collided with *Juliet* in its attempt to retreat downriver, damaging *Juliet*'s bows. Briefly disabled, *Juliet* drifted under the fire of the Confederate cannon until secured by the USS *Fort Hindman*. After making emergency overnight repairs, *Juliet* returned downstream the next morning, only to strike a snag that tore a hole beneath the waterline. Taking on water, *Juliet* stumbled into another punishing ambush. Artillery shells "completely riddled" the ship's stack, and the commanding officer later reported that other shots damaged the "hull, disabling our rudder. One struck our port crank, cutting it off, thereby knocking out both cylinder heads and totally disabling the port engine." Again, only the timely intervention of the *Fort Hindman* saved the *Juliet* from destruction. Towed out of harm's way, *Juliet* finally reached safety later in the day. In its two-day ordeal, *Juliet*'s crew suffered thirteen casualties. Twelve were wounded officers and crew, with Robert Higgins, an African American coal heaver, the only fatality. Higgins died of shrapnel wounds inflicted by the shell that disabled *Juliet*'s engine. The *Fort Hindman* also endured casualties to save the *Juliet;* among their dead was Joseph Scott, an African American ordinary seaman. Sudden ambushes also proved deadly to the crew of the USS *Prairie Bird*. Patrolling near Gaines Landing, Arkansas, in August 1864, *Prairie Bird* met sizeable Confederate resistance in the form of a "masked battery of three or four guns and a large force of musketry." Although the skirmish lasted but ten minutes and *Prairie Bird* suffered little damage, its commanding officer, Acting Master Thomas Burns, had to report four men wounded and the death of African American ordinary seaman George Matthews, "killed instantly by a piece of shell." Likewise, the USS *Commodore Read* lost an African American sailor to the suddenness of war. Raiding along Virginia's Rappahannock River in April 1864, the *Commodore Read* fended off a brief Confederate assault but lost landsman Samuel Turner in the process. One of his shipmates regretted, "He was instantly killed and his body remains in the rebel hands. . . . I miss him very much as a friend and companion."[11]

Attacks on Union ships did not always end in victory or an

escape from defeat. In the narrow confines of southern rivers, an ambush, accident, or ill-planned attack often led to the loss of the Union vessel and fatalities among its crew. For instance, Union attempts in March 1863 to run warships past the Confederate batteries at Port Hudson, Mississippi, proved fatal to the USS *Mississippi*. The largest ship of the flotilla, *Mississippi* attracted the most attention from Confederate gunners. In an attempt to hug the shore under the rebel batteries, *Mississippi* ran aground, and, failing in efforts to refloat the vessel, her captain ordered the crew to abandon ship. Two hundred twenty-three of the vessel's complement reached safety, but sixty-four men lost their lives. Four contraband sailors were among the dead— Stephen Downey, Scot Lewis, George Jackson, and Moses Obenton. An intense Confederate ambush in Florida in May 1864 led to the loss of the USS *Columbine*. Caught on the St. John's River between Confederate cannon concealed on both sides of the river, *Columbine* had little chance to avoid danger. The opening Confederate volley severed the ship's rudder chains, and the vessel drifted deeper into the ambush until grounding a short distance downriver. *Columbine's* crew, including a detachment of soldiers from the 35th USCT, staved off the Confederates briefly until the commanding officer surrendered the ship to save his exposed crew. Several sailors decided to attempt an escape and managed to reach St. Augustine. From their reports, the navy estimated the casualties from the *Columbine* at twenty. Eyewitnesses confirmed the death of several African American soldiers and one black sailor, landsman William Moran.[12]

A surprise attack also doomed the USS *Underwriter*. In a predawn raid, Confederate troops stormed the *Underwriter* while the vessel lay at anchor near New Bern, North Carolina, in February 1864. After a brief hand-to-hand struggle, four Union crewmen lay dead and the Confederates held the ship. The Union dead comprised *Underwriter's* commanding officer, Acting Master Jacob Westervelt, fireman John Fealy, ordinary seaman John Biederman, and an African American first-class boy named Alfred Banks. As with the *Columbine*, several sailors opted for the risk of escape over life in a prisoner-of-war camp and bolted for freedom. The successful escapees included African American ordinary seaman Lewis Gordon. Unable to remove *Underwriter* to a safe location, the Confederates burned the ship.[13]

Underwriter was not the only Union ship to fall to a surprise Confederate assault. In June 1864, a Confederate raid seized control of the USS *Water Witch* at Ossabaw Sound, Georgia. Like the raid on the *Underwriter*, the attackers seized the ship anchored close to shore in a predawn raid. Although the attack took most of the crew by surprise, some Union sailors tried in vain to hold their attackers at bay. Two members of *Water Witch*'s crew died in the attack, including African American landsman Jeremiah Sills. A free man before the war, Sills decided to fight rather than possibly fall into slavery and "fought most desperately" until shot dead, "while men who despised him were cowering near with idle cutlasses in the racks jogging their elbows." An African American pilot named Moses Dallas, who also died in the attack, led the successful Confederate assault.[14]

Just as sudden as a Confederate ambush was death or injury from a "torpedo," or mine, striking the hull of a warship. Lacking an effective navy, the Confederacy used torpedoes in large numbers to offset the Union's numerical advantage. The Union navy lost sixteen warships to torpedoes, and several of the underwater menaces caused African American casualties. The most notable Union navy loss to a torpedo occurred in August 1864, during the capture of Mobile Bay, Alabama. One of the few remaining ports in the South not in Union hands, the navy sought to close Mobile Bay by running past its fortifications and seizing control of the bay. On August 5, 1864, the Union squadron, commanded by Rear (later Vice) Admiral David G. Farragut, steamed into the channel with the ironclad USS *Tecumseh* and three other armored warships in the van. Their job was to immediately find and attack the Confederate ironclad CSS *Tennessee* concealed somewhere in the bay. Little more than an hour into the attack, however, *Tecumseh* struck a mine and plunged to the bottom in a matter of seconds, leaving a handful of survivors in the water. Among those entombed aboard the *Tecumseh* were African American seaman Charles J. Pemberton and landsmen Charles C. Derris, Nathaniel B. Delano, Charles Hannibal, and Peter E. Parker.[15]

The plague of torpedoes did not end with the seizure of Mobile

Bay. The route up the Blakely River to Mobile itself remained a hazardous path for Union attackers. In April 1865, a deadly torpedo attack sank the tinclad USS *Rodolph* and inflicted casualties among its African American crewmen. The *Rodolph* was towing a barge filled with salvage equipment to raise the ironclad USS *Milwaukee*, itself a mine victim, when it struck the torpedo. The lightly constructed ship split nearly in two and sank rapidly. Among the four dead crewmen were African American landsman Johnson Smith and first-class boy Jule Baltour. Four other African American sailors received serious injuries: landsman Eli Robertson (broken leg), second-class fireman William Strother (broken arm), second-class boy Moses Payne (contusions), and second-class fireman Sewell Chicquoine (scalding). Mines in the same region also claimed the tugs USS *Ida* and *Althea,* used as makeshift minesweepers. Among the dead from these two ships were African Americans Philip Williams, G. D. Andrews, and J. Glen. Torpedoes also troubled coastal regions, and Union ships on the blockade fell victim to mines. In February 1865, the USS *Harvest Moon,* flagship of Rear Admiral John Dahlgren's South Atlantic Blockading Squadron, hit a mine in Winyah Bay, South Carolina. The blast killed one man and wounded several others. Among the casualties transferred to the Norfolk Naval Hospital were four unnamed African American sailors listed only as "contrabands" recruited at Georgetown, District of Columbia.[16]

African Americans suffered numerous casualties to ambushes and mines, and still more death and injury awaited them when the navy conducted large-scale offensive operations to seize strategic objectives. For instance, black sailors shed a considerable amount of blood during the assault on Mobile Bay. Aside from the dead aboard the *Tecumseh,* two other African Americans, first-class boy Richard Ashley of the USS *Lackawanna* and landsman William Smith of the USS *Hartford,* died in the battle. Contraband Moses Jones of the USS *Oneida,* landsman James Johnston on the USS *Monongahela,* coal heavers Isaac Hewson and Job Maygett of the *Lackawanna,* first-class boy Isaac Fisher aboard the USS *Kennebec,* landsman Peter Prentiss and landsman Augustus Simmons of the *Hartford,* and landsman Samuel Hazard on the USS *Ossipee* all received wounds. Virtually all major naval conflicts resulted in African American casualties. One of the most vicious fights occurred in April 1864, when four Union warships, USS *Ceres, Miami, Southfield,* and *Whitehead,* encountered the Confederate ironclad CSS *Albemarle* on the Roanoke River near Plymouth, North Carolina. Outgunned and unable to penetrate the ironclad's armor, the Union ships fought a desperate struggle to survive. *Albemarle* managed to sink the *Southfield* but in doing so blocked the river channel, allowing the other Union ships to withdraw. The heavy Union casualties included a number of African Americans. Aboard *Ceres,* an exploding shell killed landsman Samuel Pascall and wounded landsmen Edward Giddings and Isaiah Jones. *Miami,* with African Americans composing more than half its crew, had more than a dozen wounded black sailors aboard when it retreated, and *Whitehead* suffered six wounded black seamen. The majority of casualties occurred aboard the sunken *Southfield.* Daniel Barstow, Frederick Fletcher, Joseph Gilmore, Peter Jones, Samuel Lee, Willis Norcom, Henry Reed, Isaac Richardson, James Shannon, Burrill Sharp, Peter Skinner, John Southfield, and Johnson White died or were missing and presumed dead, and Charles White was captured.[17]

Another clash with a Confederate ironclad also proved deadly for a large number of African American sailors. The CSS *Arkansas,* operating in the Yazoo River in July 1862 to stymie Union attempts to reach Vicksburg, Mississippi, from the north, had to withdraw into deeper water. In its dash down the Yazoo, the *Arkansas* burst through the Union gunboats at the mouth of the river and headed for Vicksburg. Only the USS *Lancaster,* a ponderous ram, stood in its way, and paid the price. *Lancaster* withstood several full broadsides from *Arkansas,* with at least eight rounds striking its wheelhouse and upper works. After the battle, Union salvage crews found eighty-six projectiles of various sizes lodged in the battered Union vessel. Casualties were expectedly heavy. Of the forty-three African American sailors aboard the *Lancaster,* only six were fit for duty after the battle. Most of the casualties came from scalding when a shell wrecked *Lancaster*'s boiler.[18]

Dueling with Confederate shore batteries in support of combat operations could also prove deadly. Union warships attacked Grand Gulf, Mississippi, in April 1863 in an effort to reduce the defenses south of Vicksburg. Although the attack was successful, several Union warships sustained heavy damage and casualties. Four African American sailors were wounded aboard the USS *Pittsburgh,* and landsman James Haywood died when a shell struck the gun mount he served. William H. Wright, an African American landsman of the USS *Carondelet,* also died in the Grand Gulf assault. Challenging the Vicksburg batteries in May 1863 had tragic results for the crew of the USS *Cincinnati.* Three shots penetrated *Cincinnati*'s deck in rapid succession, "two shots entered the shell room . . . coming through the fantail and ricocheting up through the . . . port side. . . . A third shot entered the magazine and flooded it almost instantly." The shelling killed several African American sailors on the *Cincinnati:* first-class boys James Wilson, Henry Freeman, Albert Williams, and Richard Howard.[19]

A survey of Union navy battle reports also reveals many African American sailors wounded in action with the enemy. For example, the captain of the USS *Valley City* reported his casualties following the capture of Elizabeth City, North Carolina. Among the wounded was James A. Young, the African American wardroom cook, with a leg contusion from a shell splinter and burns on his face and neck, both injuries listed as "not dangerous." The USS *Hartford* suffered numerous casualties during a series of attacks on the Vicksburg batteries from April to July 1862. An assault on April 24 led to severe wounds to landsmen Charles H. Banks, Theodore Douglass, and ordinary seaman Henry Manning, and landsman Randall Taliaferro's leg required an amputation at mid-thigh. Attempts at taking Vicksburg in June and July led to still more casualties among the black sailors, with most soon returning to their duties.[20]

Throughout the Civil War, African American sailors were being injured and killed aboard U.S. warships. Two black sailors, William Carroll and William Davis, aboard USS *Minnesota* were wounded when the Confederate ironclad CSS *Virginia* challenged the Union blockade at Hampton Roads, Virginia, in March 1862. Unable to return to duty, the men received a medical discharge from the service from the Washington Naval Hospital.[21] Attacking Confederate forces on the White River in

Arkansas in June 1862, steam released by a Confederate shell striking the boiler of the USS *Mound City* severely scalded coal heaver George W. Scott. In July 1863, a duel between the USS *Marblehead* and Confederate shore batteries at Gimball's Landing, South Carolina, resulted in a severe wound to black ordinary seaman Charles Taylor. Sent to the New York Naval Hospital to recuperate, Taylor received a medical discharge a month later. A similar event ended the navy career of landsman William Johnson of the USS *Massasoit*. Wounded by fragments from a Confederate shell at Howlett's House, Virginia, in January 1865, Johnson left the navy with a medical release after a three-month recovery at the Norfolk Naval Hospital. The captain of the USS *Lexington*, supporting the Red River campaign in April 1864, reported the failure of a Confederate ambush. According to the officer, "One casualty only occurred, Philip Dudley (landsman, colored), wounded in the arm, since amputated." Because of the threat of infection, even a relatively minor wound could result in death, a misfortune that fell upon several African American sailors. Wounded in September 1861 during a raid upon the rebel-occupied Pensacola Navy Yard, Edward W. Johnson of the USS *Colorado* received an immediate transfer to the New York Naval Hospital. Despite prompt medical care, Johnson died four months later. Likewise, landsman Henry A. Francis, who suffered a head wound aboard the USS *Aroostook* off Mobile Bay, Alabama, in October 1862, died despite the attention of doctors at the Boston Naval Hospital in January 1863.[22]

Under the stress of battle, many Civil War sailors rose to the occasion and demonstrated vast reserves of bravery, and African American sailors were no different. Under fire, black sailors proved their valor was the equal of anyone, and many African American seamen attracted the praise of their commanding officers. The most notable instances of bravery resulted in African American sailors' receiving the highest military award the United States can bestow, the Medal of Honor. Created in 1861 to replace the earlier "Certificate of Merit," the navy granted the award for instances of great valor and ability in the face of enemy opposition, and African American sailors received 8 of the 307 Medals of Honor issued by the navy during the Civil War. Robert Blake became the first African American sailor to receive the award for his actions on the Stono River, South Carolina, in December 1863. The USS *Marblehead* found itself under attack from concealed Confederate guns, escaping loss only through the bravery of its crew. Among the brave, Robert Blake attracted the attention of his commanding officer, Lieutenant Commander Richard W. Meade, who reported, "Robert Blake, a contraband, excited my admiration by the cool and brave manner in which he served the rifle gun." The Union operation at Mobile Bay earned four African American sailors aboard the USS *Hartford* the Medal of Honor. Landsmen William H. Brown and James Mifflin earned the medal for resolutely manning the forward shell whip despite the risk of injury. Exploding Confederate shells had twice decimated men manning the whip, but both men held their posts. Brown stayed on duty despite a severe arm wound. Landsmen Wilson Brown and John Lawson also earned the award for their insistence to stay in the fight. An exploding shell killed one of *Hartford*'s sailors, whose falling corpse knocked Brown senseless. Brown soon recovered and returned to his gun, although he was the only member of the gun crew still alive. John Lawson, manning the ammunition hoist, stayed at his post after "a shell killed or wounded the whole number" of men in the area. Lawson, thrown violently against the bulkhead and severely wounded in both legs, stayed at his post, "although begged to go below" for medical attention.[23]

In June 1864, one of the Civil War's few high seas clashes occurred off the coast of France between the USS *Kearsarge* and the Confederate raider CSS *Alabama* (see chapter 7). For their bravery in battle, seventeen of *Kearsarge*'s crew received the Medal of Honor. Among the medal recipients was Joachim Pease, an African American seaman assigned to the forward pivot gun crew, who "exhibited marked coolness" under fire. In March 1865, landsman Aaron Anderson earned the honor for his action aboard the USS *Don* in Mattox Creek, Virginia. Pinned down by Confederate fire while a member of a boat party, Anderson, lying on his back, loaded and fired the boat howitzer, "as to kill and wound many rebels." Seaman Clement Dees received the final Medal of Honor given an African American sailor in the Civil War in March 1865. Commander William G. Temple, captain of the USS *Pontoosuc*, nominated eight members of his crew who demonstrated bravery in the attack on Fort Fisher, North Carolina, in January of that year. The navy granted the award to all of the nominated men, but Clement Dees never received the medal. When the entire crew of the *Pontoosuc* transferred to the receiving ship USS *Ohio* in Boston in May 1865, Dees deserted from the service and presumably returned home. The navy declared Dees's award forfeited, but his bravery in battle remains commendable.[24]

Although a Medal of Honor was not in the offing, the navy's records are replete with instances when African American sailors exhibited great bravery. During an ambush of the USS *Valley City* on the Mississippi River, "a cutter, manned by negroes . . . under a shower of bullets and shells . . . was made fast to the tree . . . drawing the stern of the *Valley City* around so as to bring her guns to bear on the enemy." In 1864, after Confederates had captured the USS *Water Witch,* the only member of its crew to escape capture, an African American named Peter MacIntosh, managed to warn other Union vessels against falling into the same trap. An African American third-class boy aboard the USS *Louisiana,* known only as Johnny, distinguished himself during an exchange of gunfire with Confederate batteries by supplying the gun crews with powder charges when other boys feared to expose themselves. An officer's clerk bearing dispatches from USS *Hartford* "left the ship in a skiff to run the gauntlet of the rebel batteries, taking with him a contraband for oarsman. . . . Another skiff with two contrabands in it was sent away from the ship about the same time as the one first mentioned, for the purpose of distracting the attention of the enemy's pickets." Lieutenant Roswell H. Lamson of the USS *Mount Washington* cited coal heavers William Jackson and James Lody for bravery during a battle on the Nansemond River in April 1863. Although their ship suffered severe damage from entrenched Confederate artillery, only Jackson and Lody manned their posts in the engine room during the entire fight. Lamson praised the determination of his men: "There is nothing like an *American Sailor* for true grit, at least *I* think so: I would stake my life on their faithfulness."[25]

Besides the threat of injury or death, combat included the risk of capture by an enemy who did not consider African Americans as equal combatants. The capture of Union warships, such as *Underwriter* and *Water Witch,* put black sailors at risk to be lynched by a merciless adversary or, more commonly, to be sent to a Confederate prison camp. On the Tennessee River in August 1862, Confederate forces captured the transport *W. B. Terry.* The vessel's seventeen-man crew, all African Americans, became prisoners. Near Charleston, South Carolina, the USS *Isaac Smith* fell into an ambush that led to the Confederates capturing the "entire crew, consisting of 11 officers, 105 men, and 3 negroes." The USS *Matthew Vassar* lost eight men as prisoners during an ill-advised excursion in March 1863. A shore party landed to seize a possible blockade runner at North Carolina's Little River Inlet. Instead of seizing the boat, the shore party, including African American Jesse Smith, surrendered to Confederate infantry protecting the vessel.[26]

As the war progressed and more African Americans entered the service, larger numbers also became prisoners. In May 1864, the USS *Signal* and *Covington,* convoying an army transport on the Red River, fell into Confederate hands after a five-hour battle near Pierce's Landing, Louisiana. Four African Americans from the two ships, Madison Burr, Taylor Cromwell, Edward Harris, and William Melvine, landed in a Confederate prison camp. Fifteen African American sailors from the USS *Granite City* ended the war as prisoners following the capture of the vessel during the ill-fated Union assault at Sabine Pass, Texas, in May 1864. The report of the Confederate commander delineated the fifteen prisoners as "7 Northern and 8 Southern." The single largest capture of African American sailors occurred in April 1864, when the Union lost the USS *Petrel.* Disabled by Confederate batteries near Yazoo City, Mississippi, thirty-four black sailors became prisoners when the ship grounded before it could drift into Union-held waters.[27]

Early in the war, both sides attempted to establish a regular schedule of prisoner exchanges to relieve those held in confinement. Although prisoner of war exchanges were fraught with difficulties, African American sailors benefited from great exertion on the part of the navy to secure their release. The presence of African Americans themselves in the Union military created most of the disagreements between the North and South regarding prisoners of war. Early in the war, both sides were eager to recover prisoners, and an exchange cartel emerged, swapping equal numbers of prisoners between the two sides. By 1863, however, the cartel had largely ceased to function.

The cartel agreement itself was highly complex and led to confusion and distrust between the negotiators. Left unresolved was the issue of prisoners who were not normal combatants. The two sides could not agree on the prisoner status of captured surgeons, chaplains, and especially Confederate privateers, licensed by the Confederate government but illegal under international law. Under strict convention, the privateers were pirates, but the South threatened retaliation if the Union executed any. Also, the Union exchange agents tended to have short tenures and were generally unsuitable for their position. For most of the cartel's tenure Union General Benjamin Butler represented the North, despite the Confederacy's refusal to deal with him. Butler had earned the nickname "the Beast" during a stint as military governor of New Orleans, and the Confederate government considered Butler a wanted criminal. Colonel Robert Ould, a skilled lawyer and the prewar district attorney of the District of Columbia, represented the Confederate half of the cartel. His background made Ould a formidable negotiator, fully aware of all the cartel agreement's nuances.[28]

The largest hindrance to the quick exchange of prisoners, however, was Confederate law on African American Union military personnel. The Confederate government, citing prewar laws meant to prevent slave insurrection, proclaimed that any African American captured while bearing arms against the Confederacy faced punishment, including death or sale into slavery if the offender was a free black. By 1863, with large numbers of African Americans in the Union military, increasing numbers of blacks fell into the hands of the Confederates. True to their pledge, many Confederates summarily lynched captured African Americans and sold others into slavery, including northern blacks who were free before the war. Black sailors were no exception. In December 1863, landsman George Brimsmaid of the USS *Perry*, a free man from Connecticut, fell into Confederate hands at Murrell's Inlet, South Carolina. Despite Brimsmaid's prewar status as a free man and the fact he was unarmed, Southern troops lynched him. They also executed John Pinkham, a wounded white sailor unable to move from the area. Apparently, the lynching of Brimsmaid was not a singular event, and Confederate forces remained predisposed to routinely executing captured black sailors. Southern troops captured fourteen African American sailors from the USS *Queen City* near Clarendon, Arkansas, in June 1864. When the ship's surgeon inquired into the future treatment of the black sailors, the Confederate officer "supposed they would be treated as are the rest they had captured, shoot them."[29]

The Confederates labeled captured contrabands as criminals under state law, a status that made them ineligible for prisoner transfers. The South refused to discuss the issue, despite a July 1863 presidential Order of Retaliation. Under the terms of the order, Abraham Lincoln promised to put to death a Confederate prisoner for every African American executed and place at hard labor a Confederate prisoner for each African American servicemen sold into slavery. Colonel Ould bluntly informed Union exchange agents that the Confederacy would "die in the last ditch before giving up the right to send slaves back into slavery," and prisoner exchanges virtually ceased by the end of 1863.[30]

While army prisoners, black and white, languished in Confederate prisons, the navy occasionally circumvented established channels in order to reacquire its servicemen. Unwilling to leave the prisoner exchange process to the army, the navy established its own contacts with the Confederacy, allowing the successful exchange of naval prisoners beyond the reach and knowledge of official channels. The navy was willing to ignore the provisions of the cartel agreement in the absence of direct orders to obey the accord, such as off the North Carolina coast in 1862. During operations to seize control of the entrances to the Carolina Capes, the Union had collected a large number of prisoners. Union Rear Admiral Lawrence M. Goldsborough, commanding the

North Atlantic Blockading Squadron, could not spare the ships to transport the captives north. Instead, he notified Secretary Gideon Welles of his intent to parole the prisoners on the spot, in violation of the cartel rules. Goldsborough informed his sub ordinate officers: "I have decided to put the prisoners you sent down on parole at once, and hereafter I wish you would do the same thing. . . . They, by being sent here, can see and observe more of our force and doings than I care that they should do." Goldsborough informed Secretary Welles: "I have put them all on parole, as we could not conveniently dispose of them otherwise. Each, however, was made to sign a paper pledging his sacred honor that . . . he would [not] . . . take up arms against the United States."[31]

Secretary Welles could hardly criticize Goldsborough, as Welles himself evaded the cartel for the good of his seamen. By the summer of 1864, the Union's preponderance in manpower permitted them to hold prisoners rather than return them to Confederate armies. Formal exchanges ceased, and the official exchange agents could only agree to humanitarian returns of the most seriously wounded or ill prisoners—to a man, army personnel. Despite receiving reports of African American Union naval prisoners, the cartel exchanged none. The last Union naval prisoners had been swapped nearly a year earlier. Welles suspected that naval prisoners were low on the army's list of priorities and grumbled that "the number of prisoners was not large, but the omission to exchange, whether from neglect or design was . . . causing dissatisfaction." To Welles's complaints, Secretary of War Edwin Stanton explained that the South refused to exchange naval prisoners. An infuriated Welles penned an accusatory letter to Stephen Mallory, the Confederate secretary of the navy, demanding an explanation for the South's position regarding his men in their prison camps. In a courteous reply, Mallory not only denied that naval prisoners were unavailable for exchange but proposed an exchange of all naval prisoners, to be arranged between the two secretaries. Welles had no authority to conduct an exchange, but he did not hesitate to seize the opportunity. He quietly arranged transport for two hundred Confederate naval prisoners held at Fort Lafayette in New York harbor. The exchange point was to be Charleston, South Carolina, but an outbreak of yellow fever in the city forced a change in plans. The substitution occurred at the cartel's established exchange site on the James River in Virginia, where the deal caught the attention of General Butler.[32]

Both Butler and Secretary Stanton railed that Welles had arranged such a gross violation of the cartel rules and complained bitterly to President Lincoln. Stanton accused Welles of violating the Union policy of nonrecognition of the Confederacy by directly addressing Confederate Secretary Mallory as an equal representative of a hostile government. Welles responded that he had never addressed his correspondence to Mallory using the Confederate secretary's title, instead beginning his letters with "the Honorable Mr. Mallory," just as a gentleman would in any letter. Butler charged that Welles and Mallory had undermined Union efforts to reverse the Confederate position regarding African American prisoners. The basis of the charge is unclear considering that Welles had won the release of more African American prisoners in a few days than the cartel had obtained in more than a year. Lincoln, eager to restore order to his cabinet, exonerated Welles for the exchange. The president reasoned, "The navy must have its men," but admonished Welles not to attempt any other independent exchanges. Welles's efforts, however, brought the plight of naval prisoners to the army's attention, and subsequent exchanges included naval prisoners. Such an exchange occurred on November 19, 1864, when the Union swapped the crews of two Confederate privateers for 101 Union naval prisoners, including 6 African Americans, 4 from the USS *Water Witch*.[33]

Welles may have been restricted from arranging unauthorized exchanges, but he proved willing to permit his subordinates far from the cartel's control to arrange their own exchanges. In the autumn of 1864, Union Vice Admiral David G. Farragut arranged such a transfer. Farragut held a number of Confederate naval prisoners he wished to exchange for Union naval prisoners captured on the Mississippi River and held in prison camps in Texas under the authority of the Confederate army. Farragut had Welles's blessing: "The release of these prisoners is much desired, and you are authorized to make such exchange for rebel prisoners in your hands . . . as you may think proper. . . . Our navy officers and seaman in Texas have been imprisoned for a long time . . . and have doubtless suffered much. Their exchange is therefore an object . . . deserving attention." To increase his bargaining power, Welles ordered Farragut to hold all Confederate naval prisoners instead of releasing them on parole, the accepted practice in the months before Mobile Bay.[34]

In addition to the growing number of prisoners, Farragut had a tempting prize to dangle before Major General Edmund K. Smith, commanding the Confederacy's Trans-Mississippi Department: Confederate Admiral Franklin Buchanan. Captured by Farragut after the Battle of Mobile Bay in August 1864, Buchanan was the highest-ranking Confederate prisoner of war, and the South was eager to recover him. Negotiations initially did not go well. Smith, unwilling to add men to the blockade slowly starving his army into submission, initially offered only Union army captives in exchange. Forcing Smith's hand, Farragut ordered Buchanan sent to a prisoner-of-war camp if Smith did not negotiate in good faith. Under pressure from the Confederate government, Smith relented, and an unlimited exchange occurred in February 1865.[35]

To many young men, warfare is the measure of one's growth into maturity, but for African Americans the Civil War was something more. Many African Americans looked to the experience of combat during the Civil War to demonstrate their value as free citizens of the United States. By any measure, African American sailors lived up to the challenge of naval battle. By shedding their blood and proving their bravery, black sailors displayed repeatedly that they deserved the equal consideration of the government and the American people. By striving to recover captured African American sailors, the navy demonstrated its commitment to its enlisted personnel by protecting the rights and interests of its enlisted force, regardless of race. Together, African American sailors and the navy establishment worked to overcome the horrors of war.

Chapter Six

BEFORE THE BENCH

AFRICAN AMERICAN SAILORS IN THE

NAVY CRIMINAL JUSTICE SYSTEM

• Among the common images and perceptions of nineteenth-century naval service is a tradition of harsh military discipline. The liberal uses of flogging and other grotesque punishments are as much a part of naval lore as sailing vessels, ship-to-ship duels, and the rum ration. Like most popular conceptions, however, the rigorous level of navy discipline, while based upon a minimum of truth, is not entirely accurate. Even at its harshest in the early nineteenth century, discipline in the U.S. Navy was less violent than its European counterparts. By 1861 the navy had reorganized its disciplinary methods into a relatively egalitarian and humanitarian system that banned the most brutal punishments, limited the excesses of officers acting beyond navy control, and eliminated unreasonable punishments. Nowhere are the fairness and impartiality of the naval judicial system more evident than in its dealings with African American sailors. A vital source of navy manpower, African Americans received the same, and in some cases better, legal treatment than white sailors as the navy strove to maintain its flow of personnel. The very nature of the judicial system generated an atmosphere in which defendants were all treated the same, regardless of race, creating a "justice is blind" attitude that ensured equal treatment for African American offenders. Besides applying fair and equitable treatment to all of its sailors, the navy granted African American crewmen legal rights and privileges not available to free blacks in the North.

The early U.S. Navy drew upon the traditions of the British Royal Navy, inheriting a disciplinary tradition based upon the imposition of order and obedience, levying loyalty rather than developing it. Officers enforced loyalty by severe and brutal punishment meted out for infractions of naval regulations or ship's rules. Naval officers were free to impose any punishment they liked, as formal regulations and limitations on their authority did not exist. The Royal Navy had a richly deserved reputation of efficiency generated by the iron discipline of its crews, created by barbaric methods of punishment. Minor offenses were punishable by flogging, frequently thirty or more lashes. All crewmen, regardless of age or physical condition, faced the whip for their indiscretions. In 1800, for instance, twelve-year-old Horace Lane received thirty-six lashes for attempting to desert. Serious offenders faced punishment by keelhauling. Keelhauling involved pushing a bound sailor off one side of the ship and pulling him under the vessel (hauling him under the keel) to the other side. Hanging was the preferred method of capital punishment, but some noncapital punishments had the same effect. Excessive floggings, sometimes hundreds of lashes, became inadvertent capital sentences, not overtly intended to kill but almost inevitably ending the prisoner's life.[1]

The American navy sought a level of discipline equal to the British, but the Constitution restrained the level of punishment. The Fifth Amendment permitted the American military to try "cases arising in the land or naval forces," but the Eighth Amendment's ban on cruel and unusual punishment restrained the navy's ability to punish offenders. Thus, the American navy resembled its British counterparts in its dedication to sharp discipline but significantly differed in the method of applying it, with American naval officers bound by a code of naval regulations. The first formal regulations appeared in 1775, but in April 1800 Congress passed "An Act for the Better Government of the United States Navy," better known as the Navy Articles of War.[2]

The act banned keelhauling and all forms of execution except hanging (for sailors) and firing squad (for marines). Flogging still existed but was generally limited to a maximum of one hundred lashes to avoid the inadvertent deaths associated with

Royal Navy discipline, although particularly heinous crimes could earn more than one hundred lashes. The maximum number of lashes was only permissible after a formal proceeding. Floggings for shipboard offenses were limited to twelve lashes, and only certain offenses, such as drunkenness, fighting, insubordination, theft, or sleeping on watch, earned a flogging. Drunkenness was the most frequent cause for floggings in the antebellum navy, followed by neglect of duty, theft, and desertion. That figure corresponds with studies of navy courts-martial in the antebellum period, which found 37 percent of the trials were for crimes against navy authority, 18 percent for disciplinary infractions, 18 percent for desertion-related offenses, and 4 percent for violent crimes. Officers were tried in another 20 percent of the proceedings, with the remaining trials brought for more specific, single-incidence crimes.[3]

The navy also implemented a three-tiered system of legal proceedings. Shipboard courts, called "captain's masts," convened by the vessel's commanding officer, could try minor infractions. More extreme crimes (such as murder, mutiny, desertion, spying, or cowardice in battle) warranted a general court-martial. Convened only under the jurisdiction of the president, secretary of the navy, or squadron commander, the accusing officer transported the defendant to the nearest suitable site for trial by a panel of not more than thirteen officers. General courts-martial could impose any punishment, including the death sentence. Because the navy lacked its own long-term prison facility, offenders sentenced to jail terms longer than a few months went to the nearest state penitentiary, with the navy compensating the state for the prisoner's expenses. For lesser crimes, such as theft or insubordination, ship commanders could authorize summary courts-martial. Consisting of up to five members, summary courts-martial could inflict floggings commensurate to the crime, but lengthy imprisonment in the ship's brig was relatively rare, as imprisonment reduced the number of sailors available for duty.[4]

Although limited in the punishment it could inflict, the U.S. Navy was still a highly disciplined force. Commanding officers maintained order by limiting shore leave, confining the amount of idle time, and applying liberal doses of corporal punishment.

While popular officers rarely had to impose punishment, less capable commanders relied on the whip to keep their crews in line. The latter group of officers generated the navy's antebellum reputation as a brutal institution. Most commanding officers believed that stern discipline not only preserved order but was beneficial for most sailors, making them more suited for civilian life: "Discipline, too, makes him polite. There is a polish in the manners of a good sailor that would make grade with many other classes of men." Commander Samuel F. du Pont, later to command the South Atlantic Squadron during the Civil War, ordered forty-one separate floggings aboard the USS *Congress* in December 1845 alone.[5]

The navy admitted 5,936 floggings from 1846–1847, an average of fifty whippings per ship, or four per month per ship. Besides a large number of floggings, the navy was frequently guilty of inflicting the punishment for crimes that did not warrant a whipping. Among the offenses earning a flogging was skulking (hiding to avoid duty), lying, poor personal hygiene, sleeping on watch, spitting on the deck, or cursing a petty officer. Officers also flogged sailors with unauthorized implements. The Navy Articles of War mandated flogging with a cat-o'-nine-tails, a bundle of ropes attached to a wooden handle. Some officers, however, used "colts" (a thin rope that tore the skin when used), rattan canes, or other illegal implements. Besides the harsh enforcement of navy regulations, many commanding officers imposed their own strict rules for ship behavior, violations of which earned the offender a flogging. Even after the navy abolished excessive punishments, captains were still free to set rules for their own vessels and punish offenders of those rules.[6]

Violations of the navy criminal justice system attracted the attention of antebellum social reformers who sought to restrain the navy's abusive powers. Just as reformers wished to improve prisons and insane asylums, the navy was the target of a four-part reform program. The reformers wanted expanded access to religion for sailors, the creation of a career enlisted corps (to avoid excessive punishments imposed upon inexperienced sailors), an end of the liquor ration, and the restructuring of the disciplinary system. The abolition of flogging, part of a wider campaign to eliminate corporal punishment, became the centerpiece of the navy reform program. Whippings were a brutal but accepted method of disciplining not only sailors but also residents of prisons and mental asylums, and most states had no laws against husbands using corporal punishment against their own wives. Thus, the campaign against floggings appealed to many and was to have a wide effect.[7]

Events in the 1840s promoted the reform crusade. In 1842, the captain of the USS *Somers* hanged three junior officers for mutiny while on a midshipman training cruise to Africa. Commander Alexander Slidell Mackenzie held summary courts-martial for three crewmembers for plotting to murder the senior officers, maroon the midshipmen, and convert the vessel into a pirate ship. Public interest and outrage developed over the peculiar circumstances of the case. Reformers and the public alike protested the navy's "murder" of a sailor by a commanding officer without the benefit of legal counsel or jury of his peers (both of which were not permitted under the Navy Articles of War). Also, Mackenzie based the mutiny charge not upon any specific act of violence but on conflicting testimony and a few vague messages passed among the crew. Public interest was also attracted because one of the condemned, Passed Midshipman Philip Spencer, was the son of Secretary of War John C. Spencer.

Strictly speaking, Mackenzie exceeded his authority under the Navy Articles of War. Trying and executing defendants were the prerogatives of a general court-martial, convened only by the president, the secretary of the navy, or the squadron commander. The navy recognized, however, that owing to the distance from legitimate authority and the severity of the crime extraordinary legal proceedings were appropriate. A navy court of inquiry cleared Mackenzie of all charges, but he demanded and received a court-martial that also absolved him of all wrongdoing.[8]

Another questionable mutiny occurred in San Francisco in 1849. Several crewmen on a shore party from the USS *Ewing* attempted to desert to join the gold rush frenzy in the city. A shore detail overpowered Passed Midshipman William Gibson, commanding the boat crew. Two brothers, John and Peter Black, threw Gibson overboard, where he nearly drowned before reaching shore, and the sailors escaped in the cutter. Recaptured some days later, the escapees faced charges of mutiny, desertion, assaulting a superior officer, and theft of government property. As in the *Somers* incident, the navy questionably applied a charge of mutiny. The navy believed that the stolen boat, regardless of size, was still a U.S. Navy vessel, which the mutineers had seized from legitimate navy control. The court-martial also levied a charge of mutiny because Gibson had nearly died swimming to shore in his heavy cloak in treacherous currents. Despite a vigorous defense by a civilian attorney (provided as a consequence of the *Somers* incident), Captain Thomas ap Catesby Jones, commanding the Pacific Squadron, found all five defendants guilty and sentenced them to hang. His sentence, however, caused a quandary. Capital sentences carried out in U.S. waters required the consent of the president. With Washington three thousand miles away, Jones believed he could not wait. Judging that remote California was a de facto foreign station, Jones ordered the sentences carried out. The navy executed the Black brothers and sentenced the other conspirators to one hundred lashes and imprisonment at hard labor for the remainder of their terms of service. Unlike the *Somers* mutiny, however, Commander Jones did not escape retribution. With public outrage growing regarding the events in California, Secretary of the Navy William A. Graham suspended Jones from duty for five years.[9]

The *Somers* mutiny came on the heels of several highly critical disciplinary episodes during the Mexican War. The most notable occurred aboard the USS *St. Marys* in 1846. Seaman Samuel Jackson, accused and convicted of striking a superior officer, suffered the death penalty by hanging. Jackson's court-martial, although properly conducted, passed judgment very quickly and carried out the execution without consulting the Navy Department. In addition, Jackson's crime generally did not warrant the death penalty. Commodore David Conner, commanding the Gulf of Mexico Squadron, decided to make an example of Jackson to send a message to the rest of his men. Conner received formal censure from the navy, but did not lose his command. Again, the navy faced severe public criticism for appearing to punish an enlisted man beyond the legitimate limits of its authority.[10]

Stung by the growing criticism of its judicial system, the navy instituted three major reforms in its disciplinary system. First, under pressure from antebellum reformers, the navy abolished flogging in 1850, although the U.S. Army continued to flog its soldiers until 1861. In its place, the navy instituted a system of rewards to compel good behavior, rather than use the threat of violence to prevent bad conduct. The navy provided increased shore leave and promotions for good conduct and created the honorable discharge in 1855. Before that year, sailors left the service without classification, and prospective postservice employers had no way of knowing whether a former sailor had served honorably or had plagued the navy as a disciplinary problem. An honorable discharge, however, earned the departing sailor the status as a reliable member of society separate from the undisciplined tramp presumed by most Americans. Honorably discharged sailors were also entitled to a bounty of up to twenty dollars if they reenlisted in the navy. The service banned dishonorably discharged sailors forever. Strangely, many sailors opposed the flogging ban. Mariners considered flogging to be a manly form of punishment, borne silently by only the strongest individuals. Floggings, after the welts had healed, also left no permanent mark upon the offender, unlike other proposed methods of punishment like branding or tattooing. Sailors also preferred floggings to the loss of benefits, such as the suspension of the liquor ration or loss of pay and shore leave.[11]

Second, formal courts-martial were restricted in the types of cases they could hear and the forms and harshness of punishments they could inflict. General courts-martial alone could hear capital offense cases and were the only body that could inflict the death penalty. To avoid future incidents similar to the events aboard *Ewing* and *Somers,* at least three-quarters of the panel had to approve a death sentence and receive written permission from the president before carrying out the sentence. General courts-martial could also sentence offenders to either conventional prison time at a state penitentiary or hard labor at a federal construction project. Summary courts-martial were further restricted. Without the benefit of flogging, the maximum punishment a summary court could inflict was incarceration aboard ship for two months. If harsher discipline was required, an offender could face single (wrists) or double (wrists and ankles) irons on a diet of bread and water, but only for a maximum of thirty days. Summary courts-martial could also reduce an offender's rank (with corresponding reduction in pay), deprive him of shore liberty, or suspend his pay, but for no more than three months. If a sailor faced more than one charge, the panel could apply two different types of punishments. For example, in February 1862, a summary court-martial found Seaman James Murphy of the USS *Vanderbilt* guilty of assaulting a superior officer and mutinous conduct. For the assault, he suffered confinement for thirty days on bread and water. When that sentence ended, he faced sixty days of solitary confinement for the latter charge.[12]

Third, to avoid excessive punishments at captain's mast proceedings, the navy implemented a codified offense system for minor crimes. Rather than arbitrary rulings and punishments that varied from ship to ship, captains were limited in the harshness and duration of punishment for various crimes. For example, smuggling liquor on board was a Class A offense punishable by five days' solitary confinement on bread and water. Using "provoking language" to an officer was a Class F offense with a sentence of ten days' solitary confinement on bread and water. Lying to superior officer was a Class O offense liable to bring extra duties or suspension of shore leave. The new classification system obliged the navy to devise creative forms of discipline to replace the lash, and the disciplinary system thus became more humanitarian, with punishments more commensurate to the crime. The new classifications became law with the enactment of the revised Navy Articles of War in July 1862.[13]

Before the Civil War, the U.S. Navy grappled with the issue of what rights and privileges applied to its African American sailors. The primary problem was the navy's mobility. Freedom and civil liberties enjoyed by black sailors in northern ports were illegal in southern states, and the navy constantly found itself at odds with varying state laws that tried to take precedence over the navy's federal policies. A key example was the antebellum Black Seaman

Acts passed by many southern states requiring the jailing of all free black sailors during the vessel's stay in port. The laws persisted until the Civil War despite several federal circuit court opinions in suits brought by the government that ruled in favor of African American sailors. Associate Justice William Johnson, whose circuit jurisdiction included New Orleans, was especially opposed to the legislation, but without wider support from his colleagues the southern laws remained in force.[14]

The navy also debated whether African American sailors had the right to testify at navy courts-martial. The right of African American civilians to testify in court was limited to a few northern states, but the issue remained unsettled before the Civil War. The navy's unresolved attitude regarding African American court testimony included those considered competent witnesses. In *Observations on Military Law,* a handbook issued to the army and navy to aid court-martial proceedings, those banned from testifying included "idiots, madmen, and lunatics," those frequently intoxicated, "such persons as do not believe in a God" (they could not take an oath to God to truthfully testify), those guilty of legal infamy (perjury, subornation of perjury, barratry, or bribing a witness), and husbands and wives on trial together who have an "identity of interest." Those who could testify after proving their competency included children, "a person born deaf and dumb," deserters, servants in suits against their masters, and wives and husbands "in respect to any charge which affects . . . liberty or person." For both approved and unapproved witnesses extensive explanations why a person was or was not a competent witness were provided. While the manual mentioned the "objections to their competency," it made no ruling on whether African Americans were competent witnesses, simply citing two antebellum courts-martial involving African American testimony without an explanation why the testimony was accepted.[15]

The contentious issue of African American testimony in naval courts peaked at Pensacola, Florida, in May 1839 with the court-martial of Lieutenant George M. Hooe. Hooe faced charges of treating his superior officer with contempt, uttering mutinous and seditious words, and disobeying orders. Serving aboard the USS *Vandalia* of the West Indies Squadron, Hooe ordered the flogging of several men in direct violation of the commanding officer's orders banning flogging aboard his command. One of the flogged men, an African American named Daniel Waters, was a civilian employed by the captain as a cook and servant, yet Hooe had him flogged twice for perceived violations of ship's rules. During the court-martial, Waters and an African American sailor named Thomas Mitchell testified as prosecution witnesses. Found guilty, discharged from the West Indies Squadron, and sent home for reassignment, Hooe appealed to President Martin Van Buren for redress of grievance. Hooe plead his case on the grounds that the court-martial had taken place in Florida, where blacks could not legally testify against whites. Van Buren rejected Hooe's appeal on advice from Attorney General Henry D. Gilpin, who ruled the jury would have convicted Hooe without the testimony of Waters and Mitchell, as seven credible officers and white crewmen had testified against him. In addition, Gilpin ruled that courts-martial, as a separate legal entity, were not subject to state law. Hooe accepted the outcome of the court-martial, but the debate over the legitimacy of African American court-martial testimony remained unresolved.[16]

Discipline in the U.S. Army followed a generally similar pattern of development before the Civil War. The army adopted British military regulations during the American Revolution before adopting its own Articles of War in 1806. Like the navy's articles, the Army Articles of War established limitations on discipline and the structure of courts-martial and worked reasonably well before 1861. Once the Civil War began, however, the sudden growth of the army caused severe problems in its disciplinary system. The army had too few officers experienced in court-martial procedure to handle the huge influx of cases. In response, the army in 1862 established the office of judge advocate general to administer military justice (the navy did not establish a similar post until 1866). Another problem was the civilian outlook of the army's volunteer officers and recruits. Used to local courts and punishments, many soldiers balked at the army's stern discipline, resulting in an immense increase in disciplinary cases. Many volunteer officers, both as members of a court-martial and on their own, ignored provisions in the Army Articles of War limiting the types and severity of punishments they could employ, causing widespread abuse of judiciary powers.[17]

Abuse of soldiers by volunteer officers under their command often led to punishments far in excess of the worst form of navy discipline. While most punishments were relatively benign, such as digging latrines or burying dead horses, many of the ad hoc punishments inflicted upon offenders of army discipline were excessively brutal and humiliating. Despite its abolition in 1861, some army officers continued to flog those found guilty of violating regimental or camp rules. For desertion or assault, branding the offender with a hot iron (on the hip, hand, forehead, or cheek) was common. Officers punished cowardice by forcing the offender to stand atop the breastworks in full view of Confederate snipers with a sign of "coward" strung around his neck. Thieves and swindlers would be "drummed" out of the service by having their heads shaved, uniform insignia unceremoniously clipped from their uniform, and beaten severely by running a gauntlet of soldiers on their way out of camp. Minor offenders were forced to sit on rails several feet off the ground, wear barrels, or carry heavy logs for several hours, rather unsophisticated punishments but capable of reducing soldiers to "begging for mercy."[18]

Branches of the army had their own traditional punishments. Artillery officers would tie offenders spread-eagle to the spare wheel on the back of a caisson to ride uncomfortably along bumpy roads. For a more severe punishment, a wheel rotated a quarter turn forced the prisoner to hang painfully from the ropes securing his wrists and ankles. Cavalrymen found guilty of minor offenses would ride a garish wooden horse, and if drummed out of the service they would often have their prized sabers broken over their heads. The infantry often used two painful punishments, "bucking and gagging" and tying up by the thumbs. In the former, a sitting soldier would have a rifle placed under his bent knees with his hands tied under the rifle and a bayonet clenched between the teeth and tied in place. The soldier was left to sit in cramped agony for hours. A less complex, but just as painful, punishment was hanging an offender by the thumbs from a tree branch so that the prisoner's toes just touched the ground, leaving him unable to fully rest his weight on his feet.[19]

The application of the death penalty, however, was the worst abuse of the army disciplinary system. Both the Navy and Army Articles of War required a three-quarters' majority of a court-martial panel to inflict the death penalty, as well as the consent of the president. Whereas the navy followed procedures, the army frequently did not. Although President Abraham Lincoln commuted the sentences of many condemned soldiers, the army executed 267 Union soldiers during the war, mostly for desertion. The army found some of the soldiers (including five African Americans convicted of rape) guilty in proceedings other than the mandated general court-martial, at "drumhead" trials hastily called in the field. The navy, on the other hand, condemned several men, but the president commuted every sentence, and no record exists of any navy executions.[20]

Navy courts-martial went to great lengths to preserve individual rights, requiring court reporters, for instance, to transcribe every word of the proceedings for the navy's permanent records. Before the trial began, the accused met the officers sitting on the court panel, headed by the senior officer acting as judge advocate. If the offender had a complaint against any member of the panel, he could request the dismissal of the panel member. The panel would adjourn to decide the defendant's request, a demand not automatically granted. After approving the panel, the clerk of the court read the charges against the defendant into the record as well as the specifications of the charge, which detailed the crimes alleged by the prosecution, and the defendant could request defense counsel. An offender could decline counsel, retain a private attorney at his own expense, or accept the counsel of an impartial officer. Defense counsel could only advise the defendant and could not directly address the court, although counsel could submit a written defense after the trial had ended.[21]

In 1864, for instance, the lawyer representing African American landsman Joseph Johnson used an effective written appeal to save his client. Johnson, accused of desertion from a shore party, argued that the lieutenant leading his shore party granted him permission to go home to care for his ailing mother in Alexandria, Virginia. Johnson, through several letters to his commanding officer, kept the navy informed of his whereabouts. Despite this knowledge, the navy considered Johnson a deserter when he reported to his vessel for duty. In his written defense, Johnson's attorney argued that the navy had abrogated its position as the abused because the service "knew where he was and did not molest him." As the navy did not attempt to arrest a deserter at a known location, the attorney reasoned, "he was not in fact a deserter . . . and the mark should be erased." The court apparently agreed; it convicted Johnson of the lesser charge of absent without leave (AWOL).[22]

The defendant had the right to cross-examine all prosecution witnesses, with the defendant asking the questions, and produce witnesses in his own defense, although the prosecution would cross-examine all defense witnesses. Because defendants could not call themselves to the witness stand, the accused submitted a written defense to read into evidence. Once testimony had ended, the panel would retire to render a verdict and decide the appropriate punishment for entry into the court record when the trial reconvened. The panel forwarded copies of the court transcript for approval by the squadron or base commander and, in capital cases, the president.

On occasion, the squadron commander returned verdicts to the court-martial for reconsideration, usually because the punishments were not severe enough for the commander's liking. The court could take the commander's suggestion under advisement and reconvene the court for resentencing or could leave the outcome of the proceedings as originally concluded. Occasionally, squadron commanders ordered panels to lessen charges found too severe. In 1865, for instance, a court-martial on the North Atlantic Squadron found Allen Jackson, an African American coal heaver, guilty of disobeying direct orders and mutinous conduct. Initially sentenced to five years' hard labor, the panel reduced the penalty to two years. Rear Admiral David D. Porter, commanding the squadron, found the panel at fault in its assessment of the facts, ordered Jackson freed, and chastised the panel for its sloppy courtroom performance.[23]

The navy made it a point to ensure equal and fair trials and punishments, regardless of race. Whites who murdered blacks in navy uniform, for instance, rarely escaped justice. In May 1865, the Mississippi Squadron held a court-martial for James Dunlevy, a white seaman charged with the murder of an African American civilian, Simon Cleveland, at Davis Landing, Mississippi. A court martial found Dunlevy and two other officers charged with the crime not guilty, not because they were innocent but because prosecution witnesses gave conflicting accounts of the events leading to Cleveland's death. In November 1864, Charles W. Train, a white seaman aboard the USS *Arletta* on the South Atlantic Squadron, got in an argument with a black seaman, James R. Connor, while visiting a friend aboard the chartered steamer *James Douglas*. Train seized an awning stanchion and struck Connor in the head, causing his death the following day. A court-martial sentenced Train to death.[24]

An important feature of the Dunlevy and Train courts-martial, as well as many other disciplinary proceedings, was the navy policy of granting African Americans the right to testify in military trials, a right not universally granted in the North. While the states in the North that did grant African Americans the right of testimony limited the privilege to its own citizens, the navy granted the right to any sailor, regardless of race, place of origin, or prewar status. The Dunlevy court-martial heard seven African American civilians as prosecution witnesses. Of the twelve prosecution witnesses in the Train murder case, nine were African Americans. Black sailors also testified as defense witnesses. In November 1864, the North Atlantic Squadron court-martialed John Williams, an African American seaman, for desertion from a shore party. Three other African Americans on the shore party, however, testified that the coxswain in charge of the party gave Williams permission to go to a nearby store to purchase personal items for him and members of the detachment. Based upon the witnesses' testimony, the panel found Williams guilty of the lesser charge of AWOL and sentenced him to five days' solitary confinement. The sentence withstood a rebuke by Rear Admiral David D. Porter, commander of the North Atlantic Squadron, that it was insufficient. In June 1864, a court found Michael Gavican, a white sailor attached to the South Atlantic Squadron, not guilty of rape after several black crewmen confirmed Gavican's contention the woman was a prostitute "unsatisfied with the financial compensation for her services."[25]

Not only did African Americans testify in courts-martial, but the navy also took special care to protect black witnesses. A prime example came in May 1865. John Fitzpatrick, a white sailor on the North Atlantic Squadron, received a four-month prison sentence for contempt of court. Earlier in the year, a court-martial convicted Fitzpatrick of assaulting another crewmen upon the testimony of an African American witness. Before and during this court-martial, Fitzpatrick had threatened the witness with menacing gestures meant to intimidate him. Offended by Fitzpatrick's behavior in the courtroom, the court-martial panel added the additional charge of contempt and extended Fitpatrick's sentence.[26]

In sharp contrast to naval policy was the army's treatment of African American soldiers. Some white officers seemed to single out black soldiers for especially harsh discipline. In June 1864, a black soldier of the 23d USCT who disobeyed a captain was summarily shot by the officer. The army leadership disciplined African American troops peacefully protesting unequal pay, with one leader, Sergeant William Walker of the 3d South Carolina Infantry, hanged as a mutineer. In December 1863, the army tried Lieutenant Colonel Augustus W. Benedict of the 4th Infantry for inflicting cruel and unusual punishments on the troops under his command. Officers testified that Benedict had struck several men with his fists "without cause," assaulted one soldier by striking him in the face with a sword, and ordered men staked to the ground, covered in molasses to attract insects, and left there for several hours.[27]

In contrast, in October 1864, Acting Master's Mate Joseph Reid aboard the USS *Stepping Stones* of the South Atlantic Squadron was court-martialed because he "did strike with his fists James Kenny," an African American crewman. The court exonerated Reid of the crime because witnesses testified Kenny had been insubordinate. Though Reid escaped disciplinary action, the court ordered the incident reported in Reid's permanent record, disqualifying him from navy service after the war. In October 1863, a court-martial tried and found guilty Acting Volunteer Lieutenant J. W. Kittredge for beating black Ordinary Seaman John Hughes by "striking the said Hughes on the face with his fist, striking him in the mouth with a loaded revolver, and otherwise inflicting illegal punishment." The navy dismissed Kittredge from the service. Secretary of the Navy Gideon Welles added a warning to Kittredge's official record: "The Department trusts that this example will have a proper effect both on officers and seamen of the navy . . . protecting seamen from a wanton or tyrannous abuse of authority . . . [which will] conform to the requirements of discipline."[28]

The navy showed a consistently evenhanded approach to applying discipline to black sailors. Improperly criticized as having a "regulation mentality," the navy equally and fairly applied discipline to sailors of all races. In a sample of 1,420 general courts-martial and courts of inquiry conducted by the navy during the Civil War, the fairness and equality of navy judicial proceedings emerges as the most prominent feature. Quite the opposite of a regulation mentality, the navy seemed to take great pains to accommodate its African American defendants, even in certain instances inflicting punishments less severe than those imposed on white sailors.[29]

Among the 475 courts-martial defendants, 13.5 percent were African American (proportionate to the number of blacks in the general navy population) and the remainder white. Although African Americans enlisted in the navy mostly in 1863 and 1864, the distribution of African American courts-martial over the duration of the war was not significant, as the navy prosecuted both blacks and whites with equal zeal.[30] Nor was a defendant's rank a significant factor in courts-martial, with experienced sailors and raw landsmen court-martialed with equal regard.[31] African American defendants represented a higher percentage of general courts-martial in the ranks of first-class firemen, landsmen, first-class boys, third-class boys, and stewards. White offenders had higher percentages in the ranks of second-class firemen, coal heavers, seamen, ordinary seamen, and second-class boys. In courts-martial, juries found black and white offenders guilty or not guilty (panels acquitted African Americans twice as often as white defendants)[32] and applied the same types of punishments in generally equal proportions.[33] Prison terms (the mean prison sentence for African American sailors was 35.4, for whites 45.4 months) for white and black sailors were also equivalent.[34] This is especially true of defendants given the death penalty or life imprisonment, with only half as many African American sailors receiving life or capital sentences as white seamen.[35]

Other aspects of navy disciplinary policies toward African Americans, however, showed statistically significant differences between blacks and whites. Among them was the percentage of African Americans accused of certain crimes relative to the number of blacks in the navy population. While the navy charged African American sailors in 13.5 percent of courts-martial, blacks were underrepresented in the categories of desertion-related crimes (44% of African American courts-martial compared with 49% of white cases), violent crimes (2% versus 8%), and crimes against navy authority (23% versus 28%). Only in disciplinary crimes did African American sailors outnumber whites, with 31 percent of courts-martial compared with only 15 percent for white sailors.[36]

African American defendants probably appeared in court frequently for disciplinary offenses because of the similarities of navy discipline to slavery. African American sailors forced to submit to the will of white officers balked at the rigid discipline and subsequent punishments that came with rules violations. In addition, many of the punishments meted out for minor infractions (loss of liberty, extra duties, or confinement) were reminiscent of penalties inflicted by plantation owners to errant slaves, a similarity particularly uncomfortable to southern blacks in the navy.[37]

Within the specific offense categories, African American representation varied widely, particularly violent crime. Of thirty-three sailors in this category, only one was black, charged with assaulting a fellow crewman.[38] In desertion-related crimes, black sailors were overrepresented among those charged with attempting to desert and aiding desertion and those charged with desertion but found guilty of AWOL, but underrepresented in the charge of desertion and AWOL.[39] In antiauthority crimes, black sailors were overrepresented in the crime of threatening a superior officer and insubordination and underrepresented in assaulting a superior officer, mutinous conduct, contempt of court-martial, and sabotage offenses.[40] In the disciplinary offenses, however, African Americans were overrepresented in charges of theft, destroying public property, asleep at post, and deserting station.[41]

The frequency of various offenses varied by race as well, in some cases at a statistically significant level. The five most common offenses for the entire courts-martial sample were desertion, insubordination, mutinous conduct, assaulting a superior officer, and scandalous conduct. Among African Americans the five offenses appearing most often were desertion, insubordination, deserting station, scandalous conduct, and desertion reduced to AWOL. Among white defendants, the most common offenses were desertion, mutinous conduct, insubordination, assaulting a superior officer, and scandalous conduct. In short, the navy court-martialed black sailors mostly for nonviolent offenses that jeopardized navy discipline and court-martialed white sailors for violent or potentially violent crimes.

The tempo of offense categories changed during the war. In general terms, the frequency of certain crimes peaked during the middle years of the war before tapering in the latter years. Whereas antiauthority and disciplinary crimes reached their highest level in 1863, desertion-related and violent crimes did not crest until much later, in the fall of 1864. In 1861, crimes against authority and disciplinary offenses each accounted for virtually all courts-martial in that year among the general sample, with the remaining offenses related to desertion. By 1862, however, desertion-related crimes increased to 40 percent of offenses, antiauthority and disciplinary crimes composed about a quarter of the charges each, and violent crimes made up a tenth of the general court-martial sample. In 1863, antiauthority crimes totaled roughly a third of all courts-martial, followed by desertion and disciplinary offenses with a quarter each, and violent crime declined slightly in frequency. In 1864, however, desertion infractions were once again most frequent, making up more than half of all charges, followed by antiauthority offenses (20%), disciplinary offenses (12%), and violent crimes (9%). Desertion crimes continued to be a problem in 1865, growing to

60 percent of courts-martial, trailed by antiauthority infractions (20%), disciplinary offenses (15%), and violent crimes (6%).[42]

Among white sailors, the yearly distribution closely matched the general sample, as the frequency of various crimes stayed relatively the same during the war. After 1861, for instance, whites charged with antiauthority crimes ranged from a high of 36 percent in 1863 to a low of 23 percent in 1864. Whites charged with disciplinary crimes ranged from a high of 25 percent in 1862 to a low of 13 percent in 1865. Violent crimes were the most statistically stable crime category, with a difference of only 4 percent between 1862 and 1865.

Significant differences existed among the general and white sample groups, but the yearly distribution of African American sailors accused of crimes in certain categories was not statistically significant.[43] With only limited numbers of African Americans in the navy ranks in 1861, no African American courts-martial exist in the general sample. Only two black sailors were court-martialed in 1862, both for desertion-related offenses. After 1862, however, the frequency of African American courts-martial changed dramatically. Only 17 percent of 1863 African American courts-martial were for desertion, and 80 percent were an equal combination of antiauthority and disciplinary offenses. A year later, desertion-related crimes dominated African American courts-martial with 65 percent of the proceedings. In 1865, desertions were still the most common crime among African American defendants with half of the cases, but antiauthority and disciplinary offenses shared the other half. The most notable trait among African American courts-martial is the virtual absence of violent crime. With the exception of 1863, when violent offenses made up 6 percent of courts-martial, such crimes are entirely absent, in sharp contrast to the consistent trend of violent crimes among white defendants.

Specific crimes also fluctuated during the war years in the general sample. In 1861, the three most frequent crimes in the general courts-martial sample were scandalous conduct, assaulting a superior officer, and mutinous conduct. For the rest of the war, however, desertion remained the most common offense, with the second- and third-most frequent crimes changing every year. In 1862, desertion led assaulting a superior officer, mutinous conduct, and threatening a superior officer in number of cases. In 1863 desertion led, followed by assaulting a superior officer and deserting station. The percentage of desertion courts martial increased in 1864, trailed by insubordination and mutinous conduct. Desertion dominated in 1865, with insubordination and desertion reduced to AWOL as the other most frequent offenses.

Examined by year, the distribution of individual crimes by African Americans was not statistically significant.[44] No African Americans in the sample faced court-martial in 1861, and the two courts-martial in 1862 were both for desertion. In 1863, however, more African Americans faced courts-martial for deserting station than insubordination and desertion. As with whites, desertion was the most frequent crime in 1863, trailed by theft and desertion reduced to AWOL. Desertion remained the most frequent court-martial offense for African American sailors in 1865, followed by falling asleep at post and scandalous conduct.

The navy's justice system aimed to ensure discipline in its ranks, and this is evident in the mean prison sentences handed down for offenses in certain categories.[45] In the general court-martial sample, those convicted of desertion-related offenses received a mean sentence of 54.5 months in prison, followed by disciplinary crimes (37.4 months), antiauthority crimes (31.1 months), and violent crimes (28.9 months) relative to the mean sentence of 44 months for the entire court-martial sample.[46] Whites in the court-martial sample received mean sentences longer than the general court-martial sample in all categories. Desertion-related offenses earned a 54.9-month mean sentence, disciplinary crimes 43.1 months, antiauthority infractions 32.2 months, and violent crimes 30.1 months, for an overall mean sentence of 45.4 months. African Americans, however, received sentences below the mean sentence in the general sample.[47] For desertion-related offenses, African Americans received a mean sentence of 51.6 months, disciplinary infractions 24.4 months, antiauthority offenses 22.4 months, and violent crime 1 month, for a mean sentence of 35.4 months.

The mean sentence for various crimes also changed between the general sample and the white and black sailor samples. In the general sample, four crimes warranted mean sentences longer than the mean sentence of 44 months for all crimes—desertion, aiding desertion, deserting station, and assaulting a superior officer. The offenses of scandalous conduct, insubordination, assaulting a fellow crewman, threatening a superior officer, theft, and mutinous conduct all received sizeable mean sentences. By contrast, the crimes with the shortest mean sentence were destroying public property, contempt of court-martial, attempting to desert, and desertion reduced to AWOL.

Among the white court-martial sample, only two crimes were punished with mean sentences above the white mean sentence of 45.4 months: desertion and asleep at post. Other infractions, however, earned lengthy sentences that maintained the lengthy overall mean sentence, such as deserting station, assaulting a superior officer, scandalous conduct, insubordination, assaulting a fellow crew member, absent without leave, threatening a superior officer, and theft. Contempt of court-martial, desertion reduced to AWOL, and attempted desertion all earned terms of less than one year.

The relationship between the mean sentence and specific offenses for black sailors was not statistically significant. African American sailors who received mean sentences in excess of the overall mean sentence for black offenders of 35.4 months had committed one of four specific crimes: desertion, deserting station, aiding desertion, and mutinous conduct.[48] In other offenses, however, African Americans received shorter mean sentences, causing the lower overall mean sentence for infractions such as theft, assaulting a superior officer, insubordination, AWOL, scandalous conduct, and asleep at post. The offenses committed by black sailors who warranted a sentence of a year or less were desertion reduced to AWOL, attempted desertion, assaulting a fellow crewman, and destruction of public property.

The length of mean sentences greatly depended upon the jurisdiction of the court-martial. Three jurisdictions consistently handed down harsher sentences, exceeding the mean sentence of 44 months for the court-martial sample. The West Gulf

Blockading Squadron had the longest mean sentence at 58.6 months, followed closely by the Mississippi Squadron with 58.5 months and the North Atlantic Blockading Squadron at 56.1 months. All other jurisdictions, however, imposed substantially shorter sentences. Trials in the South Atlantic Blockading Squadron gave 36.4 months, the East Gulf Blockading Squadron inflicted 30.9 months, and the Philadelphia Navy Yard levied 30.4 months. Sailors received the shortest prison terms from courts-martial at the Boston Navy Yard (15.1 months), the Pacific Squadron (13.2 months), New York Navy Yard (11 months), the Atlantic Squadron (6 months), and the South American Squadron (1 month). The jurisdiction of the court-martial also determined the prison to hold the offender. Offenders in the Atlantic squadrons served their sentences in state penitentiaries, mostly at Ossining, New York, and Wethersfield, Connecticut. Those found guilty from the Mississippi Squadron faced imprisonment at the Illinois State Penitentiary in Joliet, and West Gulf Squadron convicts spent their terms at the Parish Prison in New Orleans. Key West held prisoners from the East Gulf Squadron.[49]

No jurisdiction displayed a racial bias. The white sample, with a mean sentence of 45.4 months, received longer sentences in the same three jurisdictions as the general court-martial sample. White sailors suffered the longest mean sentences in the Mississippi Squadron, followed by the North Atlantic Blockading Squadron and Western Gulf Blockading Squadron. The Philadelphia Navy Yard issued shorter mean sentences to white sailors than the general court-martial sample, but all other jurisdictions met or exceeded the average mean sentence. Prison terms on the Atlantic and South American Squadrons were the same as the general sample but were longer in the South Atlantic, Eastern Gulf, and Pacific Squadrons, Boston Navy Yard, and New York Navy Yard.

The African American sample was very different from the white court-martial sample, but those differences were not statistically significant.[50] With a general mean sentence of 35.4 months, African Americans received sentences longer than the navy's average in four jurisdictions—West Gulf Blockading Squadron, the Philadelphia Navy Yard, the Mississippi Squadron, and North Atlantic Blockading Squadron. In all other jurisdictions, however, African American sailors enjoyed mean prison terms shorter than both the general court-martial and white sample mean sentences.·

The prosecution and the defense oftened introduced additional factors into a court-martial that affected the severity of the sentence. This was especially common in desertion cases. Desertion plagued both services, but the navy had lower desertion rates than the army. The army had approximately 199,000 enlisted deserters during the war, roughly a 9 percent desertion rate.[51] The navy suffered approximately 4,600 desertions, a 4 percent rate. Roughly 93 percent of army deserters were white, and 6 percent were African American. The percentage of African Americans who deserted from the navy is impossible to determine, as the navy generally did not specify the race of its enlisted men in official documents, such as desertion records. One estimate emerges from the courts-martial sample in which 12 percent of desertion cases involved African Americans and 88 percent white, but these statistics reflect only those unfortunate deserters caught and tried.

Deserting was not easy, and the sailor on the run faced strenuous efforts to punish him. First, sailors risked bodily harm leaving the ship. The commanding officer of the USS *Sampson* reported to his superiors in May 1864, "William Johnson, landsman (colored) deserted March 30th about midnight." A sentry spotted Johnson fleeing the ship and fired at him, but "the shot missed him. He made good his escape before the sentinel could reload his musket." Another African American sailor, Richard Jackson, also deserted the *Sampson* a month later under the cover of a thunderstorm. Once on the run, deserters constantly dreaded arrest by law enforcement agents and bounty hunters intent on claiming government-issued deserter bounties. For most of the war, the government paid thirty dollars to anyone who returned deserters to military authority, and bounty hunting emerged as a cottage industry in the North. As the number of volunteers dwindled by 1864 and 1865, the navy took particular care to keep recruits in the service. By the end of the war, the navy had to escort draftees, considered the "scum of the merchant service," to their assignments under armed guard to restrain bounty jumpers. In one instance, a bounty jumper risked a plunge into New York's East River to escape his navy commitment.[52]

Desertions, especially among men on shore leave, became so numerous that the Navy Department attempted in December 1864 to make officers more accountable. Every commanding officer in the Union navy had to account for the whereabouts of every member of his crew on shore leave before going on leave himself, a system impossible to enforce.[53] The large numbers of desertions prompted the navy to make examples of the worst offenders. Among first-offense deserters in the general court-martial sample, the mean sentence was 50.7 months. Multiple offenders and "bounty jumpers"—sailors who enlisted to collect bounty money and then deserted to repeat the process—received mean sentences of 104.4 months. Among the white sailors in the sample, first-offense deserters received 50.8 months, and cases in which the prosecutor introduced especially damaging evidence averaged 108.5 months. First-offense African American deserters received mean sentences of 49.4 months, but repeat offenders suffered only 88-month mean sentences.[54] Particularly egregious cases of desertion were the most common crimes warranting a life or capital punishment. For instance, Thomas Collins and Joseph Whitehurst, from the West Gulf Blockading Squadron, received life sentences for deserting from the navy to collect an army enlistment bounty. Alvin Eldridge and Samuel Roberts, two white sailors of the Mississippi Squadron, both received the death sentence in June 1864 for deserting while on sentinel duty. The men earned the death penalty because, by deserting their lookout posts, they threatened the security of the ship and crew they left behind.[55]

Extenuating circumstances saved some African American sailors from harsh prison terms for desertion. For instance, in April 1863, Commander James Jouett of the USS *Cuyler* reported the desertion of landsman Matthew Harris near Pensacola, Florida. A few days later, however, Harris returned to the ship with his wife and children in tow. Harris had recovered his family from his erstwhile owner near Mobile, Alabama. Confessing to desertion, Harris offered to accept his punishment. After a council of officers met, Jouett voided the charges against Harris, granted him a brief leave of absence to establish his newly freed family at a contraband camp near the Pensacola Navy Yard, and cited the sailor in his official dispatches for his resourcefulness and bravery.[56]

After the war, most deserters still faced punishment for their crime. They could not apply for pensions or join veterans' fraternal organizations such as the Grand Army of the Republic until May 1900, when Congress passed an amnesty act absolving all navy deserters of their crime. One sailor who took advantage of the act was Joseph Overfield aboard the USS *Nansemond*. Given shore leave in July 1865, Overfield returned to find the ship gone. Presuming the officers had discharged the crew, Overfield went home to Buffalo, New York, not knowing the navy considered him a deserter until he tried to apply for a pension. Overfield hastily applied for amnesty; the government canceled the warrant for his arrest and granted his pension.[57]

Other crimes also earned special consideration from the navy. Sailors in the general sample accused of scandalous conduct with additional charges received mean sentences of 85.5 months, compared with the mean sentence of 5 months for first offenders. White first offenders suffered 5.3-month sentences; persistent offenders received 92.6 months. African Americans accused of their first scandalous conduct offense received 3.5-month mean sentences, compared with 36 months for subsequent offenses. Most scandalous conduct charges were either sodomy or attempted sodomy. Courts-martial punished the latter charge by dishonorable discharge, but the standard sentence for the former was ten years' hard labor.[58] Two white offenders accused of scandalous conduct were each sentenced to two years at hard labor for expressing approval of the assassination of President Lincoln. Another white sailor who applauded Lincoln's assassins suffered a life sentence at hard labor in the Dry Tortugas. The punishments were not unique; several defendants vocally supportive of John Wilkes Booth's actions faced trial in civilian criminal courts as well.[59]

Mitigating circumstances often shortened prison sentences for both blacks and whites accused of a variety of crimes. In February 1865, the West Gulf Blockading Squadron found Henry Jackson, a white coal heaver, guilty of assaulting another crewman and sentenced him to six months in prison. The panel suspended his sentence, however, after finding him mentally incompetent and sentenced him to a mental asylum instead. The same finding applied to Joseph Johns, a white seaman guilty of assault in December 1863. Mental incompetence also kept African American Washington Moody from receiving a prison sentence after his conviction on desertion charges in January 1865. The most timely instance of extenuating circumstances occurred in March 1865, after Richard Cornelius, an African American ordinary seaman on the Mississippi Squadron, avoided the death sentence given him for mutinous conduct and assaulting a superior officer in September 1863. President Lincoln, responding to clemency requests from Cornelius's family, inquired to Rear Admiral David D. Porter, who approved the death sentence when commanding the Mississippi Squadron, whether justice was satisfied by the time already served. Cornelius had been drinking at the time of the incident and otherwise had a spotless service record. Porter's written order to release Cornelius ended with the terse statement, "He has been imprisoned for 14 months, and this is enough."[60]

The impact of alcohol upon navy discipline is difficult to pin down. The termination of the liquor ration in 1862 was supposed to curb disciplinary infractions, but in reality the restriction had no significant effect.[61] In 1861, alcohol affected 86 percent of courts-martial in the sample. The percentage fell to 64 percent in 1862, and fell again to 61 percent in 1863. The percentage rose to 71 percent in 1864, moderating to 69 percent in 1865. Alcohol-related offenses were primarily a white problem, with 74 percent of white courts-martial involving alcohol in some manner, compared with only 28 percent of African American courts-martial.[62] Alcohol also was a factor in specific offense categories. In the general court-martial sample 69 percent of all desertions were alcohol related, compared with 88 percent of violent crimes, 80 percent of antiauthority crimes, and 40 percent of disciplinary offenses. Among white offenders, alcohol influenced 74 percent of desertions, compared with 88 percent of violent crimes, 86 percent of antiauthority infractions, and 46 percent of disciplinary offenses. Among African American courts-martial, however, alcohol played a smaller, statistically insignificant role.[63] Only 32 percent of desertions involved liquor, as did 27 percent of antiauthority offenses and 20 percent of disciplinary infractions. The sole violent crime committed by an African American in the sample was alcohol related.

Strangely, perhaps, defendants convicted of alcohol-related crimes received shorter mean sentences than sailors who erred while sober.[64] In the general sample, the mean sentence of alcohol-influenced offenders was 41.1 months; sober offenders received 49.4 months. Intoxicated white offenders received 41.4-month sentence, compared with the sentence for sober sailors of 56.6 months. There was no difference in sentencing for African American sailors.[65] Sentences for those under the influence of alcohol averaged 35.3 months compared with 35.4 months for sober offenders.

If any abuses of the judicial system existed, they occurred at the shipboard level. Acting on his sole authority, a captain was free to rule on infractions of ship rules without restraint. Although confined by the offense classification system from imposing excessive punishments for established offenses, captains were free to devise punishments for the ship rules. For instance, the captain of the USS *Vanderbilt* in September 1863 confined a sailor in the brig on bread and water for accidentally breaking the leg of the ship's mascot, a dog belonging to the paymaster. The captain found an African American sailor aboard the same ship guilty of stealing a blanket. His punishment was to wear "a tall canvass hat, White-washed, on his head with this inscription—'I am one of the Thieves.'" Aboard the ironclad USS *Nahant* the commanding officer, instead of court-martial, had two African American first-class boys confined in irons and incarcerated in the coal bunker for a day in hopes of scaring the two straight. Even when a boy assaulted another boy, his sentence was a week in irons instead of a court-martial. Sailors who took too long in following orders faced long hours sitting atop the tallest mast. Sailors caught spitting on the deck would have to wear spittoons about their necks.[66]

Far from navy authority, some commanding officers were guilty of excessive or illegal punishments. Rowland True aboard the *Silver Lake* remembered "seeing one fellow tied up by the thumbs for two hours for disobedience, a severe punishment" by officers who were "overbearing and fond of showing their authority, [who] often punished and ill-treated . . . when there was no necessity for it." On occasion, captains forced sailors to hang from the ratlines for several hours with the ropes under their arms, a punishment not permitted by the Navy Articles of War. In December 1860, John Murphy, a landsman in the Pacific Squadron, received an "M" brand on the hand, another banned punishment, after his conviction for mutinous conduct. Aboard the USS *Saugus*, Captain Henry Walke had two sailors "ride on the hog chain" (sit on the anchor chain suspended off the ground for several hours) for "flouring a saucy negro." The captain of the USS *Kearsarge*, John Winslow, employed a variety of punishments, including confining inebriated sailors in a canvas straitjacket until sober. The navy prohibited one particularly unpleasant form of punishment, the sweatbox, in 1863. Little bigger than a coffin, the sweatbox limited the movement of the confined sailor while the box, exposed to the sun, grew hotter with each passing hour. After learning of the apparatus, President Lincoln forbade the imprisonment of sailors in sweatboxes thereafter, although some officers were slow to respond to the order.[67]

By applying its criminal justice system fairly and equally to all its personnel, the navy reinforced its position as, for the nineteenth century, a reasonably egalitarian institution. For its time, the navy judiciary system succeeded in balancing racial concerns and strong discipline into a system that worked effectively. By giving African American sailors a legal organization designed to operate without bias, which granted them more rights than most states, and which protected them from the worst abuses of the army judicial system, black sailors could expect full legal protection.

Chapter Seven

ONE WHO WAS THERE

CHARLES B. FISHER,

UNITED STATES NAVY

• Students of the Civil War have a variety of sources to rely on, from government records to personal accounts, in a bewildering array. Those studying African American soldiers are the beneficiaries of a growing pool of books about their wartime experiences. The naval history of the Civil War is similarly replete with documentary sources. Glaringly absent in the history of African Americans in the Union navy, however, is an African American voice. With a few small exceptions, first-hand accounts by black sailors of their experiences are virtually unknown. Diaries, if any existed, were lost or destroyed as the years have passed, or sailors, not believing their experiences were worthy of print, did not offer their diaries for publication. Consequently, histories of African American sailors have had to rely on second-person observations and recollections of black sailors invariably written by white officers and crewmen. Without an African American first-person account, historians had no means of verifying historical claims or conclusions. Of the thousands of black sailors to serve in the Union navy, the experiences of only one, Charles F. Fisher, are available as a first-person account. Covering nearly three years of Fisher's life, the diary offers an excellent opportunity to compare Fisher's life in the naval service to those of other black sailors.[1]

In many ways, Charles Fisher was a typical African American sailor. Before the war, he lived in Alexandria, Virginia, a region that provided the navy with large numbers of recruits. In the sample of African American recruits, 71 claimed Alexandria as their place of origin. In addition, 478 black recruits in the sample enlisted from the District of Columbia, across the Potomac River from Alexandria. Fisher and the other recruits from Alexandria and the District of Columbia composed 3 percent of the general sample. Fisher was apparently free (though his diary makes no mention of his prewar status), and he sent letters to family and friends who lived in the North during the war. In this regard, he is also a typical African American sailor, as a majority of the enlistment sample were freemen before the war. Another hint that Fisher was not a slave came from his recruitment in Boston, Massachusetts. Were Fisher an escaped slave, he would most likely seek aid at the nearby Washington Navy Yard instead of traveling all the way to Boston to enlist. As he had no apparent restriction on his travel or place of enlistment, one can presume Fisher was not a slave.

Fisher's naval career began with his enlistment in Boston on January 15, 1862, a year Boston recorded 10 percent of all sample African American enlistments, second only to New York City's 13 percent. Fisher's age was near the average among African American recruits that year. The mean age of all African American enlistees in the sample was 24 years, and African American recruits in 1862 averaged 25.7 years. At 23, Fisher's age was common, as 23-year-olds composed about 10 percent of the general enlistment sample. Fisher was also a common African American sailor in his postwar status. The navy honorably discharged Fisher from the navy in 1865, like 74 percent of African American sailors in the sample of northern recruits. After the war, Fisher also received a pension, like 78 percent of African Americans in the pension sample.

In many ways, however, Fisher was far from the norm among African American sailors. Before the war, he was a bookbinder, a skilled laborer. In the general sample only 5 percent of African American enlistees were skilled laborers, compared with the 65 percent who were unskilled and 30 percent who listed no occupation. In 1862, the percentage of black enlistees who were skilled laborers was slightly higher than the general sample (7%). Fisher practiced other occupations before becoming a bookbinder. In 1860, Fisher served on a Mississippi riverboat named the *Fanny Bullitt,* which transported cannon and munitions to Fort Pillow, Tennessee. As a mariner before the war, Fisher joined the navy with more experience than the average black recruit. The maritime trades accounted for only 11 percent of all African American enlistments, and 9 percent of 1862 enlistments. Prewar mobility also set Fisher apart from his contemporaries. Besides his travels on the Mississippi River, Fisher mentioned visiting New Orleans and Philadelphia before the war and wrote of American cities with an air of familiarity, suggesting that Fisher, unlike most antebellum Americans, had traveled widely.[2]

Fisher also appeared to be atypical in his level of education. Besides writing poetry and eloquent entries in his diary, Fisher added elaborately detailed descriptions of the places he visited. After exploring a place, he recorded a vivid description of the town's appearance and facilities. Beyond the entertainment and recreational appeal of a city, Fisher's accounts included sites of religious, cultural, and historical significance, such as a notable cathedral, municipal house, or fortification. For instance, Fisher described his first impressions of Tangier: "The coasts are exceedingly high and bold, especially those of Spain which seems to overcrow the Moorish. . . . A hoary mountain is seen uplifting its summit from the clouds. It is Mount Abyla or, as it is called in the Moorish tongue Jebel Muza . . . it contains the tomb of a prophet of that name." At the Spanish port of La Carraca, however, Fisher was less impressed: "There is little to interest an American here unless ones tastes run on religious matters, then a visit to the Cathedral here will well repay ones trouble." Fisher was also evidently a great student of history. The city descriptions in the diary contained references to historic events, both prominent and obscure, that had occurred there. He visited Villa Da Pria, Spain, in July 1863, noting that "the Marquis of Santa Cristo in 1635 lost 500 men in an attack on this place," and in September 1863 Fisher passed Corunna, Spain, "where Sir John Moore was slain in battle with the Spaniards."[3]

Fisher was also an atypical African American sailor in other aspects of his enlistment. First, he enlisted in 1862, a year in which relatively few African Americans joined the service. The first large influx of black sailors came the next year, in the aftermath of the Emancipation Proclamation. Only 14 percent of African Americans in the recruiting sample enlisted in 1862; 32 percent joined a year later. Also, Fisher's rank was higher than most black recruits. Although enlisted officially as a landsman, like 65 percent of all African American enlistees, Fisher's commanding officer promoted him in February 1864 to wardroom cook. Responsible for acquiring provisions for the officers' dining room, the wardroom cook served the ship's officers exclusively. In addition to a wage of thirty dollars per month (two dollars more than a seaman), he was exempt from much of the drudgery of shipboard life, such as routine maintenance and standing watch at night. Fisher could also partake of the meals served to the officers, receiving food of much better quality and diversity than that served to the crew. Because supplying the officers' kitchen was his responsibility, Fisher frequently went ashore with funds from the ship's paymaster to purchase supplies, apparently trusted not to desert on one of his missions.

Few black sailors served in European waters, where Fisher was stationed. Assigned to the USS *Kearsarge,* Fisher accompanied the vessel to Europe to hunt for Confederate warships preying on Union merchant ships. While the Union navy possessed hundreds of ships, only nineteen vessels received assignments to hunt southern commerce raiders. In this capacity, Fisher spent his three years in the navy in European waters, visiting the Azores, Portugal, Spain, North Africa, Ireland, England, France, Belgium, and the Netherlands. Fisher saw a fair portion of Europe while the vast majority of African American sailors spent the war on blockade or riverine duty. Because of the nature of naval warfare during the Civil War, most sailors faced combat in the form of Confederate shore batteries and ambushes from close riverbanks. Aboard the *Kearsarge,* however, Fisher participated in one of the few ship-to-ship engagements of the Civil War, when the Union vessel caught the Confederate raider CSS *Alabama* at Cherbourg, France, in June 1864. The *Kearsarge* sank the *Alabama* in the English Channel after a one-hour gunnery duel, the only combat on the high seas between the Union and Confederate navies.[4]

Fisher's postwar life was quite different from that found by most African American sailors after they left the army. Fisher thrived in business in Washington, D.C., after the war, and he was instrumental in forming the first African American militia units in the District of Columbia. Fisher remained active in the militia organization, eventually attaining the rank of colonel before his death in 1903, at the age of 64.[5]

Fisher's diary is replete with episodes that reflect many of the same concerns as any Civil War–era sailor, regardless of race. A good example is Fisher's yearning for prize money. On July 20, 1863, *Kearsarge* intercepted the British-flagged merchant ship *Juno*, suspecting it of being a blockade-runner. Finding only "dry goods and medicine," the *Kearsarge* allowed *Juno* to proceed. Despondent at losing a rich prize, Fisher and the crew seethed at the limits of their authority in the face of *Juno*'s arrogant captain: "He was both defiant and very insulting to our Captain and everyman in the ship wished for Captain Pickering [*Kearsarge*'s commanding officer] . . . to learn him some manners—Thus went our Prize." Fisher learned later that the USS *Connecticut* seized the *Juno* while running the blockade, taking the *Kearsarge*'s prize money.[6]

Fisher and the *Kearsarge* encountered other vessels that reflected the international politics of the era. British and French warships, demonstrating their pro-Confederate leanings, frequently shadowed the Union ship. At Gibraltar in October 1862, *Kearsarge* met the British vessels HMS *Warrior* and *Black Prince*, large oceangoing ironclads, although Fisher was not impressed: "They are [armor] clad Fore and Aft but would be no match for our Monitor. She would lick a fleet of just such Ironclads." Fisher was more impressed by some French ironclads in September 1863: "the French Iron Clad Fleet . . . made a formidable appearance as they steamed into harbor. There were five iron clad rams—one frigate and one gunboat—the rams are ugly looking monsters." In May 1863, Fisher observed a French transport "bound from Mexico to Toulon." The ship had just delivered reinforcements to the French army that would soon seize power in Mexico. In the same month, however, *Kearsarge* received the salute of a Russian warship. Russia, Britain's main European rival in the late nineteenth century, improved its relations with the United States after Britain announced support for the Confederacy. In July 1864, *Kearsarge* encountered the huge steamer *Great Lastern*. The largest ship in the world at the time, *Great Eastern* was laying the first trans-Atlantic telegraph cable, the only vessel large enough to carry the miles of wire needed.[7]

Though on the other side of the Atlantic, Fisher and the other members of *Kearsarge's* crew were subject to the rigorous discipline of the U.S. Navy. The majority of infractions were alcohol related, usually sailors returning inebriated from shore leave. On two occasions, in July 1862 and September 1863, shore leave had to be suspended because of crewmen brawling ashore. The first instance was in Spain and involved local thugs. The second was at Brest, France, where *Kearsarge* was monitoring repairs on the Confederate raider *Florida*.[8] Fights had erupted between the rival crews, and the captain confined the men to ship to prevent an international incident. Attempts to halt drinking altogether were generally unsuccessful. When *Kearsarge* entered a drydock at La Carraca, Spain, to have its hull scraped, the officers and marines attempted to "blockade" the ship to prevent sailors from escaping on unauthorized shore leave. The blockade had the officers and marines "watch the men and keep them from visiting the wine shops in the yard and getting 'tight' and prevent desertion . . . Officers on duty at the bow and an old stable twenty yards away from the ship." Fisher recounted that the blockade was not very effective, with thirty or forty sailors a night escaping into town. In March 1864, *Kearsarge* found itself at the French navy yard at Boulogne. With cheap alcohol readily available, many crewmen smuggled liquor aboard the *Kearsarge* when returning from liberty. Unfortunately, the coal supply needed replenishment when the men returned, and Fisher reported, "The brig [the *Kearsarge*] has more rum than coal aboard and nearly everyman in the ship is drunk and fighting." With four men confined in irons, coaling finished the next day.[9]

On other occasions, individual sailors received punishment for returning to the ship drunk, but the captain judged the infractions as violations of the ship's rules rather than of naval regulations, which would have led to a summary court-martial. In November 1862, for instance, a gunner's mate by the name of Yeaton returned to the ship after liberty ashore; "he got drunk today and was a pitiful object to see on duty holding on to a post and talking to himself in drunken lingo. Everyone that passed him . . . would sing out . . . 'Yeaton is disabled by having a brick in his hat.' At last, the First Lieutenant sent the gunner and boatswain to lug him aboard the ship. He was put off duty."[10] Fisher witnessed only one formal legal proceeding on the *Kearsarge*. On July 28, 1862, a court-martial tried John W. Dempsey, captain of the After Guard, for mutinous conduct. The panel found Dempsey guilty, and sentenced him to a one-rank demotion, loss of one month's pay, and three months' confinement in the brig (which Fisher termed "pokie duty"). Francis Viannah, an African American seaman, replaced Dempsey as captain of the After Guard. Dempsey's offense warranted a lengthy prison term, but the navy lacked prison facilities in Europe.[11]

Desertion was the most serious disciplinary offense aboard the *Kearsarge*. Fisher recorded the desertion of only seven crewmen in his diary, but 47 (19.6 percent) of the 240 officers, sailors, and marines who crewed the ship deserted during Fisher's term of service. Fisher records in his diary the desertion of those in his immediate circle. In October 1862, a boat returned to the ship containing "Andrew J. Rowly dead drunk," but without two crewmen named Thomas Jones and Daniel Lahie, both ordinary seamen, who "had run away." In the Azores in July 1863, Fisher described a massive breakwater under construction in the harbor. The lure of working for wages on the breakwater induced three men by the name of George Read, Thomas Igo, and Charles White to desert. The work was apparently not to their liking, as Read returned in September "having gotten tired of working on the breakwater." Read escaped a court-martial for desertion. In January 1864, Fisher bluntly wrote in his diary, "Today John Netto run away." Netto, a landsman, deserted after *Kearsarge* docked in Cadiz, Spain.[12]

The most distressing desertion to Fisher was the escape of his friend Robert Scott, an African American wardroom steward.

Scott and Fisher enlisted together and were friends before the war. In July 1862, while *Kearsarge* was at Gibraltar, Scott "went ashore to get things for the mess . . . he told Ned he was not coming aboard anymore . . . [Scott] went to the English Governor and told him that he was a runaway nigger and was under the painful necessity of leaving the ship because he was ill treated, a lie, and that he . . . claimed English protection—he got it and of course we could not take him. He is a rascal and deserves hanging." The bitter feelings expressed by Fisher about a fellow African American sailor demonstrate Fisher's strong allegiances to the navy and his sense of justice. Besides the deserters, *Kearsarge*'s log noted that the captain demoted six men as a disciplinary measure during the three-year period Fisher was aboard the ship.[13]

Fisher did not escape disciplinary action and accepted punishment twice. In April 1864, Fisher's shore party was late returning to the *Kearsarge*. For his tardiness, the captain sentenced Fisher and the boat's crew to confinement in double irons, or "Double Darbies," as Fisher labeled them, on bread and water for five days. In August 1864, Fisher spent six days in the brig on bread and water for taunting the crew of the USS *Sacramento* as it passed the *Kearsarge* in the English Channel. The ship's log does not record what Fisher said to warrant the punishment.[14]

The *Kearsarge* replaced deserters with recruits from American merchant ships encountered in Europe or with foreign nationals in the ports visited by the ship. After Robert Scott's desertion, the navy recruited two men from the American clipper ship *Sunrise* to replace him, "Matthew McNully and Edward Wilt—sprightly able bodied men." In April 1863, the crew added two additional men from the "Black Ball Line Clipper *Dreadnaught*," although Fisher did not list their names. The ship needed recruits to replace crewmen lost to death, accident, or disease. Demonstrating the hazards of warships, in September 1863, Zaron Phillips "fell from the mizzen top, and broke his collar bone." Fisher was standing below decks immediately under the spot Phillips landed, making a "dull and startling sound." Five other men suffered various broken bones and amputated digits but remained aboard ship. Various ailments also plagued the crew. In April 1863, Fisher spent a few days on the "binnacle list," the daily tally of those ill and unavailable for duty. Medical facilities were inadequate for a vessel the size of *Kearsarge*. The ship carried only one surgeon and had no dedicated sick bay, forcing the ill to lie together in a corner of the berth deck. The *Kearsarge*'s surgeon was wary of of diseases endemic to North Africa, particularly malaria and yellow fever. At one point, *Kearsarge* refused contact with the USS *St. Louis,* afraid of the malaria sweeping through that vessel.[15]

Fisher recorded the deaths of four men in his diary. Mark W. Emery, buried at sea near the Azores, died of disease in August 1863, at the age of twenty-one. A few days later, Fisher reported that Clement Boener had also died, apparently from the same type of fever that claimed Emery, and the navy buried him in a church cemetery in the Azores. In addition to the two disease-related deaths, ten men, weakened by disease, received early discharge. During the June 1864 fight with the *Alabama,* the *Kearsarge* suffered only one fatality. A close friend of Fisher, "poor Bill Gowan [sic] died at three oclock." His leg badly mangled from a Confederate shell, William Gowin died of a massive infection. The fourth fatality aboard *Kearsarge* occurred in July 1862, when Edward Tibbets died in a grotesque manner. Lying at port in Algeciras, Spain, many off-duty crewmen amused themselves by fishing or swimming. Tibbets and another crewman, George Andrew, were swimming back to the ship when a shark surfaced nearby. A nearby cutter harpooning fish for dinner raced to their assistance, but the shark killed Tibbets before aid could arrive. The fifth fatality aboard *Kearsarge* occurred in March 1862, when Sabine De Santo died of pneumonia in the Azores. Curiously, Fisher does not recount De Santo's death in his diary, though he was a black officer's steward with whom Fisher would have had daily contact.[16]

The most trying experience aboard the *Kearsarge* was coping with the chronic boredom. *Kearsarge*'s mission was to hunt and sink Confederate warships. The ship found three raiders, CSS *Sumter, Rappahannock,* and *Florida,* but they were beyond reach in European ports. Union merchant ships sighted another raider, *Alabama,* on several occasions in 1862 and 1863, but searches proved fruitless. Thus, the Union vessel spent many stormy days at sea, hovering near enemy ships it could not touch. Even worse than blockading Confederate ships that might never come out to fight were the interminable stays in port with little for the sailors to do and shore leave forbidden. One such port stay, in La Carraca, Spain, was so insufferable that Fisher suspended writing in his diary for an entire month, preferring to save the pages for days in which something actually occurred. "As we are here for the winter I think there will be nothing of interest to write of," he wrote. "There is the same scenes enacted here day in and day out—so I shall skip into December or perhaps further." Because of the boredom, Fisher was frequently homesick and weary of life in the navy; "Sea sick and cold, home-sick, heart-sick, cannot write, cannot express my feelings."[17]

To break the tedium, the crew seized every entertainment opportunity available. Sailors played a variety of games, such as checkers and backgammon, although Captain John A. Winslow banned card playing when he assumed command from Captain Charles W. Pickering in April 1863. In warmer climates the sailors fished, had rowing races, or swam (at least until Edward Tibbett's death). The crew read everything they could get their hands on, especially prized mail from home. The most consistent complaint from the *Kearsarge*'s crew was the sporadic mail delivery. Religion was an important diversion for Fisher, who always noted his attendance at Sunday services, who led the services, and occasionally the topic of the sermon. Holidays provided an excuse to celebrate and break the monotony. On the Fourth of July 1862, *Kearsarge* celebrated at the Azores by decorating the ship with its flags and issuing the sailors an extra liquor ration. Crewmen reveled on the deck, including Joachim Pease, an African American sailor, "beating a drum—Daigo style."[18]

Shore leave was the best remedy for boredom, but the privilege was frequently suspended. The officers considered Fisher to be of good discipline, however, and he frequently went ashore. While other sailors made straight for the taverns and brothels, Fisher toured the city, making acquaintances along the way. When in London, Fisher struck up a friendship with soldiers of the British army's 78th Highlander Regiment, "had a nice time dancing, singing, etc. and more been [beer?] than I could drink." Another of Fisher's friends invited him to attend a masquerade ball at Cadiz, Spain: "I shall go again tonight to attend the masquerade ball. After dinner I put on my togs or in other words 'Dressed myself from top to toe and down to Dinah's I go.' . . . Each gentleman accompanies a lady and dances with her alone except he has other Ladie acquaintances in the company . . . you have to be very particular here and not stick your fingers in other folks pie for you'll get pined [pinned?] in a moment for these Spaniards are quarrelsome customers when you interfere. . . . I went with the Seniorita Pacia de Guardo. . . . Plenty of room to dance and a splendid band of forty pieces . . . the two ball rooms . . . are capable of accommodating hundreds of couples at one time. Dancing commenced at eleven and was kept up until the 'wee small Hours.'"[19]

Fisher himself entertained the crew by forming a minstrel troupe aboard the *Kearsarge*. Fisher and another African American sailor, George Williams, joined four white sailors (William Bastine, William Gowin, Martin Hoyt, and Martin Simpson) to form a band equipped with "guitars, violin cello, violin, accordeon, Tambor [tambourine], and triangle." Williams, known as "Ham Fat" for his prodigious appetite, was the star of the troupe. A talented singer and dancer, Williams performed a comedy routine that threw "the audience into fits." The minstrel troop is interesting because it challenges the premise that minstrel shows demonstrated racism against African American sailors. Although the *Kearsarge*'s band did not appear in blackface, the voluntary participation of Fisher and Williams in performances meant to elicit laughter implies that Fisher and Williams did not find the performances demeaning or degrading. Rather, the circumstances suggest that Fisher, Williams, and perhaps other black sailors found the shows rewarding diversions from the boredom of everyday existence.[20]

Kearsarge's sailors varied their diet as much as possible to introduce some novelty into their daily life, eating whatever animal crossed their paths. On several occasions, Fisher mentioned eating porpoises, although he evidently did not find them appetizing. In August 1862, "John Burns the Chief Boatswains mate succeeded in killing and getting three of the largest of them— we had for breakfast Porpoise steaks—hash and fried. It tasted something like beef but will hardly stay down." Fisher ate porpoise again in January 1864, "caught some porpoise. Fine times cutting him up and scrambling for steaks as we have been some days on salt horse [canned meat]." In October 1864, Fisher tried porpoise one last time: "We caught a porpoise from a school this morning and I cooked his liver but I cannot go it. Neither porpoise nor shark were made for human beings to eat."[21]

Alcohol broke the monotony, although Fisher at first swore off drinking: "at 4 ock [o'clock] all hands are piped up to 'splice the main brace.' I do not indulge." News of the termination of the liquor ration reached *Kearsarge* in mid-September 1862, two weeks after the ban went into effect, and many of the crew did not take the news well, casting "a Gloom over the Liquor loving ones." Despite prohibition, the officers occasionally permitted the crew bottles of beer on holidays and after particularly arduous duty. The *Kearsarge* was at sea on the Fourth of July 1863 and held no celebration. To compensate for the lack of entertainment, First Lieutenant Thomas C. Harris, *Kearsarge*'s executive officer, ordered a special meal for the crew—"a sea pie of chickens & a bottle of Pale Ale to a man." After coaling the ship in Brest, France, in September 1863, the crew received permission to purchase beer from "bum boats"—small boats alongside selling food and other goods. Fisher noted, "the Bum boat women are thick as hops and have some very good ale—quite a treat for us." Not receiving alcohol after tough duty could cause depression among the crew. Fisher recorded in April 1864, "we commenced coaling ship—there is no rum this time and the boys have all got the dumps."[22]

The boredom evaporated in June 1864, when *Kearsarge* received word from the American consul in the Netherlands that the Confederate warship *Alabama* was at Cherbourg, France. Racing to the scene, *Kearsarge* arrived as the *Alabama* was preparing to go to sea. Although other Confederate commerce raiders had been able to hide in European ports, Raphael Semmes, captain of the *Alabama,* was obliged to engage the *Kearsarge.* Earlier in the war, the French were sympathetic to the Confederacy, but with fortunes turning against the South the French were unwilling to allow the *Alabama* to stay indefinitely. Semmes had originally planned an extended stay in Cherbourg to refurbish his ship and recruit a new crew. Instead, he determined to fight the Union warship.

Although denied docking facilities, the *Alabama* could have stayed in French waters beyond the reach of the *Kearsarge*. Semmes chose to fight because he feared the arrival of more Union warships, and he faced better odds singly fighting the *Kearsarge*. Others have credited Semmes's innate aggressiveness, prompting the Confederate captain to seize a greater challenge than the unarmed merchantmen that were his usual prey. Regardless of his reasoning, Semmes informed Captain Winslow via the Confederate consul that the *Alabama* would soon emerge. On paper, the two combatants matched up evenly, with roughly the same displacement, dimensions, and firepower. *Kearsarge*'s crew, however, had frequent gunnery practice, and training on the *Alabama* was sporadic. The Union ship had fresh powder, and the Confederate powder had decayed after months at sea. Winslow was a battle-hardened veteran from the Mississippi Squadron commanding a seasoned crew. With the exception of a small Union gunboat, Semmes's crew had engaged only unarmed merchant ships, and their combat skills had eroded. Also, the Union warship was deceptively well protected. Anchor chain, draped over the hull and disguised with a wooden cover, protected the engine room from Confederate fire.

Fisher wrote that the Union crewmen showed excitement about the prospect of battle: "no man is downhearted. All the boys are in high glee. Some dancing. Some singing their Saturday songs and some spinning cuffers [telling stories] as usual." All was quiet, however, when *Alabama,* escorted by a French ironclad, cleared the Cherbourg breakwater on the morning of Sunday, June 19, 1864. Careful to avoid an international incident, Winslow positioned the *Kearsarge* well beyond French territorial waters, taking an upwind position to advance upon his approaching adversary. Seeking an advantage, *Alabama* opened fire first at twelve hundred yards, but all of its early shots missed high. A later shot struck the *Kearsarge*'s sternpost, but the faulty shell failed to explode. Had the shell detonated, *Kearsarge* could have sunk. A few minutes later, a Confederate shell exploded near *Kearsarge*'s aft pivot gun, causing the only significant damage to the Union ship. *Kearsage's* shooting, while slower than *Alabama's*, was more accurate and telling. A Union shell detonated near *Alabama's* aft pivot gun, killing most of its crew. While the Confederate aim was consistently high, the accurate Union gunnery began to riddle the *Alabama's* waterline. After an hour of incessant pounding, *Alabama* had listed noticeably to starboard. Soon after, water poured into the engine room, extinguishing the *Alabama's* boilers. With only the sails for propulsion, Semmes broke off the engagement and turned toward the French coast. The wounds to the *Alabama* were too severe, however, and she began to sink at the stern. Also, Winslow had cut off Semmes's retreat into French waters and maneuvered to rake the Confederate vessel. Semmes struck his colors (a signal of surrender) and hoisted flags requesting *Kearsarge's* assistance. Unfortunately, several shells struck the raider before Semmes's intent became clear.[23]

As Winslow sent his boats to collect *Alabama's* crew, a nearby English yacht, the *Deerhound,* also rescued survivors. Instead of turning them over to the *Kearsarge,* however, *Deerhound* steered for home, taking with it Captain Semmes and some of *Alabama's* crew. Of the 146 officers and men aboard the *Alabama,* the *Deerhound* rescued 41 (2 of them died on the trip to England), a French boat rescued 10, and the *Kearsarge* found 2 dead Confederate sailors in the water along with 68 survivors. The remaining 14 men went down with the *Alabama.* The *Kearsarge* suffered three casualties. William Gowin later died from his leg wound, John W. Dempsey, earlier court-martialed for mutinous conduct, had his right arm amputated, and Seaman James McBeth suffered a broken leg.[24]

Stationed below deck in the ammunition magazine, Fisher did not witness the engagement but reported after the battle that "except for a splitting headache I was neither frightened nor hurt." He emerged to observe "the blood from the wounded Pirates covers our berth deck and their groans are awful to hear as they lay dying on our deck." Far from the boisterous excitement before the battle, Fisher was somber. "Scarcely five hours have elapsed since they left port in their noble cruiser hoping to capture the U.S. Sloop Kearsarge and murder her crew," he wrote. "As they said before going into action they would show us no quarter, but the Lord protected us and their fate was sealed."[25]

Noticeably absent from Fisher's diary is any hint of discrimination or racism aimed at him or any other African American crewman. Nowhere in the journal did Fisher record receiving insults, labels, or special treatment by other members of the crew because of his race. The closest thing to a racial slur in the diary came from an Englishwoman in Dover. Ashore for supplies, Fisher surprised the locals when he asked directions to the nearest butcher shop: "he speaks English said a woman. . . . They have never seen Yankees before and some of the most intelligent have always thought us barbarians and it is hard to get through the crowd now that they find you are not the devil—not so black as we are painted. One Lady insisted on shaking hands with me and looking at me over and around, she said What are you, sir! I'm one of Abe Lincoln's pets ma'am I innocently replyed. Oh, yes she replyed, not knowing what I meant." Quite the opposite, in Fisher's writings *Kearsarge*'s crew seemed oblivious to the race of their shipmates. Never did he report a racist incident or slur aimed at him or any other African American crewman. On one supply run, when the water was too shallow to pull close to shore, the white sailors carried Fisher "on their shoulders to the beach as the boat could not get in close enough to the shore without wading." It is difficult to accuse sailors who would carry an African American crewman on their backs of racism.[26]

Fisher had less restraint, however, and his diary contains vitriolic comment on shipmates and the foreign nationals he encountered. One man to raise Fisher's ire was Jimmy Haley, the captain of the Forecastle. Fisher described the Irish Haley as "an old Mick . . . decidedly the ugliest man in the ship's company. He is an old growler and . . . does nothing all day but swear and quarrel with everybody who comes near him he's the Porcupine of the ship's company." Fisher also had no liking for Fireman George W. Remick, "the wickedest man in the ship's company. He swears at his food, his ration, and everything and everybody that comes in his way and all together is about the worst of the worst—he a Secesh [Confederate sympathizer] and swears Abe Lincoln is no better than Jeff Davis—and has made America a slave country and a place for no sane man to live in."[27]

Fisher also did little to hide his contempt for some of the foreigners he met. He described Spanish prisoners who worked on the docks as naturally lazy—"there are seven thousand workmen here in this navy yard and they don't do the work five hundred would do in the States. They lounge and smoke away the day in utter idleness. The tools they work with are of the most primitive character and would cut the hands and legs off an American. . . . The 'Chain Gang' is still the National Punishment of Spain. It is no punishment at all for men and guard to lay down and sleep together for hours in the day." Fisher was not particularly fond of Ireland either; "Instead of the lovely evergreen isle that we read of in story nothing pleasant meets the eye. The town and vicinity looks dreary and gray . . . squalid poverty stalks abroad in the noon days sun. Nothing is heard but Irish! Irish! I don't wonder the people leave such a miserable hole." The Netherlands was not one of Fisher's favorite ports of call: "I hope we are not going up to Dutchland again. I hate the devilish sour Krout eating Lager bloated boors." Even Brazilians of African descent earned Fisher's scorn; "They were mostly colored people and the soldiers are strapping Negroes—barefooted. . . . Every one of them are convicts and a more wicked set of men one could not imagine—naked to the waist and hairy . . . they look ferocious and are more like beasts than men."[28]

The Charles Fisher diary is an invaluable source of information about the inner thoughts and motivations of an African American sailor. Although not a typical black sailor in every respect, Fisher's rare words and opinions are one of the few means of judging what African Americans thought about their place in the navy and their perception of the world around them. Without knowing the race of the writer in advance, a reader would have little clue to his ethnicity, demonstrating that the concerns of Civil War sailors cut across racial lines. Fisher worried about money, food, when he could go home, and whether he would die in battle. The diary permits its reader to understand black sailors as human beings instead of just names in a recruiting ledger.

CONCLUSION

- During the Civil War, the U.S. Navy conducted a unique experiment in social equality. From a minimal prewar force, the Union navy developed into a powerful element of the North's war machine, but one useless without vital manpower. Driven to win the conflict between the states, the navy proved willing to grant unparalleled social and legal rights to African Americans in order to induce their enlistment and loyal service. African American sailors more than proved their bravery and commitment to the Union cause.

Determined to defeat the Confederacy, the U.S. Navy integrated thousands of African Americans into its ranks. While African American soldiers endured segregation and abuse from the army, black sailors enjoyed a wide range of freedoms. The navy provided equal pay, benefits, pensions, medical care, and living accommodations. After the war, African American sailors benefited from the government's pension system in equal regard to white veterans. When prosecuted, African Americans received fair treatment, even receiving less severe sentences than their white counterparts. Although racist attitudes endured among white sailors, not enough evidence exists to show that black sailors faced abusive racism in their everyday lives.

After the war ended, the navy continued to enlist African Americans for every enlisted rank, and for the remainder of the nineteenth century black sailors were a common sight on American warships. In the thirty years after the Civil War, the navy maintained an enlisted force of five to six thousand men, with African Americans averaging about five to seven hundred of the total (10–14%). To create a nucleus of career sailors, the navy

converted the rank of landsman into a form of naval apprentice-
ship and began giving recruits formal training on land instead of
on-the-job training at sea. Although African Americans made up
only 3 percent of apprentices in 1880, they represented 14 percent of naval trainees by 1890. During the Spanish-American war
in 1898, an African American seaman, Robert Penn, won the
Medal of Honor for bravery under Spanish fire. Around the turn
of the century, however, the navy's social climate changed
against black sailors.[1]

Three reasons were to blame for the gradual reduction of
African Americans in the U.S. Navy between 1900 and 1930.
First, the emergence of segregation, de jure in the South and de
facto in the North, led the navy and American society to over-
look the contributions of African Americans during the Civil
War and denigrate their ability to serve in the military. Racial
conflicts, increasingly common on land, began to manifest
themselves in the military service. The most notable naval race
riot occurred aboard the cruiser USS *Charleston* in 1894, when
name-calling and petty pranks erupted into a brawl that the
ship's marines contained only after "several of them had their rifles taken away from them." African Americans who made the
navy their careers still served under white officers. Three African
Americans—John H. Conyers, Alonzo McClennan, and Henry E.
Baker—entered the United States Naval Academy between 1872
and 1874. Like the first African American cadets at West Point,
however, the three suffered abuse from their white counterparts
beyond the traditional hazing and eventually left the academy.
Two African Americans, John Smith and Robert Bundy, attended
the academy in 1897 but were also forced to resign.[2]

Second, the reemergence of the U.S. Navy as a modern steel
and steam force in the 1880s altered the navy's recruiting needs.
Coastal navigators and experienced sail handlers, positions that
demanded skills that antebellum African Americans possessed in
abundance, disappeared, replaced by a need for experienced
machine operators, a skill denied blacks in the world of Jim
Crow. The demands of the new navy no longer reflected skills
possessed by African Americans. Consequently, the proportion
of African American enlistees with previous naval experience

dropped from 13 percent in 1870 to 6 percent in 1890. The percentage of African Americans assigned as mess men increased from 29 percent to 49 percent in the same years. In a sample of 125 African American sailors in 1913, 21 worked in the engine room, 6 in the commissary branch, 3 were gunner's mates, and the rest were mess men.[3]

Third, the expansion of America's empire in the early twentieth century created other sources of unskilled labor. After suppressing Filipino resistance in 1902, the navy began enlisting mess men and other menial laborers from the islands on the premise that they were more manageable. Officers considered the diminutive Filipinos "better suited for the duties of an officer's servant than one six feet or over." The number of foreign enlistments grew rapidly, and by 1914 Filipinos outnumbered African Americans in the U.S. Navy; by 1932, the ratio of Filipinos to African Americans was nearly ten to one. World War I did not halt the trend. Draftees expanded the navy's enlisted force to more than 200,000, but only 3,200 were African American, less than 2 percent of the total navy force. In 1919, with the navy again shrinking to a postwar force, the recruitment of African Americans stopped altogether. With no new enlistees, the number of African Americans in the navy declined until 1932, when they composed only one half of one percent of the navy population. In 1936 and 1937, James L. Johnson and George J. Trivers entered the Naval Academy, but fared no better than earlier African American midshipmen.[4]

After 1932, however, the social climate for African Americans in the navy changed directions. The independence of the Philippines was scheduled for 1947, and at the same time the navy reopened enlistment to African Americans, although menial jobs formerly reserved for Filipinos were the only ones available. When World War II broke out, more than five thousand African Americans were already serving in the navy, but the wider expansion of black manpower, as in the Civil War, was controversial. While the navy hierarchy opposed wider African American employment, the reality of wartime concerns overcame their objections, and in April 1942 the navy opened all ratings to African American recruits. Although still forced to fill the mess men billets first, by December 1943 blacks ranked as sailors outnumbered mess men forty-seven thousand to thirty-eight thousand. Most of the African American recruits trained in a segregated area at the Great Lakes Training Center near Chicago named Camp Robert Smalls, after the African American Civil War hero.[5]

Change continued rapidly during World War II, as the navy continued to expand African American opportunities, establishing the first officer training course for African Americans at Camp Robert Smalls. At the same time, the navy promoted thirteen senior enlisted black sailors to officer's rank. Known as the "Golden Thirteen" in subsequent years, the men were the first African American officers in navy history. By the end of the war, the navy had integrated the crews of twenty-five auxiliary ships, and the USS *Mason,* a destroyer escort, had gone to sea with an all-black crew. Unfortunately, the Port Chicago Mutiny tarnished navy attempts to improve the social position of African American sailors. Refusing to load ammunition ships under unsafe conditions, fifty African American sailors faced courts-martial and a possible capital sentence for disobeying orders to return to work. Although none received the death penalty, the mutiny's leaders faced prison terms of up to fifteen years.[6]

In the final weeks of the Second World War and thereafter, African American sailors finally received full access to the navy's career opportunities. In June 1945, the navy abolished its segregated training facilities and began integrating its recruits. In February 1946, the navy granted African Americans full access to all assignment billets, effectively desegregating the navy before President Harry Truman's order to integrate the military in 1948. In June 1945, Wesley A. Brown entered the Naval Academy and, four years later, became the first African American to graduate from the institution. In 1964, Samuel L. Gravely, one of the African Americans to attend the officer training course at Camp Robert Smalls, became the first black captain in the navy. In 1971, he became the first African American admiral.[7]

In every American war and conflict, black sailors risked their lives for a nation that did not always reward their sacrifice. The imposition of racial segregation in the navy after the Spanish-American War reflected American public attitudes regarding the ability of African Americans. The demands of the Second World War reversed the navy's position, forcing the navy again to become a means of social change. Unlike the Civil War, however, the post–World War II navy maintained its egalitarian policies. Using the participation of African Americans in the Civil War as a model, the World War II navy altered the postwar perception of African American contributions to American defense. Though America had not recognized it after the Civil War, free blacks and slaves who joined the Union navy were essential to the North's victory—and, in preserving the nation intact, their courage and heroism helped transform African Americans into citizens.

NOTES

INTRODUCTION

1. *The War of the Rebellion: A Compilation of the Official Records of the Union and Confederate Navies* (hereafter cited as *ORN*), 30 vols. (Washington, D.C.: Government Printing Office, 1880–1901), ser. 1, 6:8–10, 92; John Niven, *Gideon Welles: Lincoln's Secretary of the Navy* (New York: Oxford University Press, 1973), 392–96.

1: "AMERICA HAS SUCH TARS"

1. National Archives and Records Administration (hereafter cited as NARA), Record Group 45, "Activities of the Negro and Services in the Navy during Our Different Wars"; Benjamin Quarles, *The Negro in the American Revolution* (Chapel Hill: University of North Carolina Press, 1961), 84–85.

2. Quarles, *Negro in the American Revolution*, 86, 88; E. Merton Coulter, *A Short History of Georgia* (Chapel Hill: University of North Carolina Press, 1933), 154.

3. Samuel Eliot Morison, *John Paul Jones: A Sailor's Biography* (Boston: Little, Brown, 1959), 114; Luther Porter Jackson, "Virginia Sailors and Soldiers in the American Revolution," *Journal of Negro History* 27 (1942): 254–55; Quarles, *Negro in the American Revolution*, 19; Martin R. Delany, *The Condition, Elevation, Emigration, and Destiny of the Colored People of the United States* (Philadelphia, 1852), 73; *Journals of the Council of the State of Virginia*, vol. 3 (Richmond: Virginia Statehouse, 1790), 300.

4. Quarles, *Negro in the American Revolution*, 124–28, 152–54; Sidney Kaplan, *The Black Presence in the Era of the American Revolution* (Washington, D.C.: Smithsonian Institution, 1975), 67; John C. Fitzpatrick, ed., *The Writings of George Washington*, vol. 15 (Washington, D.C.: Government Printing Office, 1936), 488.

5. William J. Morgan, "American Privateering in America's War for Independence," *American Neptune* 36 (1976): 79–87; Robert W. Love, *History of the U.S. Navy*, vol. 1 (Harrisburg, Pa.: Stackpole, 1992), 16–17.

6. John F. Jameson, *Privateering and Piracy in the Colonial Period* (New

York: Illustrative Documents, 1923), 384–95; Brenda A. Johnston, *Between the Devil and the Sea: The Life of James Forten* (New York: Harcourt Brace, 1974).

7. Antibiastes, *Observations on the Slaves and the Indented Servants, Inlisted in the Army, and in the Navy of the United States* (Philadelphia, 1777), 1–4.

8. Marshall Smelser, *Congress Founds the Navy, 1787–1798* (South Bend, Ind.: Notre Dame University Press, 1959), 43–63.

9. Rayford W. Logan, "The Negro in the Quasi-War, 1798–1800," *Negro History Bulletin* 14 (1951): 128–32; Michael A. Palmer, *Stoddert's War: Naval Operations during the Quasi-War with France, 1798–1801* (Columbia: University of South Carolina Press, 1987), 56–60.

10. Spencer C. Tucker, *The Jeffersonian Gunboat Navy* (Columbia: University of South Carolina Press, 1993), 65–77.

11. Ira Dye, *The Fatal Cruise of the Argus: Two Captains in the War of 1812* (Annapolis: Naval Institute Press, 1994), 44–45; Harold D. Langley, "The Negro in the Navy and Merchant Service, 1789–1860," *Journal of Negro History* 52 (1967): 285. The deserters were David (possibly Daniel) Martin, John Strachan, and William Ware. The suspected deserter was Jenkin Ratford.

12. Tucker, *Jeffersonian Gunboat Navy*, 72–74.

13. Glenn Tucker, *Dawn like Thunder: The Barbary Wars and the Birth of the U.S. Navy* (Indianapolis: Bobbs-Merrill, 1963), 290–91.

14. Edward K. Eckert, *The Navy Department in the War of 1812* (Gainesville: University of Florida Press, 1973), 14.

15. Ibid., 50.

16. Delany, *Condition, Elevation, Emigration*, 83; Joseph T. Wilson, *The Black Phalanx: A History of the Negro Soldiers of the United States* (Hartford, Conn.: American Publishing, 1890), 79; Henry C. Baird, *General Washington and General Jackson on Negro Soldiers* (Philadelphia, 1863), 6–7; John Hope Franklin, *From Slavery to Freedom: A History of American Negroes* (New York: Alfred A. Knopf, 1947), 168. Lake Erie volunteers came from the Pittsburgh area.

17. Wilson, *Black Phalanx*, 78; Michael H. Goodman, "The Black Tar: Negro Seamen in the Union Navy, 1861–1865." (Ph.D. diss., University of Nottingham, 1975), 71.

18. Charles F. Adams, "The Birth of a World Power," *American Historical Review* 18 (1913): 519–20; William C. Nell, *The Colored Patriots of the American Revolution* (1855; rpt., New York: Arno Press, 1968), 313; David L. Valuska, "The Negro in the Union Navy, 1861–1865" (Ph.D. diss., Lehigh University, 1973), 7. That Hull's quotation is similar to Perry's is apparently a coincidence.

19. Jerome R. Garitee, *The Republic's Private Navy: The American Privateering Business as Practiced by Baltimore during the War of 1812* (Mid-

dletown, Conn.: Wesleyan University Press, 1977), 128, 136–37; *Baltimore Federal Gazette,* December 30, 1813, 12.

20. A Wanderer, *Journals of Two Cruises aboard the American Privateer Yankee* (New York: Macmillan, 1967), 75. The legitimacy of the journals is under scrutiny.

21. Ibid., 112–15, 120–28, 135–36, 141. The *Fly*'s cargo included 800 ounces of gold, 4 tons of ivory, various wines and luxury food items, and 200 monkeys and parrots.

22. Dye, *Fatal Cruise of the Argus,* 291–96; *Niles's Weekly Register,* February 26, 1814, 2.

23. Garitee, *Republic's Private Navy,* 130–31.

24. K. Jack Bauer, *Surfboats and Horse Marines: U.S. Naval Operations in the Mexican War, 1846–1848* (Annapolis: Naval Institute Press, 1969), 18–24.

25. Ibid., 23–25, 36.

26. Robert E. Greene, *Black Defenders of America, 1775–1973* (Chicago: Johnson Publishing, 1974), 43; W. Jeffrey Bolster, *Black Jacks: African American Seaman in the Age of Sail* (Cambridge, Mass.: Harvard University Press, 1997), 215–32; Goodman, "Black Tar," 1–15; David Connor Papers, Library of Congress, Manuscript Division, 3:323–30.

27. Logan, "Negro in the Quasi-War," 129; United States, Navy Department, *Naval Documents Related to the United States Wars with the Barbary Powers,* vol. 2 (Washington, D.C.: Government Printing Office, 1940), 479.

28. Wilson, *Black Phalanx,* 78; Michael Cohn and Michael K. H. Platzer, *Black Men of the Sea* (New York: Dodd, Mead, 1978), 122.

29. Gaddis Smith and Clark G. Reynolds, eds., "Black Seamen and the Federal Courts," *Proceedings of the North American Society of Oceanic History* 12 (1978): 7–9.

30. NARA, Record Group 45, "Captains Letters, July-October 1827," 51; Bruce Grant, *Captain of the Old Ironsides* (Chicago: Pellegrini and Cudahy, 1947), 326; James S. Buckingham, *The Slave States of America,* vol. 2 (London: Fisher and Sons, 1842), 471–73; Nathaniel P. Willis, *Summer Cruise in the Mediterranean on Board an American Frigate* (Rochester, N.Y.: Alden and Beardsley, 1856), 103.

31. Philip S. Foner, *History of the Labor Movement in the United States* vol. 1, *From Colonial Times to the Founding of the American Federation of Labor* (New York: International, 1947), 261–62; Robert S. Starobin, *Industrial Slavery in the Old South* (New York: Oxford University Press, 1970), 32.

32. Christopher McKee, *A Gentlemanly and Honorable Profession: The Creation of the U.S. Naval Officer Corps* (Annapolis: Naval Institute Press, 1991), 333.

33. Harold D. Langley, *Social Reform in the United States Navy, 1789–1862* (Urbana: University of Illinois Press, 1967), 93; Dennis J.

Ringle, *Life in Mr. Lincoln's Navy* (Annapolis: Naval Institute Press, 1998), 21. Isaac Toucey also served as the secretary of the navy during James Buchanan's administration, earning harsh criticism for his ineffective leadership during the Fort Sumter crisis.

34. Leon F. Litwack, *North of Slavery: The Negro in the Free States, 1790–1860* (Chicago: University of Chicago Press, 1961), 33.

2: "THE WANTS OF THE SERVICE"

1. William M. Fowler, *Under Two Flags: The American Navy in the Civil War* (New York: Avon Books, 1990), 47–59.

2. Bern Anderson, *By Sea and by River: The Naval History of the Civil War* (New York: Da Capo Press, 1962), 3–17; Fowler, *Under Two Flags,* 50–53.

3. Riley T. Folsom, "The United States Navy: Expansion and Reorganization, 1861–1862" (Master's thesis, University of Washington, 1970), 23, 97–98.

4. The British government declared neutrality on May 14, 1861, acknowledging the Union blockade and recognizing the Confederacy as a belligerent. See Phillip S. Paludan, *The Presidency of Abraham Lincoln* (Lawrence: University Press of Kansas, 1994), 89; Norman B. Ferris, *Desperate Diplomacy: William H. Seward's Foreign Policy, 1861* (Knoxville: University of Tennessee, 1976), 33–54.

5. D. P. Crook, *The North, the South, and the Powers, 1861–1865* (New York: Wiley, 1974), 71–98; Howard Jones, *Union in Peril: The Crisis over British Intervention in the Civil War* (Chapel Hill: University of North Carolina Press, 1992), 10–37.

6. Jay Monaghan, *Abraham Lincoln Deals with Foreign Affairs* (Indianapolis: Bobbs-Merrill, 1945), 167–69; Norman B. Ferris, *The Trent Affair: A Diplomatic Crisis* (Knoxville: University of Tennessee Press, 1977), 140–45.

7. Paludan, *Abraham Lincoln,* 83.

8. Maurice Parmelee, *Blockade and Sea Power: The Blockade, 1914–1919, and Its Significance for a World State* (New York: Crowell, 1924), 18–26.

9. Eugene M. Thomas, "Prisoner of War Exchange during the American Civil War" (Ph.D. diss., Auburn University, 1976), 3–19.

10. James L. Stokesbury, *A Short History of the Civil War* (New York: William Morrow, 1995), 35.

11. James M. McPherson, *Battle Cry of Freedom: The Civil War Era* (New York: Oxford University Press, 1988), 276–77.

12. Andrew F. Rolle, *John Charles Fremont: Character as Destiny* (Norman: University of Oklahoma Press, 1991), 205–13; McPherson, *Battle Cry of Freedom,* 353; Victor B. Howard, *Black Liberation in Kentucky: Emancipation and Freedom, 1862–1864* (Lexington: University of Kentucky Press, 1983), 3–11.

13. Edward A. Miller, *Lincoln's Abolitionist General: The Biography of David Hunter* (Columbia: University of South Carolina Press, 1997), 99–106; Ira Berlin, *Freedom: A Documentary History of Emancipation, 1861–1867,* ser. 1, 2 vols. (New York: Cambridge University Press, 1982), 1:62.

14. Hans L. Trelousse, *Benjamin Franklin Wade: Radical Republican from Ohio* (New York: Twayne Publishers, 1963), 152–53; William S. McFeely, *Frederick Douglass* (New York: W. W. Norton, 1991), 212.

15. *New York Times,* April 20, 1861, 8.

16. For a full biography of Lincoln's cabinet, see Burton J. Henrick, *Lincoln's War Cabinet* (Gloucester, Mass.: Peter Smith, 1965).

17. Ibid., 87, 105; Glyndon G. Van Deusen, *William Henry Seward* (New York: Oxford University Press, 1967), 329–30.

18. Litwack, *North of Slavery,* 32, 50–56, 75, 93–94, 154–59; Noah A. Trudeau, *Like Men of War: Black Troops in the Civil War, 1862–1865* (Boston: Little, Brown, 1998), 7; Dudley T. Cornish, *The Sable Arm: Negro Troops in the Union Army, 1861–1865* (New York: Harpers, 1966), 1–12. New York also permitted African American suffrage, but with a property requirement. The issue of African American citizenship was at the center of the infamous 1857 *Dred Scott* decision, which ruled blacks were not American citizens, although the legal debate on African American citizenship had raged since 1821.

19. *The War of the Rebellion: A Compilation of the Official Records of the Union and Confederate Armies* (hereafter cited as *ORA*), 128 vols. with atlas (Washington, D.C.: Government Printing Office, 1880–1901), ser. 3, 1:133.

20. Albert E. Cowdrey, "Slave into Soldier: The Enlistment by the North of Runaway Slaves," *History Today* 20 (1970): 710; McPherson, *Battle Cry of Freedom,* 288–89, 397–402; Philip S. Foner, *History of Black Americans,* vol. 3, *From the Compromise of 1850 to the End of the Civil War* (Westport, Conn.: Greenwood Press, 1975), 323.

21. *ORN,* ser. 1, 6:8–9, 107.

22. Cornish, *Sable Arm,* 25; *ORN,* ser. 1, 4:645, 13:109–10.

23. Samuel May, *The Fugitive Slave Law and Its Victims* (1861; rpt., New York: Books for Libraries Press, 1970), 3–5.

24. Cowdrey, "Slave into Soldier," 704–5.

25. *ORN,* ser. 1, 6:409; Foner, *History of Black Americans,* 3:338.

26. NARA, Record Group 45, Naval Records Collection of the Office of Naval Records and Library, "Miscellaneous Material Relative to Contrabands."

27. Foner, *History of Black Americans,* 3:321.

28. Thomas D. Morris, *Southern Slavery and the Law, 1619–1860* (Chapel Hill: University of North Carolina Press, 1996), 175.

29. Ibid., 171–81.

30. *ORN,* ser. 1, 6:9, 252; Ringle, *Life in Mr. Lincoln's Navy,* 13.

31. Niven, *Gideon Welles*, 396–97.

32. Canney, *Lincoln's Navy: The Ships, Men, and Organization, 1861–65* (Annapolis: Naval Institute Press, 1998), 117–21.

33. Foner, *History of Black Americans*, 3:327; Ringle, *Life in Mr. Lincoln's Navy*, 93. Recruits under the age of eighteen received the rank of "boy" (either first, second, or third class) in the antebellum navy. They performed light manual labor aboard the ship during normal operations and carried ammunition and powder charges to the guns during battle. Navy regulations forbade enlisting any crewmen under the age of 18, but children enlisted with their parent's permission. Also, the navy permitted orphans or boys from broken homes to enlist in order to learn a trade.

34. Henrietta S. Jacquette, ed., *South after Gettysburg: Letters of Cornelia Hancock, 1863–1868* (New York: Crowell, 1937), 43–44; *ORN*, ser. 1, 13:209.

35. Landsmen were recruits with no naval experience who needed instruction in naval skills. At 18, the navy generally promoted boys to landsmen. See Francis A. Lord, *They Fought for the Union* (Harrisburg, Pa.: Stackpole, 1960), 286–87.

36. The navy asked recruits their place of origin at enlistment, but often recruits omitted this information. One can guess that many enlistees who did not volunteer their place of origin were probably contrabands, although the precise number is impossible to determine.

37. Benjamin Quarles, *The Negro in the Civil War* (Boston: Little, Brown, 1953), 183; Paludan, *Abraham Lincoln*, 144.

38. McPherson, *Battle Cry of Freedom*, 500.

39. *U.S. Statutes at Large*, 12 (1862): 597; Fred A. Shannon, "The Federal Government and the Negro Soldier," *Journal of Negro History* 11 (1926): 569–71.

40. *ORN*, ser. 1, 12:334–38, 13:179–80, 14:104–12.

41. Ibid., ser. 1, 13:144–45.

42. Rebecca Paulding Meade, *Life of Hiram Paulding, Rear-Admiral, U.S.N.* (New York: Baker & Taylor, 1910), 260–63; Richard E. Winslow, *Constructing Munitions of War: The Portsmouth Navy Yard Confronts the Confederacy, 1861–1865* (Portsmouth, N.H.: Portsmouth Marine Society, 1995), 131–33, 195–96.

43. George E. Buker, *Blockaders, Refugees, and Contrabands: Civil War on Florida's Gulf Coast, 1861–1865* (Tuscaloosa: University of Alabama Press, 1993), 46–47; *ORN*, ser. 1, 13:92, 95, 110, 178–79, 195.

44. *ORN*, ser. 1, 13:95–97, 17:547–48.

45. Fred M. Mallison, *The Civil War on the Outer Banks* (Jefferson, N.C.: McFarland, 1998), 130–31.

46. *ORN*, ser. 1, 12:520–21, 13:245–46, 17:744.

47. For a full description of Union activities at Port Royal, see George

L. Hendricks, "Union Army Occupation of the Southern Seaboard, 1861–1865" (Ph.D. diss., Columbia University, 1954); Willie L. Rose, *Rehearsal for Reconstruction: The Port Royal Experiment* (Indianapolis: Bobbs-Merrill, 1964); *ORN*, ser. 1, 12:542. When first implemented, the navy organized its blockade into the Atlantic and Gulf (of Mexico) Blockading Squadrons. This system proved cumbersome and, in 1862, the Atlantic Squadron divided into the North and South Atlantic Blockading Squadrons and the Gulf Squadron split into East and West formations. The North Atlantic Squadron (based at Norfolk, Virginia) covered from Chesapeake Bay to the South Carolina border, where the South Atlantic Squadron's authority began, extending to the tip of Florida. The East Gulf Blockading Squadron (centered at Key West) watched from the tip of Florida to the base of the Florida Panhandle, and the West Gulf Squadron (headquartered at Pensacola, Florida) patrolled to the Mexican border. At the same time, naval forces on the Mississippi River emerged as the Mississippi Squadron.

48. United States, Navy Department, *Annual Report of the Secretary of the Navy, 1861* (Washington, D.C.: Government Printing Office, 1862), 87; Ringle, *Life in Mr. Lincoln's Navy*, 13. At the time of the letter, Welles reported a navy shortfall of three thousand men.

49. *ORN*, ser. 1, 17:269; Ringle, *Life in Mr. Lincoln's Navy*, 20–21.

50. *ORN*, ser. 1, 8:309.

51. Ira Berlin, *Slaves No More: Three Essays on Emancipation in the Civil War* (New York: Cambridge University Press, 1992), 30; McPherson, *Battle Cry of Freedom*, 498; Foner, *History of Black Americans*, 3:338. Lincoln first informed his cabinet, and then the American public, of his intention to issue the Emancipation Proclamation on September 22, 1862.

52. Jeffrey R. Hummel, *Emancipating Slaves, Enslaving Free Men: A History of the American Civil War* (Chicago: Open Court, 1996), 210; McPherson, *Battle Cry of Freedom*, 556; Henry Steele Commager, *Documents of American History*, 2 vols. (New York: Appleton-Century-Crofts, 1968), 1:403–5.

53. Berlin, *Slaves No More*, 199; McPherson, *Battle Cry of Freedom*, 561.

54. The North's conscription system established enlistment quotas for each state, based upon population. If a state fell short of its monthly obligation, the federal government would randomly draft men to fill the state's quota.

55. Ringle, *Life in Mr. Lincoln's Navy*, 21–22.

56. *U.S. Statutes at Large* 74 (1863): 283–86.

3: A Unique Set of Men

1. All general demographic and recruitment data for this study derives from a cumulative study of African American Civil War sailors

compiled by Professor Joseph Reidy and his staff at Howard University for the National Park Service. All statistical inferences derive from chi-square and other tests at a .05 percent level of significance. Statistical tabulations in this study are significant unless indicated otherwise.

2. The Howard University study includes African American sailors enlisted before the Civil War whose terms of enlistment did not expire before the war began.

3. *Boston Liberator,* March 24, 1865, 1.

4. For the purpose of this study the country is divided into the following recruiting regions: New England (Maine, New Hampshire, Vermont, Massachusetts, Rhode Island, and Connecticut), Mid-Atlantic (New York, New Jersey, Pennsylvania, and Delaware), Midwest (Ohio, Indiana, Illinois, Wisconsin, Michigan, Minnesota, and Iowa), West (Kansas, Utah, and California), border states (Maryland, District of Columbia, West Virginia, Kentucky, and Missouri), Northeast Confederacy (Virginia and North Carolina), Southeast Confederacy (South Carolina, Georgia, and Florida), Central Confederacy (Tennessee, Mississippi, and Alabama), trans-Mississippi (Louisiana, Arkansas, and Texas), foreign enlistees, and those enlisted aboard U.S. Navy ships without noting the location. For the purposes of this work the following regions of origin are delineated: New England (Maine, New Hampshire, Vermont, Massachusetts, Rhode Island, and Connecticut), Mid-Atlantic (New York, Pennsylvania, New Jersey, and Delaware), Midwest (Ohio, Indiana, Illinois, Iowa, Minnesota, Wisconsin, and Michigan), West (Kansas, Utah, and California), border states (Maryland, District of Columbia, West Virginia, Kentucky, and Missouri), Northeast Confederacy (Virginia and North Carolina), Southeast Confederacy (South Carolina, Georgia, and Florida), Central Confederacy (Tennessee, Alabama, and Mississippi), trans-Mississippi (Arkansas, Louisiana, and Texas), Canada, Latin America, Caribbean, Europe, African, and Pacific/Asia.

5. An additional 20.7 percent enlisted in other parts of the South, the West, or did not list their place of origin. See Berlin, *Freedom,* 2:12; United States, Secretary of the Interior, *Population of the United States in 1860: Compiled from the Original Returns of the Eighth Census* (Washington, D.C.: Government Printing Office, 1864), x, xiii.

6. Allen Parker, *Recollections of Slavery Times* (Worcester, Mass.: Burbank, 1895), 86–94.

7. Adele L. Alexander, *Homelands and Waterways: The American Journey of the Bond Family, 1846–1926* (New York: Pantheon, 1999) 1–79.

8. Richard H. Abbott, "Massachusetts and the Recruitment of Southern Negroes, 1863–1865," *Civil War History* 14 (1968): 197–210.

9. Any recruit who claimed a city with a population greater than

2,500 according to the 1860 census is "urban."

10. Although coal heavers received eighteen dollars per month (more than seamen), they are unskilled labor owing to the minimal experience needed to perform the task. The additional wages were compensation for the coal heaver's strenuous task.

11. Robert M. Browning, *From Cape Charles to Cape Fear: The North Atlantic Blockading Squadron during the Civil War* (Tuscaloosa: University of Alabama Press, 1993), 202; *Seaman's Friend*, November 1863, 83.

12. Bolster, *Black Jacks*, 178–79.

13. Philip Katcher, *Civil War Source Book* (New York: Facts on File, 1992), 179–80; *Annual Report of the Secretary of the Navy, 1861*, 18–19.

14. *Annual Reports of the Secretary of the Navy, 1861–1865* (Washington, D.C.: Government Printing Office, 1862–1866).

15. The author selected two recruiting sites at random (Philadelphia and Cairo), one in the East and one in the West. The database contains all enlistees from two months, April and August (selected at random), for the years that records are available.

16. The term petty officer comes from the French word *petit*, referring to a lesser or junior officer.

17. Lord, *They Fought for the Union*, 285–86.

18. For comparison, whites in the army were 24.4 percent professional, 19 percent skilled, 4.1 percent unskilled, and 52.5 percent farmers. See James M. McPherson, *For Cause and Comrades: Why Men Fought in the Civil War* (New York: Oxford University Press, 1997).

4: "Sick of the Sea"

1. United States, Bureau of the Census, *Historical Statistics of the United States: Colonial Times to 1970*, vol. 1 (Washington: D.C.: Government Printing Office, 1976), 728–34; NARA, Record Group 45, "An Act to Alter and Regulate the Navy Ration"; Bolster, *Black Jacks*, 178–79; *U.S. Statutes at Large* 10 (1854): 583.

2. L. B. Blair, "Dogs and Sailors Keep Off!," *United States Naval Institute Proceedings* 76 (1950): 1095–1101. Some Civil War histories, presuming the navy treated African Americans the same as the army, stated the navy paid its black personnel lower wages. An example was Allan Nevins, *The Ordeal of the Union*, 8 vols. (New York: Scribner's, 1947–1971), 2:525, when he wrote "free northern negroes and southern freedmen thus served at sea alongside white sailors, though at generally lower pay."

3. Berlin, *Slaves No More*, 214; Shannon, "Federal Government and the Negro Soldier," 581; *U.S. Statutes at Large* 13 (1864): 129–30; McPherson, *Battle Cry of Freedom*, 788–89. The pay for army troops was

the same as that for contraband laborers established under the 1862 Militia Act.

4. Berlin, *Slaves No More*, 214.

5. Langley, *Social Reform*, 242–69; Stephen E. Blanding, *Recollections of a Sailor Boy; or, The Cruise of the Gunboat Louisiana* (Providence, R.I.: E. A. Johnson, 1886), 61; Peter Josyph, *Wounded River: The Civil War Letters of John Vance Lauderdale, M.D.* (East Lansing: Michigan State University Press, 1993), 167–68.

6. *ORN*, ser. 1, 14:414–15, 444; *U.S. Statutes at Large* 1 (1864): 181–82.

7. W. R. Hooper, "Blockade Running," *Harper's New Monthly Magazine* 42 (1870): 107; *ORN*, ser. 1, 13:5.

8. Canney, *Lincoln's Navy*, 121; Edward F. Merrifield, "The Seaboard War: A History of the North Atlantic Blockading Squadron, 1861–1865" (Ph.D. diss., Case Western Reserve University, 1975), 187–89; Robert W. Daly, "Pay and Prize Money in the Old Navy, 1770–1899" *United States Naval Institute Proceedings* 74 (1948): 123.

9. NARA, Record Group 45, "Letters Received by the Secretary of the Navy, 1866–1913"; *ORN*, ser. 1, 6:342.

10. These names are from a sample of African American sailors recruited in Massachusetts derived from Massachusetts, Adjutant General's Office, *Massachusetts Soldiers, Sailors, and Marines in the Civil War*, vols. 7–8 (Norwood, Mass.: Norwood Press, 1931).

11. Paolo E. Coletta, *A Survey of U.S. Naval Affair, 1865–1917* (New York: University Press of America, 1987), 9–18.

12. Browning, *Cape Charles to Cape Fear*, 173; *ORN*, ser. 1, 12:461, 14:251, 15:300–3; William R. Trotter, *The Civil War in North Carolina*, vol. 3, *Ironclads and Columbiads: The Coast* (Winston-Salem, N.C.: J. F. Blair, 1989), 81.

13. Greene, *Black Defenders of America*, 90–91; Okon E. Uya, *From Slavery to Public Service: Robert Smalls, 1839–1915* (New York: Oxford University Press, 1971), 1–31. Although mentioned in other works on African Americans in the Union navy, the army employed Smalls for most of his war service and granted him an army pension after the war. Another African American congressman during Reconstruction, Robert B. Elliott, claimed to be a navy veteran, but no documentation has emerged to substantiate his claim. See Peggy Lamson, *The Glorious Failure: Black Congressman Robert Brown Elliott and the Reconstruction of South Carolina* (New York: W. W. Norton, 1973), 23.

14. NARA, Record Group 45, "Data Relating to Pilots Who Served during the Civil War"; *ORN*, ser. 1, 12:645–46; NARA, Record Group 25, Decklog of USS *Penguin*.

15. Megan J. McClintock, "Binding Up the Nation's Wounds: Nationalism, Civil War Pensions, and American Families, 1861–1890" (Ph.D. diss., Rutgers University, 1994), 306–8; *U.S. Statutes at Large* 5 (1862): 566–69, 608.

16. *Annual Report of the Secretary of the Navy, 1865*, 28.

17. McClintock, "Binding Up the Nation's Wounds," 306–8.

18. These names corresponded to pension files in Record Group 15 at the National Archives and Records Administration, using the "Index to Navy Pension Files, 1861–1910."

19. Donald R. Shaffer, "Marching On: African American Civil War Veterans in Postbellum America, 1865–1951 (2 vols.)" (Ph.D. diss., University of Maryland, 1996), 229.

20. Ibid., 216–24.

21. Ibid., 233–34.

22. The 343 names in the veterans' pension sample were cross-checked for a widow's pension against the "Index of Navy Dependent's Pension Files—Approved, 1861–1910" and "List of Navy Veterans for Whom There Are Navy Widows' and Other Dependents of Civil War and Later Navy Veterans, 1861–1910, Disallowed."

23. See individual name files in NARA, Record Group 15, "Index to Navy Pension Files, 1861–1910."

24. Canney, *Lincoln's Navy*, 122; Sherman L. Pompey, *Sailors and Marines of the United States Living in the Southern Branch, National Home for Disabled Soldiers, Elizabeth City County, Virginia in 1890* (Albany, Oreg., 1890), 1–6.

25. Pennsylvania State Historical Society, Unclassified Records Group, "Letter to the Widows of the Colored Soldiers and Sailors of Philadelphia"; P. Michael Jones, *Forgotten Soldiers: Murphysboro's African American Civil War Veterans* (Murphysboro, Ill.: Class Publications Committee, 1994), 72. One compensation that the government did not grant was land grants to veterans, a common benefit after the Revolutionary War and War of 1812, although to an extent the passage of the Homestead Act in 1862 opened the door for acquiring land grants in the West. See Benjamin H. Hibbard, *A History of the Public Land Policies* (Madison: University of Wisconsin Press, 1965); Nell I. Painter, *Exodusters: Black Migration to Kansas after Reconstruction* (New York: Alfred A. Knopf, 1976)

26. *St. Louis Daily Democrat*, January 24, 1862, 4.

27. The efficient collection and distribution of provisions was especially important to Gideon Welles. A former Democrat, he received an appointment as head of the navy's Bureau of Provisions and Clothing from President James K. Polk in 1846, Welles's first federal office. See Richard S. West, "Watchful Gideon," *United States Naval Institute Proceedings* 62 (1936): 1093.

28. United States, Navy Department, *Allowances Established for Vessels of the United States Navy* (Washington, D.C.: Government Printing Office, 1865), 135–36; Browning, *Cape Charles to Cape Fear,* 213. The Civil War diet differed greatly from the earlier annual diet established in 1801: 182 pounds of beef, 156 pounds pork, 52 pounds flour and rice each, 29 pounds fat, 319 pounds bread, 20 pounds cheese, 6 1/2 pounds of butter and peas each, 3 1/4 gallons of molasses and vinegar each, and 22 3/4 gallons of spirit alcohol (Eckert, *Navy Department in the War of 1812,* 46).

29. *Allowances Established for Vessels,* 177–79.

30. Alvah F. Hunter, *A Year on a Monitor and the Destruction of Fort Sumter* (Columbia: University of South Carolina Press, 1987), 31; John M. Lansden, *A History of the City of Cairo, Illinois* (Chicago: R. R. Donnelley & Sons, 1910), 128–37; Anderson, *By Sea and by River,* 216; Blanding, *Recollections of a Sailor Boy,* 67; NARA, Record Group 25, Logbook of USS *Carondelet.*

31. Browning, *Cape Charles to Cape Fear,* 215; NARA, Record Group 25, Decklog of USS *Saugus.*

32. Herbert Aptheker, *Negro Casualties in the Civil War* (Washington, D.C.: Association for the Study of Negro Life and History, 1945), 20–24.

33. Canney, *Lincoln's Navy,* 123–24.

34. Israel E. Vail, *Three Years on the Blockade: A Naval Experience* (New York: Abbey Press, 1902), 22; Robert S. Critchell, *Recollections of a Fire Insurance Man: Including His Experience in the U.S. Navy (Mississippi Squadron) during the Civil War* (Chicago: A. C. McClurg, 1909), 33–35.

35. Blanding, *Recollections of a Sailor Boy,* 108; Vail, *Three Years on the Blockade,* 47–49.

36. Blanding, *Recollections of a Sailor Boy,* 109; Henry R. Browne and Symmes E. Browne, *From the Fresh Water Navy, 1861–64: The Letters of Acting Master's Mate Henry R. Browne and Acting Ensign Symmes E. Browne* (Annapolis: Naval Institute Press, 1970), 218–19, 235.

37. Thomas Lyons diary, entries for June 2, 8, 9, and 25, 1863, Library of Congress, Manuscript Division.

38. Ringle, *Life in Mr. Lincoln's Navy,* 28–29; Gary O. Reiss, "Life aboard the Blockading Squadrons of the Union Navy during the American Civil War," (Master's thesis, St. Cloud State University, 1986), 70–73.

39. *Dictionary of American Naval Fighting Ships,* 9 vols. (Washington, D.C.: Government Printing Office, 1959–1991), 1:18; NARA, Record Group 25, Decklog of USS *Alabama* (the Union vessel *Alabama* should not be confused with the more famous Confederate raider of the same name); Stanley L. Itkin, "Operations of the East Gulf Blockade Squadron in the Blockade of Florida, 1862–1865" (Master's thesis, Florida State University, 1962), 161; *ORN,* ser. 1, 17:744–49.

40. Thomas Lyons diary, entries for June 5–22, 1863 (Lyons himself was also seriously ill during this time, and the diary abruptly ends on June 25, perhaps owing to the author's death); George G. Smith, *Leaves from a Soldier's Diary: The Personal Record of Lieutenant George G. Smith* (New York: Putnam, 1906), 1–9.

41. Ringle, "Life in Mr. Lincoln's Navy," pp. 108–110.

42. Canney, *Lincoln's Navy,* 22–23; Louis H. Roddis, *A Short History of Nautical Medicine* (New York: P. B. Hoeber, 1941), 156–57; Ringle, *Life in Mr. Lincoln's Navy,* 111.

43. The number of casualties is open to debate. I am using the statistics from the report of the provost marshal general of the army, Brigadier General James B. Fry, to Secretary of War Edwin Stanton dated March 17, 1866. Fatalities were divided into 61,362 killed in action, 34,773 died of wounds, 183,287 died of disease, 306 accidentally killed, 7 executed by court martial, and 6,749 missing and presumed dead. See Frederick Phisterer, *Statistical Record of the Armies of the United States* (1883; rpt., Carlisle, Pa.: Kallmann, 1996), 67–76.

44. Frederick H. Dyer, *A Compendium of the War of the Rebellion: Compiled and Arranged from Official Records of the Federal and Confederate Armies,* 5 vols (Des Moines: Dyer, 1908) 1:11, 18; Charles R. Cooper, *Chronological and Alphabetical Record of the Engagements of the Great Civil War . . .* (Milwaukee: Caxton Press, 1904), 168; Aptheker, *Negro Casualties in the Civil War,* 5; Phisterer, *Statistical Record,* 67.

45. The percentage includes fatalities from battle, disease, accidents, and as prisoners of war.

46. Shaffer, "Marching On," 115–17. All data originated from a random sample of 539 navy veterans from the "1890 Census of Civil War Veterans and Their Widows."

47. Chi-Square Significance = .353.

48. Chi-Square Significance = .711.

49. Canney, *Lincoln's Navy,* 149; Aptheker, *Negro Casualties in the Civil War,* 10, 12. Not all of the acting surgeons were up to the standards of the navy. The surgeon aboard the USS *Louisiana,* a Dr. Bradly, "observed that the smell of tar was very healthful and was used sometimes in fumigating hospitals" (Blanding, *Recollections of a Sailor Boy,* 113).

50. Josyph, *Wounded River,* 133; Helen T. Catterall, *Judicial Cases concerning American Slavery and the Negro,* 5 vols. (Washington, D.C.: Carnegie Institution, 1926–1937), 3:609–10; John L. Margreiter, "Anesthesia in the Civil War," *Civil War Times Illustrated* 6 (1967): 22–23; U.S. War Department, *The Medical and Surgical History of the War of the Rebellion,* 6 vols. (Washington, D.C.: Government Printing Office, 1870–1883), 1:18–23.

51. Blanding, *Recollections of a Sailor Boy,* 256–58.

52. *ORN,* ser. 1, 7:667; Alexander, *Homelands and Waterways,* 73–83.

53. NARA, Record Group 25, Decklog of USS *Red Rover;* Dennis M. Davidson, *"Red Rover:* The U.S. Navy's First Hospital Ship" (Ph.D. diss., United States Naval Academy, 1960), 22 (some dispatches refer to the *Red Rover* as the *Pinkney* in reference to Ninian Pinkney, M.D., the chief medical officer of the Mississippi Squadron); Josyph, *Wounded River,* 30–31; *ORN,* ser. 1, 7:22, 184, 531, 593, 608, 736, 22:132–33. The navy listed *Ben Morgan* at various times as a hospital, tug, store ship, or ordnance vessel.

54. Ringle, *Life in Mr. Lincoln's Navy,* 119.

55. Critchell, *Recollections of a Fire Insurance Man,* 9–10; Vail, *Three Years on the Blockade,* 90–91.

56. Robert W. Daly, *Aboard the U.S.S. Florida, 1863–65: The Letters of Paymaster William Frederick Keeler, U.S. Navy, to His Wife, Anna* (Annapolis: Naval Institute Press, 1968), 71; John W. Blassingame, *The Slave Community: Plantation Life in the Antebellum South* (New York: Oxford University Press, 1972), 37–39; Thomas Lyons diary, entry for May 4, 1863; Blanding, *Recollections of a Sailor Boy,* 140–41.

57. Blanding, *Recollections of a Sailor Boy,* 158–59; Phyllis H. Haughton, *Dearest Carrie: Civil War Letters Home* (Lawrenceville, Va.: Brunswick, 1995), 131; William C. White, *Tin Can on a Shingle* (Norwalk, Conn.: Easton Press, 1990), 50–51; Buker, *Blockaders, Refugees, and Contrabands,* 42–58; Vail, *Three Years on the Blockade,* 62–63. The *Florida* confronted by the USS *Massachusetts* is not the Confederate commerce raider of the same name.

58. Charles E. Stedman, *A Civil War Sketchbook* (San Rafael, Calif.: Presidio, 1976), 94, 100, 113; *ORN,* ser. 1, 13:143. Five white officers and an operating crew of thirty-five former slaves manned USS *Darlington,* a supply steamer tasked with supporting the *Huron.*

59. John M. Batten, *Reminiscences of Two Years in the United States Navy* (Lancaster, Pa.: Inquirer, 1881), 103; Susan G. Perkins, ed., *Letters of Capt. Geo. Hamilton Perkins, U.S.N.* (Concord, N.H.: I. C. Evans, 1886), 118; Trotter, *Civil War in North Carolina,* 3:254–55.

60. Buker, *Blockaders, Refugees, and Contrabands,* 44, 49.

61. *ORN,* ser. 1, 6:297, 9:193–95; Blanding, *Recollections of a Sailor Boy,* 250–51.

62. Bradley S. Osbon, *Cruise of the U.S. Flag-Ship Hartford, 1862–1863* (New York: L. W. Paine, 1863), 43; Critchell, *Recollections of a Fire Insurance Man,* 26, 158–59.

63. David Valuska, *The African American in the Union Navy, 1861–1865* (New York: Garland, 1993), 67.

64. Rowland True, "Life aboard a Gunboat," *Civil War Times Illustrated* 9 (1972): 38.

65. Jean H. Baker, *Affairs of Party: The Political Culture of Northern Democrats in the Mid-Nineteenth Century* (Ithaca, N.Y.: Cornell University Press, 1983), 212–20; Joseph Boskin, *Sambo: The Rise and Demise of an American Jester* (New York: Oxford University Press, 1986), 4–5.

66. Mary P. Livingston, ed., *A Civil War Marine at Sea: The Diary of Medal of Honor Recipient Miles M. Oviatt* (Shippensburg, Pa.: White Mane, 1998), 69; True, "Life aboard a Gunboat," 37; Hunter, *Year on a Monitor,* 41. African Americans and Irish immigrants frequently clashed over the lowest paying jobs in the American economy, and navy labor was no exception. In June 1863, a major riot broke out at the Brooklyn Navy Yard when black stevedores replaced some Irish laborers (Goodman, "Black Tar," 361–62).

67. James Merrill, "Men, Monotony, and Mouldy Beans: Life on a Civil War Blockader," *American Neptune* 16 (1956): 50; Livingston, *Civil War Marine at Sea,* 9; Vail, *Three Years on the Blockade,* 32; Osbon, *Cruise of the U.S. Flag-Ship Hartford,* 47; Browning, *Cape Charles to Cape Fear,* 217. One service the navy did not provide as well as the army was religion. While every army regiment employed a chaplain, the navy maintained only twenty-one "sky pilots" serving at navy yards in 1865. See Charles O. Paullin, *Paullin's History of Naval Administration, 1775–1911* (Annapolis: Naval Institute Press, 1986), 298.

5: "Energetically and Bravely—None More So"

1. Peter H. Clark, *The Black Brigade of Cincinnati* (Cincinnati: Ridder, 1864), 4–5; Quarles, *Negro in the Civil War,* 235–36; *Harper's Weekly,* November 11, 1861, 4.

2. Joseph T. Glatthaar, *Forged in Battle: The Civil War Alliance of Black Soldiers and White Officers* (New York: Free Press, 1990), 11–18; Murray M. Horowitz, "Ben Butler and the Negro." *Louisiana History* 17 (1976): 159–68.

3. Glatthaar, *Forged in Battle,* 35–61. Butler recruited the black troops after no further reinforcements were available. He informed the secretary of war, "I shall call on Africa to intervene, and I do not think I shall call in vain" (Quarles, *Negro in the Civil War,* 86–87).

4. Glatthaar, *Forged in Battle,* 182–85.

5. John William De Forest, *A Volunteer's Adventures: A Union Captain's Record of the Civil War* (New Haven, Conn.: Yale University Press, 1946), 50–51; Aptheker, *Negro Casualties in the Civil War,* 18–19; W. E. Woodward, *Meet General Grant* (New York: Liveright, 1928), 279. The 42d, 63d, 64th, 69th, 121st, 123d, and 124th U.S. Colored Troops composed the dedicated fatigue duty regiments. See Dyer, *Compendium of the War of the Rebellion,* 1733–38.

6. Trudeau, *Like Men of War,* 46–59; F. S. Bowley, *The Petersburg Mine* (Wilmington, N.C.: Broadfoot Publishing, 1995), 560–74.

7. Edmund Ross Colhoun Papers, Library of Congress, Manuscript Division. Colhoun commanded the *Saugus* from September 1864 to the end of the war.

8. *ORN,* ser. 1, 7:12–13; John S. C. Abbott, *The History of the Civil War in America . . .,* 2 vols. (Springfield, Mass.: H. Bill, 1865), 1:202. These African Americans were located in a sample of Connecticut naval recruits compiled from the names of known African American sailors and verified in *Record of Service of Connecticut Men in the Army and Navy of the United States during the War of the Rebellion,* 2 vols. (Hartford, Conn: Case, Lockwood, & Brainard, 1889).

9. *ORN,* ser. 1, 9:726–27.

10. Ibid., ser. 1, 8:110–11, 290–91.

11. Ibid., ser. 1, 26:83–85, 505; James M. McPherson, *The Negro's Civil War: How American Negroes Felt and Acted during the War for the Union* (New York: Vintage Books, 1965), 158–59.

12. *ORN,* ser. 1, 5:448–49, 19:683. Captain Melancthon Smith commanded the *Mississippi.* Lieutenant George Dewey, the naval hero of the Battle of Manila Bay in 1898, served as executive officer.

13. Ibid., ser. 1, 9:440–47.

14. Ibid., ser. 1, 15:472–82. The observer was ship's surgeon William H. Pierson. No evidence has emerged as to why Pierson believed the crew "despised" Sills.

15. *ORN,* ser. 1, 21:490–93. The destruction of the *Tecumseh* prompted requests from other officers to find a safer route. In response, Farragut bellowed his famous order, "Damn the torpedoes! Full steam ahead!"

16. Ibid., ser. 1, 22:74, 132–33; NARA, Record Group 25, Decklog of the USS *Harvest Moon;* Record Group 25, "Lists of Casualties Transferred to Norfolk Naval Hospital, January 1, 1865–June 30, 1865," book 2. In total, Confederate mines claimed seven Union vessels during the Mobile Bay fight and in subsequent operations up the Blakely River: USS *Althea, Ida, Milwaukee, Osage, Rodolph, Sciota,* and *Tecumseh.*

17. *ORN,* ser. 1, 21:409–13; Civil War Plymouth Pilgrims Descendants Society, *Ship Rosters: Battle of Plymouth* (self-published, 1998), 1–15.

18. *ORN,* ser. 1, 23:244.

19. NARA, Record Group 25, Decklog of the USS *Pittsburgh;* Connecticut Recruit Sample; *ORN,* ser. 1, 25:42–43.

20. *ORN,* ser. 1, 6:614–15; NARA, Record Group 25, Decklog of USS *Hartford,* Decklog of USS *Benton;* Osbon, *Cruise of the U.S. Flag-Ship Hartford,* 83–84.

21. These names are from a sample of African American sailors

recruited in Massachusetts derived from *Massachusetts Soldiers, Sailors, and Marines,* 7:697, 802.

22. *ORN,* ser. 1, 23:181, 26:50; NARA, Pension Record "Scott, George W."; *Massachusetts Soldiers, Sailors, and Marines,* 8:42, 224, 232, 754.

23. *ORN,* ser. 1, 15:190–91, 21.408–9, 436–37, 447–48, 451–52.

24. United States, Navy Department, *Record of the Medals of Honor Issued to the Bluejackets and Marines of the United States Navy, 1862–1877* (Washington, D.C.: Government Printing Office, 1878), 45, 54; *ORN,* ser. 1, 3:66–68, 5:534–35; NARA, Record Group 45, "Circulars and General Orders," General Order No. 59.

25. Batten, *Reminiscences of Two Years,* 74; *ORN,* ser. 1, 8:723–24, 15:472–82; Blanding, *Recollections of a Sailor Boy,* 295–97; Osbon, *Cruise of the Flagship Hartford,* 41; James M. McPherson, *Lamson of the Gettysburg: The Civil War Letters of Lieutenant Roswell H. Lamson, U.S. Navy* (New York: Oxford University Press, 1997), 95.

26. *ORN,* ser. 1, 8:584–85, 13:567, 23:332–33.

27. *Dictionary of American Naval Fighting Ships,* 2:197, 5:276–77, 6:501; *ORN,* ser. 1, 21:262–63.

28. Thomas, "Prisoner of War Exchange," 91–92.

29. *ORN,* ser. 1, 15:158–59, 26:418–19.

30. McPherson, *Battle Cry of Freedom,* 292–97; Thomas, "Prisoner of War Exchange," 181.

31. *ORN,* ser. 1, 6:631–32.

32. Gideon Welles, *Diary of Gideon Welles: Secretary of the Navy under Lincoln and Johnson,* 3 vols. (Boston: Houghton Mifflin, 1911), 2:168–69; *ORA,* ser. 2, 7:661–62; Richard S. West, *Gideon Welles: Lincoln's Navy Department* (Indianapolis: Bobbs-Merrill, 1943), 293. Like most Civil War prisoner camps, Fort Lafayette was unsuitable for its purpose. Originally meant to hold two hundred prisoners, the facility contained more than a thousand by September 1861 (*ORN,* ser. 1, 6:105, 132).

33. Welles, *Diary of Gideon Welles,* 2:170–71; R. J. M. Blackett, *Thomas Morris Chester, Black Civil War Correspondent: His Dispatches from the Virginia Front* (Baton Rouge: Louisiana State University Press, 1989), 155–62.

34. *ORN,* ser. 2, 11:605, 627.

35. Richard N. Current, ed. *Encyclopedia of the Confederacy,* 4 vols. (New York: Simon & Schuster, 1993), 1:235–37; *ORN,* ser. 1, 21:605, 764–65.

6: BEFORE THE BENCH

1. Horace Lane, *The Wandering Boy, Careless Sailor, and Result of Inconsideration: A True Narrative* (Skaneateles, N.Y.: L. A. Pratt, 1839), 23–24; James E. Valle, *Rocks and Shoals: Naval Discipline in the Age of the*

Fighting Sail (Annapolis: Naval Institute Press, 1980), 41.

2. The Uniform Code of Military Justice replaced the Articles of War in 1950.

3. *U.S. Statutes at Large* 1 (1800): 135–46; William M. Fowler, *Jack Tars and Commodores: The American Navy, 1783–1815* (Boston: Houghton Mifflin, 1984), 138; Valle, *Rocks and Shoals*, 95–96. Valle organizes his offenses into broader categories, but for the purposes of this study I have organized them into the four offense categories seen here.

4. *U.S. Statutes at Large* 1 (1800): 140.

5. Valle, *Rocks and Shoals*, 45–46, 79; Francis A. Roe, *Naval Duties and Discipline: With the Policy and Principles of Naval Organization* (New York: Van Nostrand, 1865), 136.

6. Valle, *Rocks and Shoals*, 78–81.

7. Ibid., 23; Myra C. Glenn, *Campaigns against Corporal Punishment: Prisoners, Sailors, Women, and Children in Antebellum America* (Albany: State University of New York Press, 1984), 63–83.

8. Edward L. Beach, *United States Navy: 200 Years* (New York: Holt, 1986), 177–95; Edward M. Byrne, *Military Law: A Handbook for the Navy and Marine Corps* (Annapolis: Naval Institute Press, 1970), 14–16; Joseph Di-Mona, *Great Court-Martial Cases* (New York: Grosset & Dunlap, 1972), 44–71.

9. Erwin G. Gudde, "Mutiny on the *Ewing*," *California Historical Society Quarterly* 30 (1951): 145–76; Leonard F. Guttridge, *Mutiny: A History of Naval Insurrection* (Annapolis: Naval Institute Press, 1992), 116–17.

10. Bauer, *Surfboats and Horse Marines*, 42.

11. Valle, *Rocks and Shoals*, 81–82.

12. Livingston, *Civil War Marine at Sea*, 35.

13. *U.S. Statutes at Large* 2 (1862): 601–10; *A Method of Classifying Offenses and Punishment on Board Vessels of the U.S. Navy* (Washington, D.C.: U.S. Navy Department, 1871), 6–11.

14. Smith, "Black Seamen and the Federal Courts," 7–11.

15. William C. De Hart, *Observations on Military Law, and the Constitution and Practice of Courts Martial* (New York: Wiley, 1859), 387–403. Illinois, Ohio, Indiana, Iowa, California, and Oregon all had laws barring African Americans from giving evidence against white defendants. Only Massachusetts gave African Americans the right to sit on juries judging white defendants (Litwack, *North of Slavery*, 93–94).

16. Martin Van Buren, *Negro Witness: The Case of Lieutenant Hooe* (Washington, D.C.: Government Printing Office, 1840), 3–4.

17. Edgar S. Dudley, *Military Law and the Procedure of Courts-Martial* (New York: Wiley, 1907), 5–6; Bell I. Wiley, *The Life of Billy Yank: The Common Soldier of the Union* (Indianapolis: Bobbs-Merrill, 1952), 195–96. The army significantly revised the Army Articles of War in 1875

before replacement by the Uniform Code of Military Justice in 1950.

18. Lord, *They Fought for the Union*, 207, 210–11; Bell I. Wiley, *The Common Soldier of the Civil War* (New York: Scribner's, 1973), 65.

19. Wiley, *Life of Billy Yank*, 197–204.

20. *ORA*, ser. 1, 54:56; Wiley, *Life of Billy Yank*, 205; Byrne, *Military Law*, 1–13. The army executed 3 soldiers for spying, 18 for rape, 2 for murder and rape, 1 for rape and theft, 70 for murder, and 141 for desertion. The army executed most by firing squad but hanged those who had committed crimes against civilians. The navy last executed a sailor in 1849.

21. United States, Congress, *An Act for the Better Government of the United States Navy* (Washington, D.C.: Government Printing Office, 1800), 22.

22. NARA, Record Group 45, "Claim of Lucy Ann Johnson."

23. *Act for the Better Government of the United States Navy*, 27; NARA, Record Group 45, "Records of General Courts Martial and Courts of Inquiry of the Navy Department, 1799–1867," Microforms Publication 273 (hereafter cited as NARA court-martial files), "Jackson, Allen."

24. NARA court-martial files, "Dunlevy, James," "Train, Charles W." For another analysis of the murder of Simon Cleveland, see Valuska, *African American in the Union Navy*, 72–73.

25. NARA court-martial files, "Dunlevy, James," "Train, Charles W.," "Williams, John," "Gavican, Michael."

26. Ibid., "Fitzpatrick, John."

27. Trudeau, *Like Men of War*, 228; Berlin, *Slaves No More*, 215; Wiley, *Common Soldier of the Civil War*, 112.

28. NARA court-martial files, "Reid, Joseph," "Kittredge, J. W."

29. Valuska, *African American in the Union Navy*, 71. The 475 cases came from paper files in Record Group 45, "Records of General Courts Martial of the Navy Department, 1799–1867," and Microforms Publication 273, "Records of General Courts Martial and Courts of Inquiry of the Navy Department, 1799–1867," Rolls 97 through 155. As there were no African American commissioned officers or marines, courts-martial involving these groups were not included. Also, as not every vessel assigned some categories of senior enlisted men (e.g., carpenter or sailmaker), I excluded them. The ranks included in the sample are firemen, seamen, coal heavers, ordinary seaman, landsmen, ship boys, cooks, and stewards. In cases where more than one charge was filed, only the most serious offense was noted.

30. Chi-Square Significance = .069.

31. Chi-Square Significance = .103.

32. Chi-Square Significance = .175.

33. Chi-Square Significance = .556.

34. ANOVA Significance = .133.

35. Chi-Square Significance = .742. The navy prosecuted black and white sailors in nonsignificant proportions relative to the jurisdiction in which the court-martial took place, whether in a northern navy yard, the Mississippi River, or on the blockade. About one in five trials convened at a navy yard, less than one percent in the jurisdiction of the Atlantic Squadron before its separation into two separate commands in 1862, 4.5 percent in remote stations like the Pacific and South American Squadrons, with the remainder divided among the five wartime squadrons. The navy held about 40 percent of their wartime proceedings in the North Atlantic Blockading Squadron, 10 percent in the South Atlantic Blockading Squadron, 6 percent in the East Gulf Squadron, 25 percent in the West Gulf Squadron, and 10 percent in the Mississippi River Squadron (Chi-Square Significance = .229).

36. Desertion-related crimes include desertion, attempting to desert, aiding another to desert, absent without leave, and those charged with desertion but found guilty of absent without leave. Violent crimes consist of murder, attempted murder, manslaughter, rape, assaulting a fellow crewmember, and arson. Antiauthority crimes include assaulting a superior officer, threatening a superior officer, mutinous conduct, insubordination, contempt of court-martial, and sabotage. Disciplinary crimes consist of theft, scandalous conduct, destruction of public property, asleep at one's post, and deserting one's post without proper relief.

37. Berlin, *Slaves No More*, 217.

38. The Navy Articles of War made no provision for attempted murder. Sailors who assaulted fellow crewmen faced trial under the extenuating circumstances of assault "with a deadly weapon" or "intent to kill."

39. Defendants in this crime were sailors who successfully deserted but voluntarily returned to the navy. Deserters captured at large could not qualify for the lesser charge.

40. Mutinous conduct was a more serious charge than insubordination, implying the offender was not only disobeying direct orders but also refuting the authority of a superior, hence the adjective "mutinous."

41. The navy could level scandalous conduct for virtually any breach of navy regulations or ship's rules undefined by other charges. The full offense was "scandalous conduct leading to the detriment of good moral character" and embraced such activities as profanity, failing to appear at Sunday religious services, drunkenness, poor hygiene, laziness, skulking, or sodomy.

42. Valle, *Rocks and Shoals*, 100. In 1861, the navy held 34 general courts-martial, 83 in 1862, 334 in 1863, 498 in 1864, and 471 in 1865.

43. Chi-Square Significance = .059.

44. Chi-Square Significance = .200.

45. Besides their prison sentence, those court-martialed also generally lost all pay and prize money due them at the time of conviction and during their prison sentence. For instance, a trial found a sailor named Valliant guilty of assaulting a superior officer and of drunkenness in the East Gulf Blockading Squadron in December 1863. Besides being sentenced to a year of hard labor, Valliant lost the two thousand dollars in pay and prize money he had accumulated (Buker, *Blockaders, Refugees, and Contrabands*, 25).

46. Besides those receiving prison sentences for violent crimes, 3 percent received the death penalty and 6.1 percent received a life sentence, two penalties that cannot be factored into mean prison sentences. In the entire court-martial sample, nine sailors (1.9 percent) received the death penalty, and fourteen (2.9 percent) received life sentences.

47. ANOVA Significance = .066.

48. ANOVA Significance = .194.

49. NARA, Record Group 45, "Records of Sailors Transferred to State Custody."

50. ANOVA Significance = .611.

51. Again, the statistics depend upon whom you believe. The number I used was from the final provost marshal's report of March 1866. Thomas L. Livermore, in *Numbers and Losses in the Civil War in America* (Bloomington: Indiana University Press, 1957), 48, lists desertions at 125,000; the *ORA* reported 260,339 Union desertions (ser. 3, 5:109, 600).

52. NARA, Record Group 45, "Letters to Squadron Commanders," Collection #4067, Letter 121; Lord, *They Fought for the Union*, 205; Vail, *Three Years on the Blockade*, 156–57.

53. Winslow, *Constructing Munitions of War*, 234.

54. ANOVA Significance = .109.

55. NARA court-martial files, "Collins, Thomas," "Whitehurst, Joseph," "Eldridge, Alvin," "Roberts, Samuel."

56. NARA court-martial files, "Harris, Matt."

57. *U.S. Statutes at Large* 1 (1800): 131–33; Joseph M. Overfield, *The Civil War Letters of Private George Parks* (Buffalo: Gallagher Printing, 1992), 103–4. Congress passed the original deserter amnesty law in 1882 but did not include navy deserters.

58. Charges of sodomy and attempted sodomy were primarily in the West. The sample found two attempted sodomy cases tried at the Philadelphia Navy Yard, but all other cases were in the Mississippi or Gulf Blockading Squadrons.

59. NARA court-martial files, "Brogan, Thomas," "Couliard, Daniel," "Simmons, James"; Carl Sandburg, *Abraham Lincoln: The Prairie Years and the War Years* (New York: Harcourt Brace, 1982), 726.

60. NARA court-martial files, "Jackson, Henry," "Johns, Joseph," "Moody, Washington," "Cornelius, Richard."

61. Chi-Square Significance = .281.

62. The defendant was under the influence of alcohol, was seen consuming alcohol by a prosecution witness, or used drunkenness as a mitigating factor.

63. Chi-Square Significance = .328.

64. ANOVA Significance = .077.

65. ANOVA Significance = .994.

66. Livingston, *Civil War Marine at Sea,* 12, 77; Hunter, *A Year on a Monitor,* 40–114; Blanding, *Recollections of a Sailor Boy,* 61–62. Most ironclads had no brig, so an empty coal bunker had to serve as a cell. Incarceration on the uncomfortable ironclads was particularly difficult.

67. True, "Life aboard a Gunboat," 37; Blanding, *Recollections of a Sailor Boy,* 61; NARA courts-martial files, "Murphy, John"; Thomas Lyons diary, entry for June 17, 1863; NARA, Logbook of the USS *Kearsarge;* Benjamin A. Botkin, *A Civil War Treasury of Tales, Legends, and Folklore.* (New York: Random House, 1960), 242.

7: ONE WHO WAS THERE

1. The diary of William Gould, who enlisted as a landsman in New York in 1864, also exists. The work is, as of this printing, unavailable; a descendent of Gould is preparing the diary for publication.

2. William Marvel, *The Alabama and the Kearsarge: The Sailor's Civil War* (Chapel Hill: University of North Carolina Press, 1996), 239. Confederates overran Fort Pillow, a Union outpost, in April 1864, resulting in the massacre of surrendered African American soldiers.

3. Paul E. Sluby, Sr., and Stanton L. Wormley, eds., *Diary of Charles B. Fisher* (Washington, D.C.: Columbia Harmony Society, 1983), 27, 44, 51.

4. Goodman, "Black Tar," 273.

5. NARA, Record Group 15, "Index to Navy Pension Files, 1861–1910," "Fisher, Charles B."

6. Sluby and Wormley, eds., *Diary of Charles B. Fisher,* 44, 53.

7. Ibid., 25–26, 36, 52–53, 93–94. See Jasper G. Ridley, *Maximilian and Juarez* (London: Constable Books, 1993); Albert A. Woldman, *Lincoln and the Russians* (Cleveland: World, 1952); and James Dugan, *The Great Iron Ship* (New York: Harper, 1953).

8. Ships from both sides could enter neutral ports under the recognized rules of war. If one vessel opted to leave, the neutral port could detain the other vessel for twenty-four hours to allow the leaving vessel to clear national waters before any fighting could take place.

9. Sluby and Wormley, eds., *Diary of Charles B. Fisher,* 26–27, 66. Of all their tasks, sailors found coaling the most disagreeable. Crewmen transferred loose coal in canvas gunnysacks from a supply ship aboard the receiving ship and dumped it down coal chutes for distribution through the coal bunkers. It was a dirty and laborious process, and coal dust covered the ship afterwards.

10. Ibid., 27. Yeaton later took ill, and the navy granted him a medical discharge in 1864 (Marvel, *Alabama and the Kearsarge,* 280).

11. Sluby and Wormley, eds., *Diary of Charles B. Fisher,* 14–15. Guard captains were enlisted men on larger vessels with the highest seniority placed in charge of the enlisted men in their portion of the ship. The rank conferred an additional two dollars per month. Ships typically had a captain of the Forecastle (forward part of the hull), After Guard (rear part of the hull), Lower Guard (in the holds and bilges), and Upper Guard (the rigging and yardarms). See Marvel, *Alabama and the Kearsarge,* 80, 279.

12. Sluby and Wormley, eds., *Diary of Charles B. Fisher,* 24–25, 45–46, 49, 57; Marvel, *Alabama and the Kearsarge,* 276, 278.

13. Scott was the only black sailor among the seventeen African Americans aboard *Kearsarge* to desert. See Sluby and Wormley, eds., *Diary of Charles B. Fisher,* 11–12; Marvel, *Alabama and the Kearsarge,* 273–80.

14. Sluby and Wormley, eds., *Diary of Charles B. Fisher,* 72, 96.

15. Ibid., 12, 33, 52; Marvel, *Alabama and the Kearsarge,* 26, 32, 267, 273–80. Phillips lived another fifty-one years, dying in 1914.

16. Sluby and Wormley, eds., *Diary of Charles B. Fisher,* 12–14, 46–49; Marvel, *Alabama and the Kearsarge,* 92–93, 169–70, 260, 273–80. Tibbets's real name was Edward H. Sampson, age 19. In 1861, Sampson had served aboard a merchant vessel captured by the Confederate raider CSS *Sumter* but was paroled on the condition he never fight against the Confederacy. Sampson had changed his name when he enlisted lest he face execution for violating his parole. Ironically, *Kearsarge* was in the area to keep an eye on the *Sumter* lying disabled at Cadiz, Spain (Marvel, *Alabama and the Kearsarge,* 49–50). On De Santo, see Marvel, *Alabama and the Kearsarge,* 33, 36. Of mixed race, an officer described De Santo, a Portuguese national, as a "black Portuguese."

17. Sluby and Wormley, eds., *Diary of Charles B. Fisher,* 3, 28.

18. Ibid., 10; Marvel, *Alabama and the Kearsarge,* 84–85.

19. Sluby and Wormley, eds., *Diary of Charles B. Fisher,* 59–60, 69. Visiting England after the defeat of the *Alabama,* Fisher renewed his friendship with the British soldiers; "the Highlanders are wild with joy at our return" (94).

20. Ibid., 9–10; Marvel, *Alabama and the Kearsarge,* 90.

21. Marvel, *Alabama and the Kearsarge,* 16, 57, 103.

22. Ibid., 11, 85; Sluby and Wormley, eds., *Diary of Charles B. Fisher,* 40, 51, 71.

23. Sluby and Wormley, eds., *Diary of Charles B. Fisher,* 83. *Alabama* fired 370 projectiles, but only a dozen hit the *Kearsarge* (Marvel, *Alabama and the Kearsarge,* 254).

24. Marvel, *Alabama and the Kearsarge,* 259.

25. Sluby and Wormley, eds., *Diary of Charles B. Fisher,* 88–89.

26. Ibid., 18, 64.

27. Ibid., 17.

28. Ibid., 27–28, 54, 76, 100.

CONCLUSION

1. Frederick S. Harrod, *Manning the New Navy: The Development of a Modern Naval Enlistment Force, 1899–1940* (Westport, Conn.: Greenwood Press, 1978), 8-11; Frederick S. Herrod, "Jim Crow in the Navy, 1798–1941," *United States Naval Institute Proceedings* 105 (September 1979): 46-53; Cohn and Platzer, *Black Men of the Sea,* 122.

2. "Riot on the USS *Charleston."Army and Navy Journal* 44 (1894): 563; Naval Historical Center, "Blacks and Other Minorities—Early Records": "Negroes at the United States Naval Academy"; Greene, *Black Defenders of America,* 151.

3. Harrod, *Manning the New Navy,* 11, 58; James B. Farr, *Black Odyssey: The Seafaring Traditions of Afro-Americans* (New York: Peter Lang, 1989), 143.

4. Harrod, *Manning the New Navy,* 57–62, 183–84. In 1931, there were 441 African Americans out of a navy population of 81,120; Harrod, "Jim Crow in the Navy." 49–53; Naval Historical Center, "Blacks and Other Minorities—Early Records": "Negroes at the United States Naval Academy."

5. L. D. Reddick, "The Negro in the United States Navy during World War II," *Journal of Negro History* 32 (1947): 211; Paul Stillwell, ed., *The Golden Thirteen: Recollections of the First Black Naval Officers* (Annapolis: Naval Institute Press, 1993), 263.

6. Stillwell, *Golden Thirteen,* xix–xxiv; Farr, *Black Odyssey,* 155; Robert L. Allen, *The Port Chicago Mutiny* (New York: Warner Books, 1989). See also Mary Pat Kelly, *Proudly We Served: The Men of the U.S.S. Mason* (Annapolis: Naval Institute Press, 1995).

7. Farr, *Black Odyssey,* 155; Naval Historical Center, "Blacks and Other Minorities—Early Records": "Negroes at the United States Naval Academy"; Greene, *Black Defenders of America,* 254.

BIBLIOGRAPHY

ARCHIVES

National Archives and Records Administration

Record Groups
Record Group 15, Records of the Veterans Administration
Record Group 24, Records of the Bureau of Naval Personnel
Record Group 45, Records Collection of the Office of Naval Records and Library
Record Group 52, Records of the Bureau of Medicine and Surgery
Record Group 71, Records of the Bureau of Yards and Docks
Record Group 80, General Records of the Department of the Navy
Record Group 143, Records of the Bureau of Supply and Accounts
Record Group 249, Records of the Commissary General of Prisoners

Logbooks and Ship's Records
USS *Benton;* USS *Ceres;* USS *Clara Dolson;* USS *Flag;* USS *Hartford;* USS *Harvest Moon;* USS *Howqua;* USS *Kearsarge;* USS *Miami;* USS *Milwaukee;* USS *Monitor;* USS *Oneida;* USS *Peosta;* USS *Pittsburgh;* USS *Princeton;* USS *Red Rover;* USS *Saginaw;* USS *Saugus;* USS *Sonoma;* USS *Southfield;* USS *Victory;* USS *Whitehead*

Naval Historical Center

Blacks and Other Minorities—Early Records
Navy Department Circulars, 1842–1866
Letters from Officers to Navy Department, 1840–1866
Selected Muster Roll Counts of Negroes in the Navy during the Civil War

Library of Congress, Manuscript Division

Edmund Ross Colhoun Papers
David Connor Papers
Thomas Lyons Papers
Gideon Welles Papers

NEWSPAPERS

Baltimore Federal Gazette, 1812–1813
Harper's Weekly, 1861–1865
Liberator (Boston), 1850–1866
Niles's Weekly Register (Baltimore), 1812–1814
St. Louis Daily Democrat, 1861–1865
Seaman's Friend (Baltimore), 1858–1866

WORKS CITED

Abbott, John S. C. *The History of the Civil War in America . . .* 2 vols. Springfield, Mass.: H. Bill, 1865.

Abbott, Richard H. "Massachusetts and the Recruitment of Southern Negroes, 1863–1865." *Civil War History* 14 (1968): 197–210.

Adams, Charles F. "The Birth of a World Power." *American Historical Review* 18 (1913): 517–25.

Ainsworth, F. C. *Memorandum Relative to the Probable Number and Ages of the Army and Navy Survivors of the War of the Rebellion.* Washington, D.C.: War Department, 1896.

Alexander, Adele L. *Homelands and Waterways: The American Journey of the Bond Family, 1846–1926.* New York: Pantheon, 1999.

Allen, Robert L. *The Port Chicago Mutiny.* New York: Warner Books, 1989.

Ammen, Daniel. *The Atlantic Coast.* New York: Scribner, 1883.

Ammen, D., and J. R. Soley. *The Navy in the Civil War.* 2 vols. 1900. Reprint, [Secausus, N.J.]: Blue & Grey Press, 1970.

Anderson, Bern. *By Sea and by River: The Naval History of the Civil War.* New York: Da Capo Press, 1962.

Antibiastes. *Observations on the Slaves and the Indented Servants, Inlisted in the Army, and in the Navy of the United States.* Philadelphia, 1777.

Aptheker, Herbert. *A Documentary History of the Negro People in the United States.* 3 vols. New York: Citadel Press, 1968.

———. *Negro Casualties in the Civil War.* Washington, D.C.: Association for the Study of Negro Life and History, 1945.

———. "The Negro in the Union Navy." *Journal of Negro History* 32 (1947): 169–200.

Baird, Henry C. *General Washington and General Jackson on Negro Soldiers.* Philadelphia, 1863.

Baker, Jean H. *Affairs of Party: The Political Culture of Northern Democrats in the Mid-Nineteenth Century.* Ithaca, N.Y.: Cornell University Press, 1983.

Baldwin, Leland D. *The Keelboat Age on Western Waters.* Pittsburgh: University of Pittsburgh Press, 1941.

Barker, Albert S. *Everyday Life in the Navy: Autobiography of Rear Admiral*

Albert S. Barker. Boston: Badger, 1928.

Bartlett, Irving H. *From Slave to Citizen: The Story of the Negro in Rhode Island.* Providence, R.I.: Urban League of Greater Providence, 1954.

Batten, John M. *Reminiscences of Two Years in the United States Navy.* Lancaster, Pa.: Inquirer, 1881.

Bauer, K. Jack. *Surfboats and Horse Marines: U.S. Naval Operations in the Mexican War, 1846–1848.* Annpolis: Naval Institute Press, 1969.

Beach, Edward L. *The United States Navy: 200 Years.* New York: Holt, 1986.

Belz, Herman. "Law, Politics, and Race in the Struggle for Equal Pay during the Civil War." *Civil War History* 22 (1976): 197–213.

Benedict, G. G. *Vermont in the Civil War: A History of the Part Taken by the Vermont Soldiers and Sailors in the War for the Union, 1861–5.* 2 vols. Burlington, Vt.: Free Press Association, 1886.

Bennett, Frank M. *The Steam Navy of the United States.* Pittsburgh: Warren, 1896.

Berent, Irwin M. *The Crewmen of the U.S.S. Monitor: A Biographical Directory.* Raleigh, N.C.: Department of Cultural Resources, 1984.

Beringer, Richard E. *Why the South Lost the Civil War.* Athens: University of Georgia Press, 1991.

Berlin, Ira, ed. *The Black Military Experience.* New York: Cambridge University Press, 1982.

———. *Freedom: A Documentary History of Emancipation, 1861–1867.* Ser. 1. 2 vols. New York: Cambridge University Press, 1982.

———. *Slaves No More: Three Essays on Emancipation in the Civil War.* New York: Cambridge University Press, 1992.

Berry, Mary F. *Military Necessity and Civil Rights Policy: Black Citizenship and the Constitution, 1861–1868.* Port Washington, N.Y.: Kennikat Press, 1977.

Bibb, Henry. *Narrative of the Life and Adventures of Henry Bibb, American Slave.* Miami: Mnemosyne, 1969.

Bilby, Joseph G. *Forgotten Warriors: New Jersey's African American Soldiers in the Civil War.* Hightstown, N.J.: Longstreet House, 1993.

Blackett, R. J. M. *Thomas Morris Chester, Black Civil War Correspondent: His Dispatches from the Virginia Front.* Baton Rouge: Louisiana State University Press, 1989.

Blair, L. B. "Dogs and Sailors Keep Off!" *United States Naval Institute Proceedings* 76 (1950): 1095–1103.

Blanding, Stephen E. *Recollections of a Sailor Boy; or, The Cruise of the Gunboat Louisiana.* Providence, R.I.: E. A. Johnson, 1886.

Blassingame, John W. *The Slave Community: Plantation Life in the Antebellum South.* New York: Oxford University Press, 1972.

Bolster, William J. "African American Seaman: Race, Seafaring Work, and Atlantic Maritime Culture." Ph.D. diss., Johns Hopkins University, 1992.

Bolster, W. Jeffrey. *Black Jacks: African American Seaman in the Age of Sail.* Cambridge, Mass.: Harvard University Press, 1997.

Boskin, Joseph. *Sambo: The Rise and Demise of an American Jester.* New York: Oxford University Press, 1986.

Botkin, Benjamin A. *A Civil War Treasury of Tales, Legends, and Folklore.* New York: Random House, 1960.

Bowley, F. S. *The Petersburg Mine.* Wilmington, N.C.: Broadfoot Publishing, 1995.

Boyer, Samuel P. *Naval Surgeon: The Diary of Dr. Samuel Pellman Boyer.* Bloomington: Indiana University Press, 1963.

Boynton, Charles. *The History of the Navy during the Rebellion.* 2 vols. New York: Appleton, 1868.

Bracey, John H. *Free Blacks in America, 1800–1860.* Belmont, Calif.: Wadsworth Publishing, 1971.

Bradford, James C., ed. *Captains of the Old Steam Navy: Makers of the American Naval Tradition, 1840–1880.* Annapolis: Naval Institute Press, 1986.

Brawshaw, Wesley. *The Volunteer's Roll of Honor: A Collection of the Noble and Praiseworthy Deeds Performed in the Cause of the Union by Heroes of the Army and Navy of the United States.* Philadelphia: Barclay Press, 1864.

Brewer, James H. *The Confederate Negro: Virginia's Negro Craftsmen and Military Laborers, 1861–1865.* Durham, N.C.: Duke University Press, 1969.

Brodkin, Allan K. "The Negro Seaman Acts." Master's thesis, University of Texas, 1960.

Brown, William W. *The Negro in the American Rebellion, His Heroism, and His Fidelity.* Miami: Mnemosyne Publishing, 1969.

Browne, Henry R. and Symmes E. Browne. *From the Fresh Water Navy, 1861–64: The Letters of Acting Master's Mate Henry R. Browne and Acting Ensign Symmes E. Browne.* Annapolis: United States Naval Institute, 1970.

Browning, Robert M. *From Cape Charles to Cape Fear: The North Atlantic Blockading Squadron during the Civil War.* Tuscaloosa: University of Alabama Press, 1993.

Bruce, John E. *Defense of the Colored Soldiers Who Fought in the War of the Rebellion.* New York: Yonkers, 1919.

Buckingham, James S. *The Slave States of America.* 2 vols. London: Fisher and Sons, 1842.

Buker, George E. *Blockaders, Refugees, and Contrabands: Civil War on Florida's Gulf Coast, 1861–1865.* Tuscaloosa: University of Alabama Press, 1993.

Butler, Benjamin F. *Butler's Book: A Review of His Legal, Political, and Military Career.* Boston: Atwater Publishers, 1892.

———. *Private and Official Correspondence of Gen. Benjamin F. Butler during the*

Period of the Civil War. 5 vols. Norwood, Mass.: Plimpton Press, 1917.

Byrn, John D., Jr. *Crime and Punishment in the Royal Navy: Discipline on the Leeward Islands Station, 1784–1812.* Aldershot, U.K.: Scholar Press, 1989.

Byrne, Edward M. *Military Law: A Handbook for the Navy and Marine Corps.* Annapolis: United States Naval Institute, 1970.

Caldara, Hugh. "The Federal Navy on Western Rivers, 1861–1863." Master's thesis, Wesleyan University, 1981.

Canney, Donald L. *Lincoln's Navy: The Ships, Men, and Organization, 1861–65.* Annapolis: Naval Institute Press, 1998.

———. *The Old Steam Navy.* 2 vols. Annapolis: Naval Institute Press, 1990–1993.

Catterall, Helen T. *Judicial Cases concerning American Slavery and the Negro.* Washington, D.C.: Carnegie Institution, 1936.

Chapin, Eugene. *By-Gone Days; or, The Experiences of an American.* Boston: Boston Publishers, 1898.

Chapelle, Howard I. *The History of the American Sailing Navy.* New York: W. W. Norton, 1949.

Civil War Plymouth Pilgrims Descendants Society. *Ship Rosters: Battle of Plymouth.* Plymouth, N.C., 1998

Clark, Peter H. *The Black Brigade of Cincinnati.* Cincinnati: Ridder, 1864.

Cochran, Hamilton. *Blockade-Runners of the Confederacy.* Indianapolis: Bobbs-Merrill, 1958.

Cohn, Michael, and Michael K. H. Platzer. *Black Men of the Sea.* New York: Dodd, Mead, 1978.

Coletta, Paolo E. *A Survey of U.S. Naval Affairs, 1865–1917.* New York: University Press of America, 1987.

———. *American Secretaries of the Navy.* 2 vols. Annapolis: Naval Institute Press, 1980.

Commager, Henry Steele. *Documents of American History.* 2 vols. New York: Appleton-Century-Crofts, 1968.

Confederate States of America, Bureau of Exchange. *Official Correspondence between the Agents of Exchange, Together with Mr. Ould's Report.* Richmond: Sentinel Job Office, 1864.

Confederate States of America, Navy Department. *Regulations for the Navy of the Confederate States.* Richmond: Macfarlane & Ferguson, 1862.

Coombe, Jack D. *Thunder along the Mississippi: The River Battles That Split the Confederacy.* New York: Serpedon, 1996.

Cooper, Charles R. *Chronological and Alphabetical Records of the Engagements of the Great Civil War . . .* Milwaukee: Caxton Press, 1904.

Cornish, Dudley T. *The Sable Arm: Negro Troops in the Union Army, 1861–1865.* New York: Harpers, 1966.

Coulter, E. Merton. *A Short History of Georgia.* Chapel Hill: University of

North Carolina Press, 1933.

Cowdrey, Albert E. "Slave into Soldier: The Enlistment by the North of Runaway Slaves." *History Today* 20 (1970): 704–15.

Cox, J. Lee and Michael A. Jehle. *Ironclad Intruder: USS Monitor.* Philadelphia: Philadelphia Maritime Museum, 1988.

Critchell, Robert S. *Recollections of a Fire Insurance Man: Including His Experience in the U.S. Navy (Mississippi Squadron) during the Civil War.* Chicago: A. C. McClurg, 1909.

Croffut, W. A. and John M. Morris. *The Military and Civil History of Connecticut.* New York: Ledyard, 1868.

Crook, D. P. *Diplomacy during the American Civil War.* New York: Wiley, 1975.
———. *The North, the South, and the Powers, 1861–1865.* New York: Wiley, 1974.

Cruden, Robert. *The War That Never Ended: The American Civil War.* New York: Prentice-Hall, 1973.

Current, Richard N., ed. *Encyclopedia of the Confederacy.* 4 vols. New York: Simon & Schuster, 1993.

Daly, Robert W. *Aboard the USS Florida, 1863–65: The Letters of Paymaster William Frederick Keeler, U.S. Navy, to His Wife, Anna.* Annapolis: United States Naval Institute, 1968.

———. "Pay and Prize Money in the Old Navy, 1770–1899." *United States Naval Institute Proceedings* 74 (1948): 967–71.

Davidson, Dennis M. "*Red Rover:* The Navy's First Hospital Ship." Ph.D. diss., United States Naval Academy, 1960.

Davis, Lenwood G. and George Hill. *Blacks in the American Armed Forces, 1776–1983.* Westport, Conn.: Greenwood Press, 1985.

De Hart, William C. *Observations on Military Law, and the Constitution and Practice of Courts Martial.* New York: Wiley, 1859.

De Forest, John William. *A Volunteer's Adventures: A Union Captain's Record of the Civil War.* New Haven, Conn.: Yale University Press, 1946.

Delany, Martin R. *The Condition, Elevation, Emigration, and Destiny of the Colored People of the United States.* Philadelphia, 1852.

Despain, Jeffrey W. "Operations of the Western Gulf Blockading Squadron and the Department of the Gulf in the Gulf of Mexico, 1862–1864." Master's thesis, U.S. Army Command and General Staff College, Fort Leavenworth, Kans., 1996.

Dibble, Ernest F. *War Averters: Seward, Mallory, and Fort Pickens.* Wilmington, Del.: Gulf Coast Collection, 1978.

Dictionary of American Naval Fighting Ships. 9 vols. Washington, D.C.: Government Printing Office, 1959–1991.

DiMona, Joseph. *Great Court-Martial Cases.* New York: Grosset & Dunlap, 1972.

Doughty, Thomas H. *Selected Documents and Papers Relating to His Service in the Union Navy during the Civil War.* Annapolis: United States

Naval Academy Library, 1863.

Drury, Clifford M. *United States Navy Chaplains, 1778–1945*. Washington, D.C.: Government Printing Office, 1948.

Dudley, Edgar S. *Military Law and the Procedure of Courts-Martial*. New York: Wiley, 1907.

du Pont, Samuel F. *Official Dispatches and Letters of Rear Admiral Du Pont, U.S. Navy, 1846–48 and 1861–63*. Wilmington, Del.: Ferris Brothers, 1883.

Dupuy, R. Ernest and Trevor N. Dupuy. *The Compact History of the Civil War*. New York: Warner Books, 1993.

Durkin, Joseph T. *Confederate Navy Chief: Stephen R. Mallory*. Columbia: University of South Carolina Press, 1997.

Dye, Ira. *The Fatal Cruise of the Argus: Two Captains in the War of 1812*. Annapolis: Naval Institute Press, 1994.

Dyer, Brainard. "The Treatment of Colored Union Troops by the Confederates, 1861–1865." *Journal of Negro History* 20 (1935): 273–86.

Dyer, Frederick H. *A Compendium of the War of the Rebellion: Compiled and Arranged from Official Records of the Federal and Confederate Armies*. 5 vols. Des Moines: Dyer, 1908.

Eckert, Edward K. *The Navy Department in the War of 1812*. Gainesville: University of Florida Press, 1973.

Eisenbarth, Robert K. "The Construction and Administration of the Union Navy." Master's thesis, Butler University, 1953.

Eller, E. M. *The Civil War at Sea*. 3 vols. New York: Holt, Rinehart, Winston, 1962.

An Essay on Flogging in the Navy. New York: Pudney, 1849.

Farr, James B. *Black Odyssey: The Seafaring Traditions of Afro-Americans*. New York: Peter Lang, 1989.

Ferguson, L. Gilbert. "A Study of Civil War Prisoner Policy." Master's thesis, Mississippi College, 1994.

Ferris, Norman B. *Desperate Diplomacy: William H. Seward's Foreign Policy, 1861*. Knoxville: University of Tennessee Press, 1976.

———. *The Trent Affair: A Diplomatic Crisis*. Knoxville: University of Tennessee Press, 1977.

Fitzpatrick, John C., ed. *The Writings of George Washington*. 30 vols. Washington, D.C.: Government Printing Office, 1936.

Folsom, Riley T. "United States Navy: Expansion and Reorganization, 1861–1862." Master's thesis, University of Washington, 1970.

Foner, Philip S. *History of Black Americans*. Vol. 3, *From the Compromise of 1850 to the End of the Civil War*. Westport, Conn.: Greenwood Press, 1975.

———. *History of the Labor Movement in the United States*. Vol. 1, *From Colonial Times to the Founding of the American Federation of Labor*. New York: International, 1947.

Fowler, William M. *Jack Tars and Commodores: The American Navy, 1783–1815.* Boston: Houghton Mifflin, 1984.

———. *Under Two Flags: The American Navy in the Civil War.* New York: Avon Books, 1990.

Fox, Gustavus V. *Confidential Correspondence of Gustavus Vasa Fox, Assistant Secretary of the Navy, 1861–1865.* New York: De Vinne Press, 1971.

Fox, William F. *Regimental Losses in the American Civil War.* Albany: Albany Publishing Company, 1889.

Franklin, John Hope. *The Emancipation Proclamation.* Garden City, New York: Doubleday, 1963.

———. *From Slavery to Freedom: A History of American Negroes.* New York: Alfred A. Knopf, 1947.

Frederickson, George M. *The Black Image in the White Mind.* New York: Harper, 1971.

Freel, Margaret W. *Our Heritage: The People of Cherokee County, North Carolina, 1540–1955.* Asheville, N.C.: Miller Printing, 1957.

Fretwell, Jacqueline K. *Civil War Times in St. Augustine.* St. Augustine: St. Augustine Historical Society, 1986.

Gabriel, Richard A. and Karen S. Metz. *A History of Military Medicine.* New York: Greenwood Press, 1992.

Gardiner, Robert, ed. *The Advent of Steam: History of the Ship.* London: Conway Maritime Press, 1993.

———. *Steam, Steel, and Shellfire: History of the Ship.* London: Conway Maritime Press, 1992.

Garitee, Jerome R. *The Republic's Private Navy: The American Privateering Business as Practiced by Baltimore during the War of 1812.* Middletown, Conn.: Wesleyan University Press, 1977.

Gerteis, Louis S. *From Contraband to Freedman: Federal Policy toward Southern Blacks, 1861–1865.* Westport, Conn.: Greenwood Press, 1973.

Gibson, Charles D. *Assault and Logistics: Union Army Coastal and River Operations, 1861–1866.* Camden, Maine: Ensign Press, 1995.

———. *Dictionary of the Transports and Combatant Vessels, Steam and Sail, Employed by the Union Army, 1861–1868.* Camden, Maine: Ensign Press, 1995.

Glatthaar, Joseph T. *Forged in Battle: The Civil War Alliance of Black Soldiers and White Officers.* New York: Free Press. 1990.

Glenn, Myra C. *Campaigns against Corporal Punishment: Prisoners, Sailors, Women, and Children in Antebellum America.* Albany: State University of New York Press, 1984.

Glover, Robert W. "The West Gulf Blockade, 1861–1865." Ph.D. diss., North Texas State University, 1974.

Gooding, James H. *On the Altar of Freedom: A Black Soldier's Civil War Let-*

ters from the Front. Amherst: University of Massachusetts Press, 1991.

Goodman, Michael H. "The Black Tar: Negro Seamen in the Union Navy, 1861–1865." Ph.D. diss., University of Nottingham, 1975.

Gosnell, Harpur A. *Guns on the Western Waters: The Story of the River Gunboats in the Civil War.* Baton Rouge . Louisiana State University Press, 1949.

Grant, Bruce. *Captain of the Old Ironsides.* Chicago: Pellegrini and Cudahy, 1947.

Greene, Robert E. *Black Defenders of America, 1775–1973.* Chicago: Johnson Publishing, 1974.

Grimsley, Mark. *The Hard Hand of War: Union Military Policy towards Southern Civilians, 1861–1865.* New York: Cambridge University Press, 1995.

Gudde, Erwin G. "Mutiny on the *Ewing.*" *California Historical Society Quarterly* 30 (1951): 145–76.

Guthrie, James M. *Campfires of the Afro-American.* Philadelphia: Afro-American Press, 1899.

Guttridge, Leonard F. *Mutiny: A History of Naval Insurrection.* Annapolis: Naval Institute Press, 1992.

Hamilton, Frank H. *A Practical Treatise on Military Surgery.* New York: Bailliere Brothers, 1861.

Hammersly, Thomas H. S. *General Register of the United States Navy and Marine Corps.* Washington, D.C.: Hammersly, 1882.

Hanaford, Phebe A. *Field, Gunboat, Hospital, and Prison; or, The Thrilling Records of Heroism, Endurance, and Patriotism Displayed in the Union Army and Navy during the Great Rebellion.* Boston: C. M. Dinsmoor, 1866.

Hargrove, Hondon B. *Black Union Soldiers in the Civil War.* Jefferson, N.C.: McFarland Press, 1988.

Harris, Thomas L. *The Trent Affair.* Indianapolis: Bobbs-Merrill, 1896.

Harrod, Frederick S. "Integration of the Navy, 1941–1978." *United States Naval Institute Proceedings* 105 (October 1979): 40–47.

———. "Jim Crow in the Navy, 1798–1941." *United States Naval Institute Proceedings* 105 (September 1979): 46–53.

———. *Manning the New Navy: The Development of a Modern Naval Enlisted Force, 1899–1940.* Westport, Conn.: Greenwood Press, 1978.

Haughton, Phyllis H. *Dearest Carrie: Civil War Letters Home.* Lawrenceville, Va.: Brunswick, 1995.

Hayes, John D. "Sea Power in the Civil War." *United States Naval Institute Proceedings* 87 (1961): 60–69.

Heitman, Francis B. *Historical Register and Dictionary of the United States Army: From Its Organization September 29, 1789, to March 2, 1903.* 2 vols. Washington, D.C.: Government Printing Office, 1903.

Hendricks, George L. "Union Army Occupation of the Southern Seaboard, 1861–1865." Ph.D. diss., Columbia University, 1954.

Hesseltine, William B. *Civil War Prisons: A Study in War Psychology.* New York: Ungar Publishing, 1930.

Hibbard, Benjamin H. *A History of the Public Land Policies.* Madison: University of Wisconsin Press, 1965.

Higginson, Thomas W. *Army Life in a Black Regiment.* Boston: Fields and Osgood, 1870.

——. *Massachusetts in the Army and Navy during the War of 1861–65.* 2 vols. Boston: Wright and Potter, 1900.

Hill, Frederick S. *Twenty Years at Sea; or, Leaves From my Old Log-Books.* Boston: Houghton-Mifflin, 1893.

Hinds, John W. *Invasion and Conquest of North Carolina: Anatomy of a Gunboat War.* Shippensburg, Pa.: Burd Street Press, 1998.

Hooper, W. R. "Blockade Running." *Harper's New Monthly Magazine* 42 (1870): 16–22.

Horowitz, Murray M. "Ben Butler and the Negro." *Louisiana History* 17 (1976): 159–68.

Howard, Victor B. *Black Liberation in Kentucky: Emancipation and Freedom, 1862–1864.* Lexington: University of Kentucky Press, 1983.

Hummel, Jeffrey R. *Emancipating Slaves, Enslaving Free Men: A History of the American Civil War.* Chicago: Open Court, 1996.

Hunter, Alvah F. *A Year on a Monitor and the Destruction of Fort Sumter.* Columbia: University of South Carolina Press, 1987.

Illinois, Adjutant General's Office. *Record Requests for Discharge Certificates.* Springfield: Illinois State House, 1868.

——. *Roll of Honor: Record of Burial Places of Soldiers, Sailors, Marines, and Army Nurses of All Wars of the United States Buried in the State of Illinois.* 2 vols. Springfield: Illinois Adjutant General's Office, 1929.

——. *Roster of Illinois Men in the U.S. Navy during the Civil War.* Springfield: Illinois State House, 1867.

Illinois, Military State Agent, *Records of Illinois Soldier's Claims.* 4 vols. Springfield: Illinois State House, 1875.

——. *Disallowed Charges on Illinois War Claims.* Springfield: Illinois State House, 1867.

Itkin, Stanley L. "Operations of the East Gulf Blockading Squadron in the Blockade of Florida, 1862–1865." Master's thesis, Florida State University, 1962.

Jackson, Luther Porter. "Virginia Sailors and Soldiers in the American Revolution." *Journal of Negro History* 27 (1942): 254–55.

Jacquette, Henrietta S., ed. *South after Gettysburg: Letters of Cornelia Hancock, 1863–1868.* New York: Crowell, 1937.

Jameson, John F. *Privateering and Piracy in the Colonial Period.* New York: Illustrative Documents, 1923.

Johnston, Brenda A. *Between the Devil and the Sea: The Life of James Forten.* New York: Harcourt Brace, 1974.

Jones, Howard. *Union in Peril: The Crisis over British Intervention in the Civil War.* Chapel Hill: University of North Carolina Press, 1992.

Jones, P. Michael. *Forgotten Soldiers: Murphysboro's African American Civil War Veterans.* Murphysboro, Ill.: Class Publications Committee, 1994.

Jones, Virgil C. *The Civil War at Sea.* 3 vols. New York: Holt, Rinehart, and Winston, 1962.

Journals of the Council of the State of Virginia. 3 vols. Richmond: Virginia Statehouse, 1790.

Josyph, Peter. *The Wounded River: The Civil War Letters of John Vance Lauderdale, M.D.* East Lansing: Michigan State University Press, 1993.

Kalata, Eric J. "A Categorical Analysis of Desertion during the American Civil War." Bachelor's thesis, Lake Forest College, 1992.

Kaplan, Sidney. *The Black Presence in the Era of the American Revolution.* Washington, D.C.: Smithsonian Institution, 1975.

Katcher, Philip. *The Civil War Source Book.* New York: Facts on File, 1992.

———. *Union Forces of the American Civil War.* London: Arms and Armour Press, 1989.

Keeler, William F. *Aboard the USS Monitor, 1862: The Letters of Acting Paymaster William Frederick Keeler, U.S. Navy.* Annapolis: Naval Institute Press, 1964.

Kelly, Mary Pat. *Proudly We Served: The Men of the U.S.S. Mason.* Annapolis: Naval Institute Press, 1995.

Keys, Thomas B. *The Uncivil War: Union Army and Navy Excesses in the Official Records.* Biloxi, Miss.: Beauvoir Press, 1991.

Knox, Dudley W. *A History of the United States Navy.* New York: Putnam, 1936.

Kohn, Richard H. *The United States Military under the Constitution of the United States, 1789–1989.* New York: New York University Press, 1991.

Lamson, Peggy. *The Glorious Failure: Black Congressman Robert Brown Elliott and the Reconstruction of South Carolina.* New York: W. W. Norton, 1973.

Lane, Horace. *The Wandering Boy, Careless Sailor, and Result of Inconsideration: A True Narrative.* Skaneateles, N.Y.: L. A. Pratt, 1839.

Lang, George. *Medal of Honor Recipients, 1863–1994.* 2 vols. New York: Facts on File, 1995.

Langley, Harold D. *A History of Medicine in the Early U.S. Navy.* Baltimore: Johns Hopkins University Press, 1995.

———. "The Negro in the Navy and Merchant Service, 1798–1860." *Journal of Negro History* 52 (1967): 273–86.

———. *Social Reform in the United States Navy, 1789–1862.* Urbana: University of Illinois Press, 1967.

Lansden, John M. *A History of the City of Cairo, Illinois.* Chicago: R. R. Donnelley & Sons, 1910.

Lee, Stephen P. *General Orders of the Mississippi Squadron: Acting Rear Admiral S. P. Lee, Commanding.* St. Louis: Studley, 1865.

Levy, Uriah P. *Manual of Internal Rules and Regulations for Men of War.* New York: Van Nostrand, 1862.

List of Persons, Residents of the State of Wisconsin, Reported as Deserters from the Military or Naval Service of the United States. Madison, Wisc.: Atwood, 1869.

Litwack, Leon F. *North of Slavery: The Negro in the Free States, 1790–1860.* Chicago: University of Chicago Press, 1961.

Livermore, George. *Negroes as Slaves, Citizens, and Soldiers.* New York: Franklin, 1968.

Livermore, Thomas L. *Numbers and Losses in the Civil War in America.* Bloomington: Indiana University Press, 1957.

Livingston, Mary P., ed. *A Civil War Marine at Sea: The Diary of Medal of Honor Recipient Miles M. Oviatt.* Shippensburg, Pa.: White Mane, 1998.

Lockman, Robert F. *Attitudes toward the Navy of First Term Blacks and Whites in the Fleet.* Arlington, Va.: Institute of Naval Studies, 1977.

Logan, Rayford W. "The Negro in the Quasi-War, 1798–1800." *Negro History Bulletin* 14 (1951), 128–32.

Lonn, Ella. *Desertion during the Civil War.* Gloucester, Mass.: P. Smith, 1966.

———. *Foreigners in the Union Army and Navy.* Baton Rouge: Louisiana State University Press, 1951.

Lord, Francis A. *They Fought for the Union.* Harrisburg, Pa.: Stackpole, 1960.

Love, Robert W. *History of the U.S. Navy.* 2 vols. Harrisburg, Pa.: Stackpole, 1992.

McCarten, Francis. *Description and Cruise of USS Augusta.* N.p., 1876.

———. *Description and Cruise of USS Metacomet.* N.p., 1876.

———. *In Peace and War; or, Seven Years in the U.S. Navy.* N.p., 1876.

McCarthy, Agnes. *Worth Fighting For: A History of the Negro in the United States during the Civil War and Reconstruction.* New York: Doubleday, 1965.

McCartney, Clarence E. *Mr. Lincoln's Admirals.* New York: Funk & Wagnalls, 1956.

McCline, John. *Slavery in the Clover Bottoms: John McCline's Narrative of His Life during Slavery and the Civil War.* Knoxville: University of Tennessee Press, 1998.

McClintock, Megan J. "Binding Up the Nation's Wounds: Nationalism, Civil War Pensions, and American Families, 1861–1890." Ph.D. diss., Rutgers University, 1994.

McFeely, William S. *Frederick Douglass.* New York: W. W. Norton, 1991.

McKay, Ernest A. *The Civil War and New York City.* Syracuse: Syracuse

University Press, 1990.

McKee, Christopher. *A Gentlemanly and Honorable Profession: The Creation of the U.S. Naval Officer Corps.* Annapolis: Naval Institute Press, 1991.

Maclay, Edgar S. *A History of the United States Navy from 1775 to 1893.* New York: D. Appleton, 1894.

McPherson, James M. *Battle Cry of Freedom: The Civil War Era.* New York: Oxford University Press, 1988.

———. *For Cause and Comrades: Why Men Fought in the Civil War.* New York: Oxford University Press, 1997.

———. *Lamson of the Gettysburg: The Civil War Letters of Lieutenant Roswell H. Lamson, U.S. Navy.* New York: Oxford University Press, 1997.

———. *The Negro's Civil War: How American Negroes Felt and Acted during the War for the Union.* New York: Vintage Books, 1965.

Mahan, Alfred Thayer. *The Gulf and Inland Waters.* 1883. Reprint, Freeport, N.Y.: Books for Libraries Press, 1970.

Mallison, Fred M. *The Civil War on the Outer Banks.* Jefferson, N.C.: McFarland, 1998.

Mallory, Stephen R. *Corporal Punishment in the Navy.* Washington, D.C.: Congressional Globe Office, 1852.

Margreiter, John L. "Anesthesia in the Civil War." *Civil War Times Illustrated* 6 (1967): 22–27.

Marvel, William. *The Alabama and the Kearsarge: The Sailor's Civil War.* Chapel Hill: University of North Carolina Press, 1996.

Massachusetts, Adjutant General's Office, *Massachusetts Soldiers, Sailors, and Marines in the Civil War.* Vols. 7–8. Norwood, Mass.: Norwood Press, 1931.

Massachusetts, Bureau of Statistics. *A List of the Soldiers, Sailors, and Marines of the Civil War Surviving and Resident in Massachusetts on April 1, 1915.* Boston: Wright & Potter, 1916.

May, Samuel. *The Fugitive Slave Law and Its Victims.* 1861. Reprint, Freeport, N.Y.: Books for Libraries Press, 1970.

Mays, Joe H. *Black Americans and their Contributions toward Union Victory in the American Civil War.* New York: University Press of America, 1984.

Meade, Rebecca Paulding. *Life of Hiram Paulding, Rear-Admiral, U.S.N.* New York: Baker & Taylor, 1910.

Merrifield, Edward F. "The Seaboard War: A History of the North Atlantic Blockading Squadron, 1861–1865." Ph.D. diss., Case Western Reserve University, 1975.

Merrill, James M. "Men, Monotony, and Mouldy Beans: Life on a Civil War Blockader." *American Neptune* 16 (1956): 134–46.

———. *The Rebel Shore: The Story of Union Sea Power in the Civil War.* Boston: Little, Brown, 1957.

Mervine, Charles K. *Jottings by the Way: A Sailor's Log, 1862 to 1864.* Philadelphia: Pennsylvania Historical Society, 1947.

Milligan, John D. "The Federal Fresh-Water Navy and the Opening of the Mississippi River: Its Organization, Construction, and Operations through the Fall of Vicksburg." Ph.D. diss., University of Michigan, 1961.

———. *Gunboats down the Mississippi.* Salem, N.H.: Ayer, 1965.

Michigan, Adjutant-General's Department. *Record of Service of Michigan Volunteers in the Civil War, 1861–1865.* 42 vols. Kalamazoo: Ihling Brothers, 1905.

Miller, Edward A. *Lincoln's Abolitionist General: The Biography of David Hunter.* Columbia: University of South Carolina Press, 1997.

Moebs, Thomas T. *Black Soldiers, Black Sailors, Black Ink: Research Guide on African Americans in U.S. Military History, 1526–1900.* Williamsburg, Va.: Moebs Publishing, 1994.

Monaghan, Jay. *Abraham Lincoln Deals with Foreign Affairs.* Indianapolis: Bobbs-Merrill, 1945.

———. *The Diary of James T. Ayers: Civil War Recruiter.* Springfield: Illinois State Historical Society, 1947.

Morgan, William J., "American Privateering in America's War for Independence." *American Neptune* 36 (1976): 472–90.

Morison, Samuel Eliot. *John Paul Jones: A Sailor's Biography.* Boston: Little, Brown, 1959.

Morris, Thomas D. *Southern Slavery and the Law, 1619–1860.* Chapel Hill: University of North Carolina Press, 1996.

Murdock, Eugene C. *One Million Men: The Civil War Draft in the North.* Madison: State Historical Society of Wisconsin, 1971.

Nalty, Bernard C. *Strength for the Fight: A History of Black Americans in the Military.* New York: Free Press, 1986.

Nalty, Bernard C. and Morris J. MacGregor, eds. *Blacks in the Military: Essential Documents.* Wilmington, Del.: Scholarly Resources, 1981.

———. *Blacks in the United States Armed Forces: Basic Documents.* 13 vols. Wilmington, Del.: Scholarly Resources, 1977.

Names of Officers, Soldiers, and Sailors in Rhode Island Regiments. Providence, R.I.: Providence Press, 1869.

Nell, William C. *The Colored Patriots of the American Revolution.* 1855. Reprint, New York: Arno Press, 1968.

Nelson, Dennis D. *The Integration of the Negro into the U.S. Navy.* New York: Farrar, Straus, and Young, 1951.

Nesser, Robert W. *Statistical and Chronological History of the U.S. Navy.* New York: Macmillan, 1909.

Nevins, Allan. *Ordeal of the Union.* 8 vols. New York: Scribner's, 1947–1971.

Niven, John. *Connecticut for the Union: The Role of the State in the Civil War.* New Haven, Conn.: Yale University Press, 1965.

———. *Gideon Welles: Lincoln's Secretary of the Navy.* New York: Oxford University Press, 1973.

Nordhoff, Charles. *Nine Years a Sailor.* Cincinnati: Moore Publishing, 1857.

Ohio, Adjutant General's Office. *Naval Records of Ohio Personnel.* Columbus: State Publishing, 1867.

———. *Record of Naval Credits Filed by the Cincinnati Provost Marshal.* Columbus: State Publishing, 1864.

———. *Record of Ohio Civil War Service Medals Sent.* Columbus: State Publishing, 1912.

———. *Report of Expunged Civil War Desertion Charges.* Columbus: State Publishing, 1889–1893.

Ohio, Roster Commission. *Official Roster of the Soldiers of the State of Ohio in the War of the Rebellion, 1861–1866.* Akron: Werner, 1886–1895.

Osbon, Bradley S. *Cruise of the Flag-Ship Hartford, 1862–1863.* New York: L. W. Paine, 1863.

———. *Hand Book of the United States Navy.* New York: Van Nostrand, 1864.

Overfield, Joseph M. *The Civil War Letters of Private George Parks.* Buffalo: Gallagher Printing, 1992.

Painter, Nell I. *Exodusters: Black Migration to Kansas after Reconstruction.* New York: Alfred A. Knopf, 1976.

Palmer, Michael A. *Stoddert's War: Naval Operations during the Quasi-War with France.* Columbia: University of South Carolina Press, 1987.

Paludan, Phillip S. *The Presidency of Abraham Lincoln.* Lawrence: University Press of Kansas, 1994.

Parker, Allen. *Recollections of Slavery Times.* Worcester, Mass.: Charles W. Burbank, 1895.

Parks, George. *The Civil War Letters of Private George Parks.* Buffalo: Gallagher Printing, 1992.

Parmelee, Maurice. *Blockade and Sea Power: The Blockade, 1914–1919, and Its Significance for a World State.* New York: Crowell, 1924.

Paullin, Charles O. *Paullin's History of Naval Administration, 1775–1911.* Annapolis: United States Naval Institute, 1986.

Perkins, Susan G., ed. *Letters of Capt. Geo. Hamilton Perkins, U.S.N.* Concord, N.H.: I. C. Evans, 1886.

Phisterer, Frederick. *Statistical Record of the Armies of the United States.* 1883. Reprint, Carlisle, Pa.: Kallmann, 1996.

Pierce, Edward L. *The Contrabands at Fortress Monroe.* Boston: Ticknow, 1861.

Pleadwell, Frank L. *Ninian Pinkney, M.D., Surgeon, United States Navy.* Washington, D.C.: Annals of Medical History, 1929.

Plumb, Robert J. "Yankee Paymaster." *United States Naval Institute Proceedings* 93 (1977): 51–57.

Pompey, Sherman L. *Sailors and Marines of the United States Living in the Southern Branch, National Home for Disabled Soldiers, Elizabeth City County, Virginia in 1890.* Albany, Oreg., 1985.

Porter, David D. *General Orders of the Mississippi Squadron: Rear Admiral D. D. Porter, Commanding.* St. Louis: Studley, 1865.

——. *Naval History of the Civil War.* New York: Sherman, 1886.

Post, Charles A. "A Diary of the Blockade in 1863." *United States Naval Institute Proceedings* 54 (1918): 2333–50.

Powell, Judy. *Eastern Shore of Maryland: 1890 Census of Civil War Veterans.* Roanoke, Tex.: J. Powell, 1993.

Pratt, Marion D. *Illinois Men in the Union Navy during the Civil War.* Springfield: Illinois State Library, 1962.

Pressly, Thomas J. *Americans Interpret Their Civil War.* Princeton: Princeton University Press, 1954.

Proceeding of the Naval Court Martial in the Case of Alexander Slidell Mackenzie (1844). 1844. Reprint, Delmar, N.Y.: Scholar's Facsimiles, 1992.

Quarles, Benjamin. *The Negro in the Civil War.* Boston: Little, Brown, 1953.

Rasner, Gustav C. "The Effect of the Breakdown of the Prisoner Parole and Exchange Cartel of 22 July, 1862, on Conditions in Civil War Prisons." Master's thesis, Baylor University, 1986.

Rawick, George P., ed. *The American Slave: A Composite Autobiography.* 19 vols. Westport, Conn.: Greenwood, 1972.

Record of Service of Connecticut Men in the Army and Navy of the United States during the War of the Rebellion. 2 vols. Hartford, Conn.: Case, Lockwood, & Brainard, 1889.

Reddick, L. D. "The Negro in the United States Navy during World War II." *Journal of Negro History* 32 (1947): 201–19.

Redkey, Edwin S. *A Grand Army of Black Men: Letters from African American Soldiers in the Union Army, 1861–1865.* New York: Cambridge University Press, 1992.

Reed, Beverly T. *Military Pension Applications, 1875–1889.* Toledo: Buchanan & MacGahan Law Firm, 1997.

Reiss, Gary O. "Life aboard the Blockading Squadrons of the Union Navy during the American Civil War." Master's thesis, St. Cloud State University, 1986.

Remey, George C. *Reminiscences of the Blockade of Charleston, S.C.* New York: Remey, 1914.

Reynolds, Clark G. *Navies in History.* Annapolis: Naval Institute Press, 1998.

Rhode Island, Adjutant-Generals' Office. *Official Register of Rhode Island Officers and Soldiers Who Served in the United States Army and Navy, from 1861 to 1866*. Providence, R.I.: State Publishing, 1866.

Rhode Island, Laws and Statutes. *An Act for the Relief of Honorably Discharged Indigent Ex-Union Soldiers, Sailors, and Marines*. Providence, R.I.: State Publishing, 1889.

Ringle, Dennis. "Life in Mr. Lincoln's Navy." Master's thesis, Eastern Michigan University, 1997.

———. *Life in Mr. Lincoln's Navy*. Annapolis: Naval Institute Press, 1998.

"Riot on the USS *Charleston*." *Army and Navy Journal* 44 (1894): 563

Robbins, Coy D. *African American Soldiers from Indiana with the Union Army in the Civil War, 1863–1865*. Bloomington, Ind.: Robbins, 1989.

Roddis, Louis H. *A Short History of Nautical Medicine*. New York: P. B. Hoeber, 1941.

Roe, Francis A. *Naval Duties and Discipline: With the Policy and Principles of Naval Organization*. New York: Van Nostrand, 1865.

Rolle, Andrew F. *John Charles Fremont: Character as Destiny*. Norman: University of Oklahoma Press, 1991.

Rose, Willie L. *Rehearsal for Reconstruction: The Port Royal Experiment*. Indianapolis: Bobbs-Merrill, 1964.

Rowland, Leslie S. "Emancipation and the Black Military Experience during the American Civil War: A Documentary History (3 vols.)." Ph.D. diss., University of Rochester, 1991.

Rubin, Lester and William S. Swift. *Negro Employment in the Maritime Industries: A Study of Racial Policies in the Shipbuilding, Longshore, and Offshore Maritime Industries*. Wharton: University of Pennsylvania Press, 1974.

Rye, Scott. *Men and Ships of the Civil War*. Stamford, Conn.: Longmeadow Press, 1994.

Sandburg, Carl. *Abraham Lincoln: The Prairie Years and the War Years*. New York: Harcourt Brace, 1982.

Sands, Francis P. *A Volunteer's Reminiscences of Life in the North Atlantic Blockading Squadron, 1862*. Washington, D.C.: Military Order of the Loyal Legion, 1894.

Scharf, J. Thomas. *A History of the Confederate States Navy*. New York: Crown Press, 1977.

Schlesinger, Arthur M. "A Blue Jacket's Letters Home, 1863–1864." *New England Quarterly* 1 (1928): 554–67.

Schweninger, Loren. *Black Property Owners in the South, 1790–1915*. Urbana: University of Illinois Press, 1990.

Scofield, Walter K. *Life in a U.S. Civil War Blockading Squadron, From the Diary of a Naval Surgeon*. Coral Gables, Fla.: Coral Gables Press, 1950.

Secret, Jeanette B. *Iverson Granderson: First Class "Colored" Boy, Union Navy (1863–1865)*. Bowie, Md.: Heritage Books, 1998.

Shaffer, Donald R. "Marching On: African American Civil War Veterans in Postbellum America, 1865–1951 (2 vols.)." Ph.D. diss., University of Maryland, 1996.

Shannon, Fred A. "The Federal Government and the Negro Soldier." *Journal of Negro History* 11 (1926): 563–83.

Sharrock, Charles E. *Civil War Medal of Honor Recipients.* Denver: Sharrock, 1995.

Silverstone, Paul H. *Warships of the Civil War Navies.* Annapolis: Naval Institute Press, 1989.

Simpson, Edward. *A Treatise on Ordnance and Naval Gunnery.* New York: Simpson, 1862.

Slagle, Jay. *Ironclad Captain: Seth Ledyard Phelps and the United States Navy, 1841–1864.* Kent, Ohio: Kent State University Press, 1996.

Sloan, Irving J. *The American Negro: A Chronology and Fact Book.* Dobbs Ferry, N.Y.: Oceana Publications, 1968.

Sluby, Paul E., Sr., and Stanton L. Wormley, eds. *Diary of Charles B. Fisher.* Washington, D.C.: Columbia Harmony Society, 1983.

Smelser, Marshall. *Congress Founds the Navy, 1787–1798.* South Bend, Ind.: Notre Dame University Press, 1959.

Smith, Gaddis, and Clark G. Reynolds, eds. "Black Seamen and the Federal Courts." *Proceedings of the North American Society of Oceanic History* 12 (1978): 1–23.

Smith, George G. *Leaves from a Soldier's Diary: The Personal Record of Lieutenant George G. Smith.* New York: Putnam, 1906.

Smyth, William H. *The Sailor's Word-book: An Alphabetical Digest of Nautical Terms.* London: Blackie and Son, 1867.

Soley, James R. *The Blockade and the Cruisers.* New York: Scribner's, 1881.

Speer, Lonnie R. *Portals to Hell: Military Prisons of the Civil War.* Mechanicsburg, Pa.: Stackpole Books, 1997.

Stansbury, George F. *The Life of a "Lie-Out"; or, Adventures of a Rover.* Weedsport, N.Y.: G. W. Churchill's Press, 1899.

Starobin, Robert S. *Industrial Slavery in the Old South.* New York: Oxford University Press, 1970.

Stedman, Charles E. *The Civil War Sketchbook of Charles Ellery Stedman, Surgeon, United States Navy.* San Rafael, Calif.: Presidio Press, 1976.

Steiner, Paul E. *Disease in the Civil War: Natural Biological Warfare in 1861–1865.* Springfield, Ill.: Charles C. Thomas, 1968.

Sterling, Dorothy. *Captain of the Planter: The Story of Robert Smalls.* New York: Doubleday, 1958.

Stevens, A. Parsons. *The Military History of Ohio.* New York: H. H. Hardesty, 1886.

Still, William N. *Iron Afloat: The Story of the Confederate Armorclads.* Columbia: University of South Carolina Press, 1985.

Still, William N., John M. Taylor, and Norman C. Delaney. *Raiders and Blockaders: The American Civil War Afloat.* Washington, D.C.: Brassey's, 1998.

Stillwell, Paul, ed. *The Golden Thirteen: Recollections of the First Black Naval Officers.* Annapolis: Naval Institute Press, 1993.

Stivers, Reuben E. *Privateers and Volunteers: The Men and Women of Our Reserve Naval Forces, 1766 to 1866.* Annapolis: Naval Institute Press, 1975.

Stokesbury, James L. *A Short History of the Civil War.* New York: William Morrow, 1995.

Swierenga, Robert P. *Beyond the Civil War Synthesis: Political Essays of the Civil War Era.* Westport, Conn.: Greenwood Press, 1975.

Symonds, Craig L. *Charleston Blockade: The Journals of John B. Marchand, U.S. Navy, 1861–1862.* Newport, R.I.: Naval War College Press, 1976.

Syrett, John. "The Confiscation Acts: Efforts at Reconstruction during the Civil War." Ph.D. diss., University of Minnesota, 1971.

Tap, Bruce. *Over Lincoln's Shoulder: The Committee on the Conduct of the War.* Lawrence: University Press of Kansas, 1998.

Thomas, Eugene M. "Prisoner of War Exchange during the American Civil War." Ph.D. diss., Auburn University, 1976.

Thompson. *The Story of a Strange Career.* New York: Appleton, 1902.

Thompson, Robert M. and Richard Wainright. *Correspondence of Gustavus V. Fox.* New York: De Vinne Press, 1920.

Thornbrough, Emma L. *Indiana in the Civil War Era, 1850–1880.* Indianapolis: Indiana Historical Society, 1965.

Trefousse, Hans L. *Benjamin Franklin Wade: Radical Republican from Ohio.* New York: Twayne Publishers, 1963.

Trotter, William R. *The Civil War in North Carolina.* Vol. 3, *Ironclads and Columbiads: The Coast.* Winston-Salem, N.C.: J. F. Blair, 1989.

Trudeau, Noah A. *Like Men of War: Black Troops in the Civil War, 1862–1865.* Boston: Little, Brown, 1998.

True, Rowland S. "Life aboard a Gunboat." *Civil War Times Illustrated* 9 (1972): 36–43.

Tucker, Glenn. *Dawn like Thunder: The Barbary Wars and the Birth of the U.S. Navy.* Indianapolis: Bobbs-Merrill, 1963.

Tucker, Spencer C. *The Jeffersonian Gunboat Navy.* Columbia: University of South Carolina Press, 1993.

Turner, Robert R. *Virginia's Union Veterans: Eleventh Census of the United States, 1890.* Manassas, Va.: R. R. Turner, 1994.

United States, Adjutant General's Office. *General Court Martial Orders.* Washington, D.C.: War Department, 1860.

United States, Army. *Articles of War, for the Government of the Armies of the United States.* Washington, D.C.: Government Printing Office, 1877.

United States, Bureau of the Census. *Historical Statistics of the United States: Colonial Times to 1970.* Washington, D.C.: Government Printing Office, 1976.

United States, Congress. *An Act for the Better Government of the United States Navy.* Washington, D.C.: Government Printing Office, 1800 and 1862.

United States, Congress. *Acts and Resolutions Relating to the Navy.* Washington, D.C.: Government Printing Office, 1870.

United States, Naval War Records Office. *List of Log Books of U.S. Vessels, 1861–1865, on File in the Navy Department.* Washington, D.C.: Government Printing Office, 1891.

United States, Navy Department. *Allowances Established for Vessels of the United States Navy.* Washington, D.C.: Government Printing Office, 1865.

———. *Annual Reports of the Secretary of the Navy, 1861–1865.* Washington, D.C.: Government Printing Office, 1862–1866.

———. *A Method of Classifying Offences and Punishments on Board Vessels of the United States Navy.* Washington, D.C.: Government Printing Office, 1871.

———. *Naval Documents Related to the United States Wars with the Barbary Powers.* Vol. 2. Washington, D.C.: Government Printing Office, 1940.

———. *Navy Registers of the United States, 1860–1865.* Washington, D.C.: Government Printing Office, 1860–1865.

———. *Orders, Regulations, and Instructions for the Administration of Law and Justice in the United States Navy.* Washington, D.C.: Government Printing Office, 1870.

———. *Record of the Medals of Honor Issued to the Bluejackets and Marines of the United States Navy, 1862–1877.* Washington, D.C.: Government Printing Office, 1878.

———. *Regulations for the Government of the United States Navy: 1863.* Washington, D.C.: Government Printing Office, 1863.

United States, Navy Department, Office of the Judge Advocate General. *Index-Digest of Court-Martial Orders for the Year Ending December 31, 1864.* Washington, D.C.: Government Printing Office, 1865.

United States, Office of the Solicitor of the Treasury. *Prize Cases in New York.* Washington, D.C.: Government Printing Office, 1864.

United States, Secretary of the Interior. *Population of the United States in 1860: Compiled from the Original Returns of the Eighth Census.* Washington, D.C.: Government Printing Office, 1864.

———. *Statistics of the United States (Including Mortality, Property, Etc.) in 1860: The Eighth Census.* Washington, D.C.: Government Printing Office, 1866.

United States, War Department. *An Estimate for Collection and Payment of Bounty, Prize Money, and Other Claims of Colored Soldiers and Sailors.*

Washington, D.C.: Government Printing Office, 1880.

———. *Estimates from the Paymaster General for the Collection and Payment of Bounty, Prize Money, and Other Claims of Colored Soldiers and Sailors.* Washington, D.C.: Government Printing Office, 1878.

———. *The Medical and Surgical History of the War of the Rebellion.* 6 vols. Washington, D.C.: Government Printing Office, 1870–1883.

Uya, Okon E. *From Slavery to Public Service: Robert Smalls, 1839–1915.* New York: Oxford University Press, 1971.

Vail, Israel E. *Three Years on the Blockade: A Naval Experience.* New York: Abbey Press, 1902.

Valle, James E. "The Disciplinary System of the United States Navy, 1800–1861." Ph.D. diss., University of Delaware, 1979.

———. *Rocks and Shoals: Naval Discipline in the Age of the Fighting Sail.* Annapolis: Naval Institute Press, 1980.

Valuska, David L. *The African American in the Union Navy, 1861–1865.* New York: Garland, 1993.

———. "The Negro in the Union Navy, 1861–1865." Ph.D. diss., Lehigh University, 1973.

Van Buren, Martin. *Negro Witnesses: The Case of Lieutenant Hooe.* Washington, D.C.: Government Printing Office, 1840.

Van Deusen, Glyndon G. *William Henry Seward.* New York: Oxford University Press, 1967.

Vermont, Adjutant and Inspector General's Office. *Revised Roster of Vermont Volunteers and Lists of Vermonters Who Served in the Army and Navy of the United States during the War of the Rebellion, 1861–1866.* Montpelier, Vt.: Watchman, 1892.

Vlock, Laurel F. and Joel A. Levitch. *Contraband of War: William Henry Singleton.* New York: Funk and Wagnalls, 1970.

The War of the Rebellion: A Compilation of the Official Records of the Union and Confederate Armies. 128 vols. with atlas. Washington, D.C.: Government Printing Office, 1880–1901.

The War of the Rebellion: A Compilation of the Official Records of the Union and Confederate Navies. 30 vols. Washington, D.C.: Government Printing Office, 1894–1922.

Wanderer, A. *Journals of Two Cruises aboard the American Privateer Yankee.* New York: Macmillan, 1967.

Weisenburger, Francis P. *Columbus during the War.* Columbus: Ohio State University Press, 1963.

Welles, Gideon. *Diary of Gideon Welles: Secretary of the Navy under Lincoln and Johnson.* 3 vols. Boston: Houghton Mifflin, 1911.

Wesley, Charles H. *Negro-Americans of Ohio in Civil War History.* Wilberforce, Ohio: Central State College, 1962.

Wesley, Charles H. and Patricia W. Romero. *Negro Americans in the Civil War: From Slavery to Citizenship.* New York: Publishers Company, 1967.

West, Richard S. *Gideon Welles: Lincoln's Navy Department.* Indianapolis: Bobbs-Merrill, 1943.

———. *Mr. Lincoln's Navy.* New York: Longmans and Green, 1957.

———. "The Navy and the Press during the Civil War." *United States Naval Institute Proceedings* 63 (1937): 33–41.

———. *The Second Admiral: A Life of David Dixon Porter, 1813–1891.* New York: Coward & McCann, 1937.

———. "Watchful Gideon." *United States Naval Institute Proceedings* 62 (1936): 1091–97.

Westwood, Howard C. *Black Troops, White Commanders, and Freedmen during the Civil War.* Carbondale: Southern Illinois University Press, 1992.

———. "Captive Black Union Soldiers in Charleston." *Civil War History* 28 (1982): 29–44.

White, William C. *Tin Can on a Shingle.* Norwalk, Conn.: Easton Press, 1990.

Wiley, Bell I. *The Common Soldier of the Civil War.* New York: Scribner's, 1973.

———. *The Life of Billy Yank: The Common Soldier of the Union.* Indianapolis: Bobbs-Merrill, 1952.

———. *Southern Negroes, 1861–1865.* New Haven, Conn.: Yale University Press, 1938.

Williams, George W. *A History of the Negro Troops in the War of the Rebellion, 1861–1865.* New York: Bergman Publishers, 1968.

Willis, Nathaniel P. *Summer Cruise in the Mediterranean on Board an American Frigate.* Rochester, N.Y.: Alden and Beardsley, 1856.

Wilson, Joseph T. *The Black Phalanx: A History of the Negro Soldiers of the United States.* Hartford, Conn.: American Publishing, 1890.

Williams, Harry. "The Navy and the Committee on the Conduct of the War." *United States Naval Institute Proceedings* 65 (1939): 1751–55.

Winslow, Richard E. *Constructing Munitions of War: The Portsmouth Navy Yard Confronts the Confederacy, 1861–1865.* Portsmouth, N.H.: Portsmouth Marine Society, 1995.

Winthrop, William. *Military Law.* 2 vols. Washington, D.C.: W. H. Morrison, 1886.

Wisconsin, Secretary of State. *Census Enumeration of Soldiers and Sailors of the Late War Residing in Wisconsin June 1885.* Madison, Wisc.: Democrat Printing, 1886.

Wood, Richard E. "The Operations of the North Atlantic Blockading Squadron, 1861–1865." Master's thesis, Florida State University, 1969.

Woodford, Frank B. *Father Abraham's Children: Michigan Episodes in the Civil War.* Detroit: Wayne State University Press, 1961.

Woodward, W. E. *Meet General Grant.* New York: Liveright, 1928.

INDEX

Medal of Honor, 129–30, 131, 183
Medical care: for African American sailors, 17, 100–108; in merchant service, 105–6; for Union Army, 105. *See also* Disease
Melvine, William, 132
Memphis, Tenn., health center at, 106
Mental incompetence, prison term and, 163
Merchant sailors, 65; demand for, 12; opportunities for, 19–20; recruitment of African American into Navy, 65, 66–67; segregation of, 83
Merchant ships: African American sailors on, 12, 22; and impressment, 12–13; medical care on, 105–6; recruitment of sailors from, 173
Messes, 97, 98, 112, 113
Mexican War, 19–20; African American sailors in, 19–21; blockade during, 19–20; disciplinary episodes during, 143; naval battles during, 116
Mifflin, James, 130
Military projects: employment of slaves on Confederate, 36, 39, 42, 44; use of contrabands on Union, 42–43
Militia Act (1792), 20–21
Militia Act (1862), 45, 49–50, 50, 56
Miller, Matthew, 120
Milliken's Bend, La., 120
Minstrel troupes, 113, 176
Mississippi, seccession of, 30
Mississippi Squadron: Confederate ambushes on, 122–23; medical care for, 104, 105; navy justice system on, 150–51, 158–60, 163; supplies for, 96

Missouri edict, 31–32, 33
Mitchell, Thomas, 147
Mobile Bay, Ala.: assault on, 107, 125, 126, 129, 130, 137; capture of, 125–26
Moody, Wash., 163
Moore, Elis, 122
Moore, Joyce, 122
Moran, William, 124
Morris Island, S.C., capture of, 119
Moss, George, 111
Multiple desertions, 161
Murphy, James, 145
Murphy, John, 165
Murrell's Inlet, S.C., 134
Mutinous conduct, 142–44, 155, 156, 165, 169, 172, 185

Nansemond River, battle on, 131
Napoleonic Wars, 12
National Forces Act (1863), 53, 56
National Home for Disabled Soldiers (Elizabeth City, Va.), 94
Naval experience, and rank, 75, 76
Naval medical school, 104–5
Navy. *See* Continental navy; U.S. Navy
Navy Articles of War, 139–40, 141, 142, 145, 149, 165
Navy criminal justice system: abuses of, at shipboard level, 164; African American sailors in, 138–65, 182; alcohol and infractions in, 163–64, 171–72; appeals in, 149–50; captains' masts in, 140, 145; and contempt, 152; codified offense system in, 145; and Constitution, 139; death penalty in, 29, 133–34, 140, 143, 149, 161; defense witnesses in, 151–52; disciplinary methods in, 138–39,